# Acing

## Federal Income Tax

## Tax

**A Checklist Approach to
Federal Income Tax**

### Samuel A. Donaldson

*Professor of Law*

*University of Washington
School of Law*

*Series Editor*
### A. Benjamin Spencer

**THOMSON**

**WEST**

Mat #40545313

Thomson/West have created this publication to provide you with accurate and authoritative information concerning the subject matter covered. However, this publication was not necessarily prepared by persons licensed to practice law in a particular jurisdiction. Thomson/West are not engaged in rendering legal or other professional advice, and this publication is not a substitute for the advice of an attorney. If you require legal or other expert advice, you should seek the services of a competent attorney or other professional.

© 2008 Thomson/West
    610 Opperman Drive
    St. Paul, MN 55123
    1–800–313–9378

Printed in the United States of America

**ISBN:** 978–0–314–17683–7

# Introduction

--------

**M**any law students approach the first course in federal income taxation with some degree of anxiety. They worry that the course will be too dry, too technical, or too mathematical for their tastes. Justifiably, the course at most law schools enjoys the reputation as being more rigorous than the average law course. A student in the introductory federal income tax course cannot simply spend under an hour painting 10–15 pages of a casebook in different highlight colors and be prepared for class. Instead, the student must also read some very dense statutory and regulatory provisions and then, in most classes, apply those complex rules to a fact pattern designed to test comprehension, analysis, and synthesis.

After a few weeks, most students come to realize that the federal income tax course is among the most refreshing in the law school curriculum. At long last: a course with *answers*! No more "well, it depends on what the trier of fact concludes," and no more of the amorphous "it's okay if it's reasonable but not okay if it's unreasonable" stuff. Students also realize that (gasp) the Internal Revenue Code can actually be understood, if only you have the patience and perseverance to read a particular provision as many times as it takes for it to sink in and become clear. One of the most rewarding experiences of law school can be that "aha moment," when the fog lifts and the once-indecipherable rule makes sense. And the basic income tax course will have many of these moments.

But by the time exam preparation rolls around, students again become anxious. It turns out that the real challenge of the introductory federal income tax course is not so much any particular rule or concept—it's the *volume* of material covered and the *connections* from one concept to the next that students often find hard to master. Students crave some methodical approach that will help them maneuver through the numerous tax issues that can be raised in the simplest of fact patterns, primarily to make sure they miss nothing obvious. That's where this book comes in.

This book is not intended to be a hornbook, treatise, or even a nutshell on federal income tax. Instead, it is intended to serve as an organizational tool for you, the tax student. This book offers a series of ten checklists you can use as a guide for answering exam questions. Using the "yes or no" checklist approach common to the *Acing* series, the checklists in this book will help you identify the relevant issues you can discuss in your answers to exam questions. Each checklist is wrapped by some very brief explanatory text for context and a few sample problems with answers to illustrate how the checklist can be used to systematically answer an exam question.

Don't waste your time with this book if you are looking for a substitute for your daily class preparation. In fact, this book assumes you have a fairly good understanding of the material. What this books offers is a method for *organizing* your knowledge into a usable framework. You might want to use the checklists as the framework for your own "outline" of the course. Wouldn't it be nice for once to have an outline that could actually assist you in writing an answer to an exam question instead of some tome that merely assigns letters and numbers to your class notes? Now you can have a useful map of the course that will guide your analysis as you answer an exam question. With a properly constructed outline using these checklists as the skeleton, you have a better shot at writing a comprehensive and reasoned analysis that reaches a solid conclusion.

Keep in mind that every federal income tax course is different. They use different texts and are taught by professors with different backgrounds and interests. Some topics that seem to get a lot of attention in this book might get little or no attention in your own class. Likewise, this book may say nothing at all about one or more of your professor's pet topics. You can still use this book as a model for constructing your own checklists for those topics you just know will be on the exam even though they are not mentioned at all on these pages. By creating your own checklists, you will synthesize the material yourself, see better whether there are gaps in your knowledge, and discover connections between topics that you might have missed.

*

# **T**able of **C**ontents

# Introduction

**M**any law students approach the first course in federal income taxation with some degree of anxiety. They worry that the course will be too dry, too technical, or too mathematical for their tastes. Justifiably, the course at most law schools enjoys the reputation as being more rigorous than the average law course. A student in the introductory federal income tax course cannot simply spend under an hour painting 10–15 pages of a casebook in different highlight colors and be prepared for class. Instead, the student must also read some very dense statutory and regulatory provisions and then, in most classes, apply those complex rules to a fact pattern designed to test comprehension, analysis, and synthesis.

After a few weeks, most students come to realize that the federal income tax course is among the most refreshing in the law school curriculum. At long last: a course with *answers*! No more "well, it depends on what the trier of fact concludes," and no more of the amorphous "it's okay if it's reasonable but not okay if it's unreasonable" stuff. Students also realize that (gasp) the Internal Revenue Code can actually be understood, if only you have the patience and perseverance to read a particular provision as many times as it takes for it to sink in and become clear. One of the most rewarding experiences of law school can be that "aha moment," when the fog lifts and the once-indecipherable rule makes sense. And the basic income tax course will have many of these moments.

But by the time exam preparation rolls around, students again become anxious. It turns out that the real challenge of the introductory federal income tax course is not so much any particular rule or concept—it's the *volume* of material covered and the *connections* from one concept to the next that students often find hard to master. Students crave some methodical approach that will help them maneuver through the numerous tax issues that can be raised in the simplest of fact patterns, primarily to make sure they miss nothing obvious. That's where this book comes in.

This book is not intended to be a hornbook, treatise, or even a nutshell on federal income tax. Instead, it is intended to serve as an organizational tool for you, the tax student. This book offers a series of ten checklists you can use as a guide for answering exam questions. Using the "yes or no" checklist approach common to the *Acing* series, the checklists in this book will help you identify the relevant issues you can discuss in your answers to exam questions. Each checklist is wrapped by some very brief explanatory text for context and a few sample problems with answers to illustrate how the checklist can be used to systematically answer an exam question.

Don't waste your time with this book if you are looking for a substitute for your daily class preparation. In fact, this book assumes you have a fairly good understanding of the material. What this books offers is a method for *organizing* your knowledge into a usable framework. You might want to use the checklists as the framework for your own "outline" of the course. Wouldn't it be nice for once to have an outline that could actually assist you in writing an answer to an exam question instead of some tome that merely assigns letters and numbers to your class notes? Now you can have a useful map of the course that will guide your analysis as you answer an exam question. With a properly constructed outline using these checklists as the skeleton, you have a better shot at writing a comprehensive and reasoned analysis that reaches a solid conclusion.

Keep in mind that every federal income tax course is different. They use different texts and are taught by professors

with different backgrounds and interests. Some topics that seem to
get a lot of attention in this book might get little or no attention in
your own class. Likewise, this book may say nothing at all about one
or more of your professor's pet topics. You can still use this book as
a model for constructing your own checklists for those topics you
just know will be on the exam even though they are not mentioned
at all on these pages. By creating your own checklists, you will
synthesize the material yourself, see better whether there are gaps
in your knowledge, and discover connections between topics that
you might have missed.

*

# CHAPTER 1

# The Tax Ladder

An individual's federal income tax liability is determined under IRC § 1. It generally provides that one's tax liability is a function of two variables: filing status and taxable income. This opening Chapter considers how one determines the applicable filing status and how one computes taxable income. Armed with these two variables, the computation of tax liability is a simple matter of multiplication and addition using the correct rate table in IRC § 1(a)–(d).

## THE TAX LADDER REVIEW

*Filing Status.* Taxpayers must choose the correct filing status in order to determine the tax liability associated with their taxable income. There are four possible choices: married filing jointly (which includes certain surviving spouses), head of household, unmarried, and married filing separately.

*Married Filing Jointly.* Married couples have been able to combine their incomes on a single return since 1948. It all stemmed from *Poe v. Seaborn*, 282 U.S. 101 (1930), where the Supreme Court held that because the laws of community property states consider the earnings of one spouse to belong to the community, couples in community property states could divide a spouse's earnings equally between them for federal income tax purposes. Thus, half of the income earned by a spouse in a community property state was reportable by the other spouse. Because of the progressive tax rates in IRC § 1, one-earner couples in community property states enjoyed a lower total tax liability than similarly-situated couples in common-law states. In response, Congress permitted spouses filing a joint return to combine their incomes no matter whether they lived in community property states or common-law property states. Accordingly, the tax table in IRC § 1(a) expands the size of each of the lower tax brackets so that couples in all states will be treated more or less equally. "Married filing jointly" status is also available to a "surviving spouse."

*Head of Household.* If an individual qualifies as a "head of household," he or she uses the tax table in IRC § 1(b). IRC § 2(b) defines a head of household as one who both maintains his or her home as the principal residence of a dependent and is neither married nor a surviving spouse. The qualification rules here are somewhat more relaxed than is the case for surviving spouses seeking the continued benefit of the IRC § 1(a) tax table.

*Unmarried.* Unmarried individuals who do not qualify as a head of household or a surviving spouse use the tax table contained in IRC § 1(c). It should be no surprise that the tax table in IRC § 1(b) for heads of households is more generous than the table in IRC § 1(c); after all, the incomes of heads of household are by definition supporting more individuals than the incomes of unmarried individuals with no dependents.

*Married Filing Separately.* Although the joint return often produces a better tax result, married couples may opt to file separate returns for a taxable year. As one would expect, the tax brackets in IRC § 1(d), the table for married couples filing separately, are exactly half the size of the brackets applicable to joint returns in IRC § 1(a). What may be somewhat surprising, however, is the fact that there are different brackets for unmarried taxpayers than for married taxpayers who file separately. Unmarried taxpayers enjoy wider tax brackets, meaning they pay less tax on the same amount of income. This result might be justified on the grounds that married couples enjoy an economy of scale by sharing certain household expenses that unmarried taxpayers also incur. Giving unmarried individuals slightly fatter tax brackets might be a fair accommodation to reflect this economic reality. That assumption might hold less weight today, as more unmarried couples cohabitate and thus share many of the same economies of scale as married couples.

*Taxable Income.* IRC § 63 reveals *two* methods for computing "taxable income." The first, in IRC § 63(a), states that taxable income means "gross income minus the deductions allowed by this chapter (other than the standard deduction)." This definition contains three other specific terms: (1) gross income; (2) deductions; and (3) the standard deduction.

*Gross Income.* IRC § 61(a) defines gross income as "all income from whatever source derived," and then lists 15 examples of gross income items. The language "all income from whatever source derived" parallels the language used in the Sixteenth Amendment to the United States Constitution: "The Congress shall have the power to lay and collect taxes on incomes, from whatever source derived, without apportionment among the several States, and without regard to any census or enumeration." By providing that gross income is "all income from whatever source derived," Congress clearly intends to exert the full measure of its authority to tax income. Thus, anything that is "income" is potentially subject to taxation. Chapter 2 provides a more comprehensive discussion of the subject of gross income.

The broad sweep of IRC § 61(a) is limited by exceptions provided elsewhere in the Code. As discussed in Chapter 3, certain Code provisions exclude from gross income items that would otherwise constitute income. Thus, with respect to each potential item of income, a taxpayer must first determine whether the item constitutes "income" within the meaning of the Sixteenth Amendment (Chapter 2). If so, the taxpayer must treat the item as gross income unless it is specifically excluded from gross income in whole or in part under some other provision of the Code (Chapter 3).

*Deductions.* There is no formal definition of "deductions." IRC § 161 merely provides that only deductions specifically authorized by the Code may be used to compute taxable income. As this provision implies, not every taxpayer expenditure is deductible; a taxpayer must have statutory authority for every deduction. The basics of deductions are explored in Chapter 4. One of the themes of that Chapter is that while expenses incurred in business and investment activities are deductible, personal and living expenses are not. Chapter 5, however, concerns several of the deductions for personal expenditures.

*An Alternative Method for Computing Taxable Income.* IRC § 63(b) contains an alternate formula for computing taxable income as, in relevant part, "adjusted gross income, minus the standard deduction and the deduction for personal exemptions." Here, in addition to the "standard deduction," we have two more special terms: (1) adjusted gross income; and (2) personal exemptions.

Note that every taxpayer can choose between the IRC § 63(a) formula and the IRC § 63(b) formula to compute taxable income. Naturally, taxpayers will choose the formula that produces the smaller amount of taxable income. Generally, if a taxpayer's various deduction items for a year do not exceed the standard deduction, the taxpayer will choose to use the standard deduction and the IRC § 63(b) formula. If the deductions exceed the standard deduction, the taxpayer should use the IRC § 63(a) formula and itemize all of the deductions to reduce the tax liability.

*Adjusted Gross Income.* IRC § 62(a) defines adjusted gross income as gross income minus 21 specifically identified deductions. Note that IRC § 62(a) does not by itself authorize deductions; it merely lists those deductions that are used to compute adjusted gross income. The deductions listed in IRC § 62(a) are sometimes called **above-the-line deductions** because they are used in computing adjusted gross income. (Adjusted gross income is "the line.") It is important to note too that *all* taxpayers can claim the deductions listed in IRC § 62(a). Taxpayers using the IRC § 63(a) formula are entitled to these deductions, for they claim "all deductions" other than the standard deduction. Meanwhile, taxpayers employing the IRC § 63(b) formula use "adjusted gross income" as the starting point for the computation of taxable income. Accordingly, above-the-line deductions are the best kind of deductions.

*Personal Exemptions.* Taxpayers who do not itemize get to claim the "personal exemptions" authorized by IRC § 151. Because the personal exemptions are deductions, even taxpayers who do choose to itemize deductions can claim personal exemptions. Thus, the IRC § 151 personal exemptions are also available to all taxpayers. But because the IRC § 151 personal exemptions are not listed in IRC § 62(a), these deductions cannot be taken "above the line;" in other words, they cannot be used to compute adjusted gross income. They must be taken into account *after* a taxpayer has determined adjusted gross income.

*Standard Deduction and Itemized Deductions.* Whether to itemize all deductions depends upon the amount of the standard deduction. If the standard deduction is roughly equal to the amount of a taxpayer's itemized deductions, the taxpayer might choose the standard deduction simply to avoid the hassle of itemizing each of the deductions. If the standard deduction clearly exceeds the amount of itemized deductions, the choice is easy. The **standard deduction** amount is set forth in IRC § 63(c) (the amount is adjusted annually for inflation). It is comprised of a "basic standard deduction" and, where appropriate, an "additional standard deduction." IRC § 63(d) states that **itemized deductions** are all deductions other than above-the-line deductions and personal exemptions. Of course, since a taxpayer cannot claim both itemized deductions and the standard deduction, the standard deduction is not an itemized deduction. Itemized deductions are often referred to as "below-the-line deductions," as they are taken into account after the determination of adjusted gross income.

*Limitations on Itemized Deductions.* IRC §§ 67 and 68 impose separate limitations on the amount of itemized deductions that a taxpayer may claim in a taxable year. IRC § 67(a) states that a taxpayer can deduct "miscellaneous itemized deductions" only to the extent that such deductions (in the aggregate) exceed two percent of the taxpayer's adjusted gross income. IRC § 67(b) defines miscellaneous itemized deductions as all itemized deductions *other than* the twelve deductions listed in IRC § 67(b). Thus, the twelve itemized deductions listed are "regular itemized deductions" not subject to the "two-percent haircut" of IRC § 67(a).

Under IRC § 68(a), affluent taxpayers with taxable incomes in excess of an "applicable amount" will lose up to 80 percent of their total itemized deductions (both regular itemized deductions and what is left of the miscellaneous itemized deductions after the two-percent haircut of IRC § 67(a)). Four itemized deductions are spared from the IRC § 68 phase-out: the deduction for medical expenses, the deduction for investment interest, the deduction for casualty or theft losses related to property held for investment or personal use, and the deduction for gambling losses. See IRC § 68(c). Under current law, the phase-out of itemized deductions under IRC § 68(a) will terminate in 2010. Until then, the amount of the reduction has been substantially curtailed, as the checklist for this Chapter explains.

*Assembling the Tax Ladder.* Having looked at the components of both the IRC § 63(a) formula for computing taxable income and the IRC § 63(b) formula, one can construct a single, comprehensive formula that all taxpayers can use. Because the formula looks like a ladder, it is sometimes referred to as the "tax ladder:"

---

Gross Income [§ 61(a)]
Less: Deductions Listed in § 62(a)
Equals: Adjusted Gross Income
Less: Personal Exemptions
& Less: EITHER Standard Deduction [§ 63(c)]
OR Itemized Deductions [§ 63(d)]
Equals: Taxable Income

---

*Credits.* After computing taxable income, taxpayers consult the applicable table in IRC § 1(a)–(d) to determine tentative tax liability. Then, taxpayers may claim various credits against this tentative tax liability. Any tax liability remaining after application of the appropriate credits is the taxpayer's final tax liability.

It is important to note that taxpayers generally prefer credits to deductions, because credits reduce tax liability dollar for dollar, while deductions only save tax equal to the amount of the deductions multiplied by the taxpayer's marginal tax rate (the rate at which the last dollar of taxable income is taxed).

There are a number of credits, but a few are worth brief mention here. First, IRC § 21 offers a limited credit for certain expenses related to the care of a dependent. Generally, a taxpayer can credit anywhere from 20 percent to 35 percent of such costs against the taxpayer's federal income tax liability. The applicable percentage will depend upon the taxpayer's adjusted gross income: the higher the adjusted gross income, the lower the percentage. In any case, the maximum credit amount available under IRC § 21 is $3,000 (or $6,000, if the taxpayer household contains more than one dependent). Creditable expenses include not only those incurred for actual physical care of the dependent but also ancillary "household" services like meal preparation and cleaning. This **household and dependent care credit** is "nonrefundable." This means that if the amount of the credit, after application of all relevant limitations, exceeds the taxpayer's pre-credit federal income tax liability, the excess is not paid to the taxpayer. Nonrefundable credits can only reduce or eliminate liability for tax; by definition, they cannot create a balance due to the taxpayer.

Second, there are two nonrefundable **education credits** for certain expenses related to higher education. The Hope Scholarship Credit is available for tuition and related expenses incurred during the first two years of postsecondary education. See IRC § 25A(b) and Chapter 5. Under the Lifetime Learning Credit, the qualified tuition and related expenses beyond the first two years of undergraduate study are creditable as long as they relate to any course of instruction (at most colleges and universities) designed to develop or improve the student's job skills. See IRC § 25A(c) and Chapter 5.

Finally, there is the **credit for income taxes withheld on wages**. Anyone who has received a paycheck knows how this works. Amounts withheld from wages are credited against the taxpayer's pre-credit tax liability to determine if enough tax was collected through the withholding process. See IRC § 31(a). As you may know from personal experience, this credit is refundable: if the federal income tax withheld from the paychecks exceeds the taxpayer's pre-credit tax liability, the excess tax withheld is refunded to the taxpayer (but without interest).

## THE TAX LADDER CHECKLIST

This checklist will walk through the steps necessary to determine an individual's filing status and compute his or her taxable income. Before proceeding through this checklist, be sure you know the taxpayer's gross income (Chapters 2 and 3) and the deductions the taxpayer may claim (Chapters 4 and 5) for the taxable year. Keep in mind that income includes gain from property transactions (Chapters 6, 7, and 9) and that a loss from a property transaction might also be deductible (Chapters 6, 7, 8, and 9). For issues concerning the timing of income and deduction items, see Chapter 10. Accordingly, although this is the first checklist in this book, this will likely be the last checklist you would consult with respect to a particular fact pattern.

### A. FILING STATUS

Use this Part A to determine the taxpayer's filing status for the taxable year at issue.

1. **Married**—Was the taxpayer married on the last day of the taxable year at issue, or, if not, did the taxpayer's spouse die during the taxable year at issue?

    a. **Yes**—If yes, then the taxpayer may choose either to file a joint return with his or her spouse and compute tax liability under IRC § 1(a) or file a separate return and compute tax liability under IRC § 1(d). IRC § 7703(a). Generally it will be preferable for the spouses to file a joint return because the tax brackets in IRC § 1(a) for joint return filers are fatter than the tax brackets in IRC § 1(d) for separate filers. Also, various Code provisions provide reduced benefits to married couples filing separately than the benefits provided to joint filers. One drawback to filing a joint return is that both spouses agree to be jointly and severally liable for any tax deficiency allocable to the return. IRC § 6013(d)(3). If the taxpayer suspects that his or her spouse is secreting income or fabricating deduction items, a separate return may be advisable. See IRC § 6015 for special relief rules where an innocent spouse had no knowledge or reason to know of a deficiency attributable to his or her spouse when the joint return was filed.

b. **No**—If no, then continue in this Part A.

2. **Surviving Spouse**—Is the taxpayer a "surviving spouse" for the taxable year?

    a. **Definition**—A surviving spouse is someone who is not married at the end of the taxable year at issue, whose spouse died in either of the two prior taxable years, and who furnishes more than half of the cost to maintain a home that is also the principal residence of his or her child or stepchild. IRC § 2(a).

    b. **Yes**—If yes, then the taxpayer is eligible to use the tax table for joint return filers in IRC § 1(a). IRC § 1(a)(2).

    c. **No**—If no, then continue in this Part A.

3. **Maintaining Home for Dependent**—Does the taxpayer maintain as his or her home a household which also serves for the majority of the taxable year at issue as the principal place of abode for an unmarried "qualifying child" of the taxpayer or for a parent or other "dependent" of the taxpayer?

    a. **Qualifying Child and Dependent**—These terms have the same meaning as in B(3) of this checklist.

    b. **Yes**—If yes, then the taxpayer qualifies as a "head of household" and may compute tax liability using the tax table in IRC § 1(b). IRC § 2(b).

    c. **No**—If no, then the taxpayer must file as an "unmarried" individual and must use the tax table in IRC § 1(c).

## B. TAXABLE INCOME

Use this Part B to compute a taxpayer's taxable income for the year.

1. **Gross Income**—What is the taxpayer's gross income for the taxable year? See Chapters 2, 3, 6, 7, and 9 for the definition of gross income, a discussion of several of the various exclusions from gross income, and the impact of gains from property transactions. Continue in this Part B.

2. **Above-the-Line Deductions**—Does the taxpayer have any of the deductions listed in IRC § 62(a)? See Chapters 4, 5, 6, 7, 8, and 9 for discussion of the various deductions a taxpayer may claim, including losses from property transactions.

a. **Yes**—If yes, subtract those deduction items listed in IRC § 62(a) from the taxpayer's gross income. The resulting amount is the taxpayer's "adjusted gross income." IRC § 62(a). Continue in this Part B.

b. **No**—If no, then the taxpayer's "adjusted gross income" is the same amount as the taxpayer's "gross income." IRC § 62(a). Continue in this Part B.

3. **Personal Exemptions**—Does the taxpayer have a deduction for personal exemptions for the taxable year? The deduction for personal exemptions is equal to the number of exemptions available to the taxpayer times the exemption amount.

a. **Number of Exemptions**—Under IRC § 151(b), a taxpayer can claim one exemption equal to the exemption amount (listed in IRC § 151(d)(1) and adjusted annually for inflation) for himself or herself. (Spouses filing a joint return may claim two exemptions per Treas. Reg. § 1.-151–1(b).) In addition, a taxpayer may claim an exemption for his or her spouse, but only if the couple files separately and the taxpayer's spouse has no gross income and is not the "dependent" of another. Under IRC § 151(c), the taxpayer may claim one exemption for each "dependent." Generally, two types of people can be dependents: "qualifying relatives" and "qualifying children."

b. **Qualifying Relatives**—Qualifying relatives are those individuals who meet the following five requirements: (i) they have one of seven listed relationships to the taxpayer or are a member of the taxpayer's household; (ii) the taxpayer provides over half of the their total support; (iii) each of their gross incomes is less than the exemption amount; (iv) they are citizens or residents of the United States or residents of Canada or Mexico; and (v) they do not file a joint return with a spouse. IRC § 152(d).

c. **Qualifying Children**—Qualifying children are those individuals who meet a different five-part test: (i) they are a child (biological or adopted son, biological or adopted daughter, stepson, stepdaughter, eligible foster child or any descendent of such a child) or sibling (brother, sister, stepbrother, stepsister, half brother, half sister, or any descendant of such a sibling) of the taxpayer; (ii) they are under age 19 (or under age 24 and a full-time student); (iii) with some exceptions, they are citizens or residents of the United States or residents of Canada or Mexico who do not file joint returns with their spouses; (iv) their principal place of abode for more than half of the year is the same as the taxpayer's; and (v) they have not provided over half of their own support. IRC § 152(c).

d. **Exemption Amount**—The exemption amount is $2,000, but this amount is adjusted annually for inflation. Be sure to use the correct inflation-adjusted exemption amount for the year at issue. If the taxpayer's adjusted gross income exceeds the applicable "threshold amount" listed in IRC § 151(d)(3)(C), the exemption amount is reduced under the following formula:

---

1. Adjusted gross income: 1. _____
2. Threshold amount listed in IRC § 151(d)(3)(C): 2. _____
3. Subtract line 2 from line 1: 3. _____
4. Divide line 3 by $2,500 and enter result here, rounding up all fractions to nearest whole number: 4. _____
5. Multiply line 4 by 2 and enter result here (if this number exceeds 100, enter 100): 5. _____
6. Multiply line 5 by 0.333 and enter result here: 6. _____

*The amount in line 6 is the percentage by which the exemption amount is to be reduced. Note this applies only for 2008 and 2009. Under current law, no reduction to the exemption amount will occur as of 2010.*

---

e. **Yes**—If yes, the total deduction for personal exemptions (the exemption amount, as adjusted under IRC § 151(d)(3), multiplied by the number of exemptions to which the taxpayer is entitled) is subtracted from adjusted gross income. IRC § 63(a), (b). Continue in this Part B.

f. **No**—If no, then continue in this Part B.

4. **Regular Itemized Deductions**—Does the taxpayer have any "regular itemized deductions" for the taxable year?

    a. **Definition**—A regular itemized deduction is any of the 12 deduction items listed in IRC § 67(b).

    b. **Yes**—If yes, these regular itemized deductions will be added to the deductible portion of the taxpayer's "miscellaneous itemized deductions" for the taxable year in order to determine whether to itemize or claim the standard deduction. Continue in this Part B.

    c. **No**—If no, then continue in this Part B.

5. **Miscellaneous Itemized Deductions**—Does the taxpayer have any "miscellaneous itemized deductions" for the taxable year at issue?

    a. **Definition**—A miscellaneous itemized deduction is any deduction *except* those listed in IRC § 62(a) (the above-the-line deductions considered in B(2) above), the personal exemptions (considered in B(3) above) and those listed in IRC § 67(b) (the "regular itemized deductions" considered in B(4) above). IRC §§ 63(d); 67(b).

    b. **Yes**—If yes, then subtract two percent of the taxpayer's adjusted gross income from the aggregate amount of miscellaneous itemized deductions. The resulting amount (if greater than zero) is the deductible portion of the taxpayer's miscellaneous itemized deductions. IRC § 67(a). Continue in this Part B.

    c. **No**—If no, then continue in this Part B.

6. **Overall Limitation on Itemized Deductions**—Does the taxpayer's adjusted gross income exceed the "applicable amount" set forth in IRC § 68(b)? The applicable amount is $100,000 ($50,000 for a married person filing a separate return), but these figures are adjusted annually for inflation. Be sure you are using the correct dollar amount for the taxable year at issue.

    a. **Yes**—If yes, then the total amount of itemized deductions for the taxable year must be reduced. IRC § 68(a). Use the following formula to make the necessary reduction:

1. Total amount of deductions for medical expenses, investment interest, casualty or theft losses to property held for investment or personal use, and gambling losses:  1. _____

2. Total amount of all other regular itemized deductions from B(4) above:  2. _____

3. Deductible portion of miscellaneous itemized deductions from B(5) above:  3. _____

4. Add line 2 and line 3 and enter result here:  4. _____

5. Multiply line 4 by 80% and enter result here:  5. _____

6. Adjusted gross income:  6. _____

7. Multiply line 6 by 3% and enter result here:  7. _____

8. Enter the smaller of line 5 and line 7 here:  8. _____

9. Multiply line 8 by 0.333 and enter result here:  9. _____

10. Subtract line 9 from line 4 and enter result here:  10. _____

11. Add line 1 and line 10 and enter result here:  11. _____

*The amount in line 11 is the total amount of itemized deductions that the taxpayer may claim for taxable years beginning in 2008 or 2009. As of 2010, current law provides that IRC § 68(a) will not apply, and this entire B(6) may be disregarded.*

    b. **No**—If no, then continue in this Part A.

**7. Standard Deduction v. Itemized Deductions**—Does the taxpayer's standard deduction amount exceed the total amount of itemized deductions that the taxpayer may claim for the taxable year after any applicable adjustments in B(6) above?

    a. **Standard Deduction Amount**—The standard deduction amount is the sum of the "basic standard deduction" and the "additional standard deduction." The basic standard deduction is $6,000 for married couples filing jointly, $4,400 for heads of households, and $3,000 for everyone else, although these amounts are adjusted annually for inflation. IRC § 63(c)(2), (4). Accordingly, be sure you have the correct standard deduction amount for the taxable years at issue. The additional standard deduction amount is $600 for a taxpayer who is age 65 or over by the end of the taxable year, $600 for a taxpayer who is blind at the end of the taxable year, and $1,200 for a taxpayer is both age 65 or over and blind at the end of the taxable year. IRC § 63(c)(3), (f). These numbers increase to $750, $750, and $1,500, respectively, for unmarried taxpayers. IRC § 63(f)(3).

b.  **Yes**—If yes, then subtract both the standard deduction amount and the personal exemptions deduction from B(3) above from the taxpayer's adjusted gross income. The result is the taxpayer's "taxable income." To compute the taxpayer's pre-credit tax liability, plug the taxable income figure into the appropriate tax rate table in IRC § 1(a)–(d).

c.  **No**—If no, then subtract both the total amount of itemized deductions that the taxpayer may claim for the taxable year after any applicable adjustments in B(6) above and the personal exemptions deduction from B(3) above from the taxpayer's adjusted gross income. The result is the taxpayer's "taxable income." To compute the taxpayer's pre-credit tax liability, plug the taxable income figure into the appropriate tax rate table in IRC § 1(a)–(d).

## ILLUSTRATIVE PROBLEMS

The following problems are designed to show how the checklist helps in analyzing a question involving the computation of a taxpayer's taxable income.

## ■ PROBLEM 1.1 ■

T is unmarried and has one child, age 10, who resides with T throughout 2008 and for whom T provides all support. T and T's child are both United States citizens. T's gross income for 2008 is $100,000. T's only deduction items for 2008 are $3,000 in mortgage interest (deductible under IRC § 163), $2,000 in moving expenses (deductible under IRC § 217), and $200 for tax return preparation and advice (deductible under IRC § 212(3)). What is T's taxable income for 2008, ignoring any inflation adjustments provided under the Code?

## Analysis

T will file as a head of household for 2008. T is neither married nor a surviving spouse, but T's home is also a household for an unmarried "qualifying child" throughout the year. The child is a "qualifying child" because the child is a United States citizen under age 19 who shares the same principal place of abode with T throughout the year and who does not provide over half of his or her own support. IRC § 152(c). Accordingly, T qualifies as a head of household under IRC § 2(b). This means T can use the tax rate table in IRC § 1(b) for 2008.

The facts state that T's gross income is $100,000. T's adjusted gross income is the gross income less any of the deductions listed in IRC § 62(a). Here, the only above-the-line deduction is the $2,000 in moving expenses (IRC § 62(a)(15)), meaning T's adjusted gross income is $98,000.

T can claim a personal exemption for T and for T's child, again because the child is a "qualifying child." The exemption amount in IRC § 151(d)(1) is $2,000, and the problem indicates that inflation adjustments are not to be considered. Therefore, T's deduction for personal exemptions will be $4,000. The income-based phase-out to the exemption amount does not apply on these facts because T's adjusted gross income is beneath the threshold amount of $125,000. IRC § 151(d)(3)(C).

The $3,000 mortgage interest deduction is a "regular item-ized deduction," IRC § 67(b)(1), but the $200 tax return prepara-tion deduction is a "miscellaneous itemized deduction" (it is de-scribed in neither IRC § 62(a) nor IRC § 67(b)). This is significant because under IRC § 67(a), T's miscellaneous itemized deductions are deductible only to the extent they exceed two percent of T's adjusted gross income. As explained above, T's adjusted gross income is $98,000, and two percent of that amount is $1,960. Since the only miscellaneous itemized deduction is well below that figure, the entire deduction is disallowed. T's $3,000 mortgage interest deduction is unaffected by IRC § 67, and IRC § 68 does not apply either because T's adjusted gross income does not exceed the $100,000 "applicable amount."

T's total itemized deductions, therefore, is $3,000. The standard deduction amount, ignoring inflation adjustments, is $4,400 for a head of household. Accordingly, T should choose the standard deduction instead of itemizing. T's taxable income will, therefore, be $89,600: the $98,000 of adjusted gross income minus $4,000 in personal exemptions and the $4,400 standard deduction.

---

## ■ PROBLEM 1.2 ■

---

T and S, both United States citizens, are married and have no children. T's gross income for 2008 is $100,000 and S's gross income for 2008 is $30,000. They have only two deductions between them: $5,000 in mortgage interest (deductible under IRC § 163) and $2,500 in property taxes on their home (deductible under IRC § 164). What is the taxable income for T and S for 2008, ignoring any inflation adjustments provided under the Code?

### Analysis

T and S will likely choose to file a joint return for 2008. They are eligible to do so assuming they are married on the last day of 2008. By filing jointly, they will be able to let more income be taxed at the lower rates because the tax brackets in IRC § 1(a) are twice as large as those in IRC § 1(d). Accordingly, this analysis assumes T and S elect to file a joint return.

Their combined gross income, under the facts, is $130,000. Neither of their deduction items is an above-the-line deduction, so their adjusted gross income is also $130,000. They can claim personal exemptions (one for T and one for S) on their joint return per Treas. Reg. § 1.151–1(b). The exemption amount is $2,000. The phase-out in IRC § 151(d)(3) does not apply to T and S because their adjusted gross income is below the $150,000 threshold applicable to joint filers. Therefore, their deduction for personal exemptions will be the full $4,000 (unadjusted for inflation, as the problem states).

Both of their deductions are regular itemized deductions. See IRC § 67(b)(1) for the interest and IRC § 67(b)(2) for the taxes. Therefore, the two-percent haircut in IRC § 67(a) will not apply. However, because their adjusted gross income of $130,000 exceeds the $100,000 applicable amount in IRC § 68(b)(1), the IRC § 68 limitation applies. Under this rule, T and S must reduce their itemized deductions by lesser of 3% of $30,000 (the excess of their adjusted gross income over the IRC § 68(b)(1) applicable amount) or 80% of $7,500 (their total itemized deductions otherwise allowable). In this case, the lesser of the two products is $900. But for 2008, the reduction is limited to one-third of this amount, or $300. Thus, their itemized deductions for 2008 will be reduced from $7,500 to $7,200.

Because their itemized deductions ($7,200) exceeds the standard deduction available to T and S ($6,000 under IRC § 63(c)), they should choose to itemize their deductions. The taxable income shown on the joint return of T and S will be $118,800, which is their $130,000 adjusted gross income less the $4,000 in personal exemptions and the $7,200 in itemized deductions.

## POINTS TO REMEMBER

- Once you know a taxpayer's taxable income and filing status, you can use the applicable tax rate table in IRC § 1(a)–(d) to compute the taxpayer's tentative tax liability. The final tax liability is then determined by subtracting any credits to which the taxpayer may be entitled. The checklist does not discuss the credits to any extent because most federal income tax courses do not focus on them. The review text, however, provides a limited discussion of some of the more significant credits.

- Above-the-line deductions are the best kind of deductions because they are available to all taxpayers, no matter whether they itemize or claim the standard deduction.

- Regular itemized deductions are better than miscellaneous itemized deductions because the latter are subject to the "two-percent haircut" of IRC § 67(a).

- All itemized deductions and the deduction for personal exemptions are subject to income-based phase-outs. If the taxpayer's adjusted gross income is sufficiently high, a taxpayer in 2008 and 2009 could lose up to 1/3 of the deduction for personal exemptions and up to 26.67 percent of the total amount of itemized deductions.

- You can assume all taxpayers in all problems are United States citizens; if they are not, the facts of the problem will so indicate.

# CHAPTER 2

# Gross Income

As explained in Chapter 1, the starting point for the determination of taxable income is the computation of "gross income." This Chapter covers the Code's definition of the term as well as the administrative implementation and judicial interpretation of the concept.

## GROSS INCOME REVIEW

IRC § 61(a) defines gross income as "all income from whatever source derived." This definition is unhelpful, but it has significance. The Sixteenth Amendment to the United States Constitution gives Congress the power "to lay and collect taxes on *incomes, from whatever source derived,* without apportionment among the several states and without regard to any census or enumeration" (emphasis added). By defining gross income as "all income from whatever source derived," Congress clearly states its intention to exercise the full measure of the power granted to it by the Sixteenth Amendment.

The problem with the definition of gross income in IRC § 61(a) is that it does not define "income." Nor does any other Code provision, and the regulations are conspicuously silent on this point as well. Economists tend to define income as the sum of a taxpayer's consumption plus his or her change in wealth over a particular period. *See* Robert M. Haig, *The Concept of Income—Economic and Legal Aspects*, in THE FEDERAL INCOME TAX 1, 7 (Robert M. Haig, ed. 1921), reprinted in Am. Econ. Ass'n, READINGS IN THE ECONOMICS OF TAXATION 54 (Richard A. Musgrave & Carl Shoup, eds. 1959); Henry C. Simons, PERSONAL INCOME TAXATION 50 (1938). As a matter of economic theory, this is a helpful start, but it is not suitable as a real-life measure of income because of the practical complexities that would be involved in administering it. (Measuring fluctuations in the value of a taxpayer's assets each year, for instance, would add enormously to a taxpayer's compliance burden.)

Courts have therefore supplied more workable definitions. In *Eisner v. Macomber*, 252 U.S. 189 (1920), for example, the Court held that a shareholder did not have gross income from a "stock dividend" (a transaction under which a shareholder in a corporation receives additional shares of stock in the company based on the number of shares the shareholder already owns) because such a transaction did not represent a "gain derived from capital, from labor, or from both combined." The notion that income had to represent a gain from capital, labor, or both lasted for over three decades.

The contemporary test for income, however, comes from *Commissioner v. Glenshaw Glass Company*, 348 U.S. 426 (1955). In that case, the Supreme Court held that punitive damages received by the taxpayer were part of the taxpayer's gross income. The taxpayer argued that punitive damages did not represent "gain from capital or labor," as required by the *Macomber* case. But the Court held that the *Macomber* standard was not the only test for income. The taxpayer had gross income in this case because "[h]ere we have instances of undeniable accessions to wealth, clearly realized, and over which the taxpayers have complete dominion." This has become the standard by which one determines whether an item represents income that, therefore, must be included in gross income.

Congress has in some cases gone out of its way to make sure that certain items are included in gross income, even though most of these items would constitute income under the *Glenshaw Glass* test already. Many of these specific rules of income inclusion are found in IRC §§ 71–90, and the checklist in this Chapter considers several of the more significant rules.

Likewise, Congress, the courts, and the Internal Revenue Service have identified receipts that arguably may be income under the *Glenshaw Glass* test but that, for various policy reasons, should not be included as part of a taxpayer's gross income. The exclusion provisions of the Code are studied in Chapter 3 of this book, but the checklist in this Chapter considers several of the common law income exclusions.

Accordingly, one should always begin the gross income analysis by determining whether a particular item is income under the *Glenshaw Glass* case (Part A of the checklist) or whether the item is specifically included in gross income by statute, regulation or other law (Part B of the checklist). If so, one should then consider whether the item has been excluded from gross income, either by common law (Part C of the checklist) or by an express Code provision (Chapter 3). Finally, if an item represents gross income, it may be worth considering the proper taxpayer to report the income. Taxpayers are often tempted to assign income to related persons in lower tax brackets so as to keep the money in the family while paying less tax. Part D examines the basic rules for determining who has to report the income item at issue.

## GROSS INCOME CHECKLIST

This checklist will assist in determining whether a particular item is gross income to the taxpayer.

### A. GENERAL TEST FOR INCOME

The *Glenshaw Glass* Court held that an item is "income" if it represents an instance of "undeniable accessions to wealth, clearly realized, and over which the taxpayer [has] complete dominion."

This Part A of the checklist breaks down the test for income from *Glenshaw Glass* into three discrete components. Remember that all three components must be met in order to conclude that the taxpayer has income.

1. **Accession to Wealth**—Does the item add to the taxpayer's wealth?

    a. **Yes**—If yes, continue in this Part A.

    b. **No**—If no, the item is not income and therefore not part of the taxpayer's gross income.

2. **Clearly Realized**—Has the taxpayer realized the benefit of the addition to wealth?

    a. **Realization**—A taxpayer "realizes" the benefit of an addition to wealth if the taxpayer has received something severable for his or her use or benefit. The realization element here primarily serves to distinguish items of income from the mere appreciation in the value of pre-existing assets. So while a taxpayer's receipt of $1,000 cash as compensation for services is a clearly realized accession to wealth, the fact that a taxpayer's personal investment portfolio of stocks and securities grows by $1,000 is not income because there has been no "realization" of the growth in value. Note that realization does not require the receipt of cash or a sale of an asset. A taxpayer has realized an accession to wealth, for example, by accepting a vehicle as compensation for services performed by the taxpayer.

    b. **Yes**—If yes, continue in this Part A.

    c. **No**—If no, the item is not income and therefore not part of the taxpayer's gross income.

3. **Complete Dominion**—Does the taxpayer have full ownership and control over the addition to wealth?

    a. **Yes**—If yes, then the item is "income" and, unless an exception in Part C of this checklist applies, the item is includible in the taxpayer's gross income.

    b. **No**—If no, the item is not income and therefore not part of the taxpayer's gross income.

   c. **Illegal Receipts**—A taxpayer is considered to have complete dominion over an item even if the taxpayer received it illegally. *James v. United States*, 366 U.S. 213 (1961). The fact that the taxpayer does not have a claim of right to the item does not control its inclusion in gross income; it is sufficient that the taxpayer presently has the possession and control over the item.

## B. SPECIFIC ITEMS OF INCOME

Although most of the items in this Part B are income under the *Glenshaw Glass* test discussed in Part A of this checklist, it will help to mention the authorities that specifically include these items in a taxpayer's gross income.

   1. **Treasure Trove**—Did the taxpayer discover the item and take possession of it?

      a. **Yes**—If yes, the value of the "treasure trove" is included in gross income. Treas. Reg. § 1.61–14(a). In *Cesarini v. United States*, 296 F.Supp. 3 (N.D. Ohio 1969), for example, the court held that money found inside a piano purchased at an auction sale was gross income to the taxpayers in the year they discovered the money inside the piano.

      b. **No**—If no, continue in this Part B.

   2. **Barter Exchange**—Did the taxpayer participate in a barter exchange (swapping property or services in exchange for other property or services)?

      a. **Yes**—If yes, the fair market value of the property or services received in the exchange is included in gross income. *Revenue Ruling 79–24*. Fair market value is generally the price at which an item would trade between a willing buyer and a willing seller, neither acting under compulsion to buy or sell, and both having knowledge of all material facts. Treas. Reg. § 20.2031–1(b).

      b. **No**—If no, continue in this Part B.

   3. **Prizes and Awards**—Did the taxpayer receive the item as a prize or award?

a.   **Yes**—If yes, the item is included in the taxpayer's gross income unless either of the exceptions described in (c), (d) or (e) below applies. IRC § 74(a).

b.   **No**—If no, then continue in this Part B.

c.   **Exception for Certain Awards Donated to Charity**—Gross income does not include the value of any prize or award given primarily in recognition of religious, charitable, scientific, educational, artistic, literary, or civic achievement, provided: (i) the taxpayer was chosen without any action on the taxpayer's part to enter the contest; (ii) the taxpayer is not required to render substantial future services as a condition to receiving the award; and (iii) the prize is transferred to a governmental or charitable organization. IRC § 74(b).

d.   **Employee Achievement Awards**—A taxpayer need not include the value of an employee achievement award in gross income to the extent the employer's cost in providing the award does not exceed the amount the employer may deduct for furnishing the award. IRC § 74(c). An employee achievement award is any item of tangible personal property awarded to an employee by and employer in a meaningful presentation for length of service or safety achievement and not as disguised compensation. IRC § 274(j)(3)(A).

e.   **Qualified Scholarships**—A taxpayer need not include in gross income any prize or award that constitutes a "qualified scholarship" under IRC § 117. See Chapter 3 for more about the IRC § 117 exclusion.

4.   **Alimony**—Did the taxpayer receive alimony?

a.   **Alimony Defined**—For purposes of this rule, IRC § 71(b)(1) defines "alimony" as a payment in cash that meets these three requirements: (i) the payment is received by (or on behalf of) the taxpayer under a divorce or separation instrument (specially defined in IRC § 71(b)(2)) that does not designate the payment as non-alimony; (ii) if the taxpayer and the payor are legally separated, they are not members of the same household at the time of payment; and (iii) the payor has no liability to continue making payments or any substitute for payments after the taxpayer's death.

b. **Yes**—If yes, the alimony must be included in the taxpayer's gross income.

c. **No**—If no, then continue in this Part B.

d. **Child Support**—Payments for child support are not considered to be payments of alimony. IRC § 71(c)(1). Therefore, such amounts are not included in gross income. To the extent the amount of any cash payment to the taxpayer will be reduced upon the occurrence of a contingency related to a child, such amount will be considered child support and not alimony. IRC § 71(c)(2). If the taxpayer receives a payment for alimony and child support that is less than the amount required to be received under the divorce or separation instrument, the taxpayer is deemed to receive all of the required child support before receiving any portion of the alimony. IRC § 71(c)(3).

e. **Watch Out for Alimony Recapture**—If the amount of alimony received by the taxpayer in the first two years of alimony payments substantially exceeds the payments received in later years, the taxpayer receiving the payments may have a deduction under IRC § 71(f) for the "excess front-loading" of payments in the first two years. Here are formulas for determining whether this "alimony recapture" applies and, if so, the amount of the taxpayer's deduction:

---

STEP ONE: Compute the excess payments for the second calendar year in which alimony payments are made.
1. Alimony in the second post-
   separation year:                        1. _____
2. Alimony in third post-separation
   year:                                  2. _____
3. Add $15,000 to line 2:                 3. _____
4. Subtract line 3 from line 1:           4. _____

---

*The amount in line 4 is the excess payment for the second post-separation year; the taxpayer receiving the alimony can deduct this amount in the third post-separation year.*

<u>STEP TWO</u>: Compute the excess payments for the first calendar year in which alimony payments are made.

  5. Alimony in the first post-separation
      year:                                 5. _____
  6. Enter the amount in line 1 here:     6. _____
  7. Enter the amount in line 4 here:     7. _____
  8. Subtract line 7 from line 6:        8. _____
  9. Enter the amount in line 2 here:     9. _____
10. Enter the average of the amounts in
     lines 8 and 9:                       10. _____
11. Add \$15,000 to line 10:         11. _____
12. Subtract line 11 from line 5:      12. _____

*The amount in line 12 is the excess payment for the first post-separation year; the taxpayer receiving the alimony can deduct this amount in the third post-separation year.*

---

5. **Third Party Satisfaction of Taxpayer's Liability**—Did a third party pay or otherwise satisfy an obligation of the taxpayer?

   a. **Yes**—If yes, then the taxpayer has gross income unless a specific exclusion provision applies. See Chapter 3. To determine the amount included in gross income, pretend the third party paid the taxpayer directly and that the taxpayer then used that payment to satisfy the liability. Thus, for example, if the taxpayer's employer pays the taxpayer's federal income tax liability directly to the Internal Revenue Service, the taxpayer has gross income equal to the amount paid to the Service by the employer. *Old Colony Trust Company v. Commissioner*, 279 U.S. 716 (1929).

   b. **No**—If no, then continue in this Part B.

6. **Discharge of Indebtedness**—Was a debt of the taxpayer discharged or canceled to any extent?

   a. **Yes**—If yes, the taxpayer has gross income equal to the amount discharged unless a specific exclusion provision applies. IRC § 61(a)(12); *United States v. Kirby Lumber Company*, 284 U.S. 1 (1931). See Chapter 3.

b. **No**—If no, then continue in this Part B.

7. **Annuities**—Did the taxpayer receive a payment under an annuity, endowment, or life insurance contract?

    a. **Yes**—If yes, then the amount of the payment is included in gross income except for that portion of the payment equal to the exclusion ratio. IRC § 72(a). Go to part (c) below to determine the exclusion ratio.

    b. **No**—If no, then continue in this Part B.

    c. **Exclusion Ratio**—The exclusion ratio is the ratio determined by dividing the "investment in the contract" by the "expected return under the contract." IRC § 72(b)(1). The investment in the contract is generally equal to the total amount of premiums and other consideration paid for the contract less any amounts received under the contract before the annuity starting date. IRC § 72(c)(1). The expected return under the contract is generally equal to the aggregate amounts receivable under the contract in the form of an annuity. IRC § 72(c)(3). If the total amount receivable under the contract depends on the life expectancy of one or more individuals, the expected return is determined by multiplying the recipient's life expectancy by the annual amount receivable under the contract. See Treas. Reg. § 1.72–9, Table V for a table of life expectancy figures based on the age of the recipient.

    d. **Limitation on the Exclusion Ratio**—Once the taxpayer has recovered his or her entire investment in the contract through application of the exclusion ratio in prior years, all subsequent annuity payments under the same contract are fully includible in gross income. IRC § 72(b)(2). If the taxpayer dies before all of the investment in the contract has been recovered, the taxpayer's final return may claim a deduction for that portion of the investment in the contract which was not recovered. IRC § 72(b)(3)(A).

8. **Compensation for Services**—Did the taxpayer receive the item as compensation for services?

a. **Yes**—If yes, then the item must be included in gross income. IRC § 61(a)(1). Note that any form of compensation is subject to this rule, including fees, wages, commissions, fringe benefits, and tips. Treas. Reg. § 1.61–2(a)(1).

b. **No**—If no, then continue in this Part B.

c. **Property Transferred in Connection with Performance of Services**—Under IRC § 83(a), a taxpayer has gross income if property is transferred to the taxpayer or to a third party in connection with services performed by the taxpayer if either of the following conditions is met:

   i. **No Substantial Future Services Required**—The recipient's rights to the property are not conditioned upon the performance of substantial future services by anyone. IRC § 83(c)(1).

   ii. **Property is Transferable**—The rights of any transferee are not conditioned on the future performance of substantial services by anyone. IRC § 83(c)(2).

If neither of these conditions exist, IRC § 83(a) does not apply. Nonetheless, the taxpayer may elect to include the value of the property received (less any amount paid for the property) in the year of receipt by making an election under IRC § 83(b). Such an election is advisable if the taxpayer anticipates that the value of the property will surge between the year of receipt and the year in which one of the two conditions above is met.

If a taxpayer has gross income under IRC § 83(a), the amount included is equal to the fair market value of the property received less any amount paid for the property. Importantly, when IRC § 83(a) applies, the taxpayer has gross income in the year of receipt.

d. **Payments to Third Party as Compensation**—Remember that payments by a third party on behalf of the taxpayer for services performed by the taxpayer are treated as compensation paid to the taxpayer. *Old Colony Trust Company v. Commissioner*, 279 U.S. 716 (1929).

9.  **Advance Payments**—Has the taxpayer received the item as an advance payment for goods or services to be rendered in the future?

    a.  **Yes**—If yes, the taxpayer must include the amount of the advance payment in gross income, generally in the year of receipt. *Commissioner v. Indianapolis Power & Light Company*, 493 U.S. 203 (1990). See Chapter 10 for more on this issue.

    b.  **No**—If no, then the item is not required to be included in gross income.

C.  ITEMS NOT INCOME

1.  **Imputed Income**—Does the accession to wealth stem from the taxpayer's own efforts or from the use of the taxpayer's own property?

    a.  **Yes**—If yes, the accession to wealth represents "imputed income" and will not be included in gross income. While economic theory would conclude that imputed income is like any other form of gross income (in that it is either consumed or enhances the taxpayer's net worth), Congress and the Internal Revenue Service recognize the insurmountable practical obstacles inherent in enforcing the taxation of imputed income. As a result, benefits from growing one's own garden vegetables, occupying one's own home on a rent-free basis, or (in the case of a lawyer, at least) writing one's own will are not subject to taxation.

    b.  **No**—If no, then continue in this Part C.

2.  **Bargain Purchase**—Did the taxpayer benefit from purchasing an interest in property at a price below its fair market value?

    a.  **Yes**—If yes, the taxpayer will not be required to include the amount of the discount in gross income. It is well accepted that a taxpayer need not include the benefit of a bargain purchase in gross income. If the bargain purchase was income, there would be less of an incentive for taxpayers to seek bargains and this would make market transactions less efficient. Thus, for example, a taxpayer does not have gross income from purchasing a painting worth $1,000 at a garage sale for $20. Instead, the taxpayer will have a basis in the painting of $20; when the taxpayer later sells the painting, the gain may be subject to tax. See Chapter 6.

b. **No**—If no, then continue in this Part C.

3. **Unrealized Appreciation**—Does the accession to wealth represent an increase in the value of a property interest that the taxpayer did not sell or otherwise dispose of during the taxable year?

   a. **Yes**—If yes, there is no gross income yet. As explained in Part A of this checklist, taxpayers do not have income from the mere increase in the value of property owned during the year. The appreciation will not be taxed until there is a "realization event" with respect to the property (i.e., a sale or other disposition of part or all of the property). Thus, for example, a taxpayer does not have gross income if stocks purchased at the beginning of the year for $1,000 have a value of $1,800 at the end of the year.

   b. **No**—If no, then continue in this Part C.

4. **Free Samples**—Did the taxpayer receive the item as a free sample or through some promotional activity by the provider?

   a. **Yes**—If yes, then the taxpayer does not have gross income. Although there is no firm authority, it is well accepted that a taxpayer does not have gross income from "free samples" provided by a manufacturer, distributor, or retailer because the primary benefit of the sample inures to the provider. When a company provides a free sample of its product to a taxpayer, it hopes that the taxpayer will like the product enough to purchase additional quantities of the product in the future. The incremental accession to the taxpayer's wealth is far outweighed by the promotional benefit to the provider.

   b. **No**—If no, then continue in this Part C.

5. **Loans**—Did the taxpayer borrow the amount received under a consensual arrangement under which the taxpayer has an obligation to repay the lender?

a. **Yes**—If yes, the transaction is a loan and the taxpayer does not have gross income from the transaction. A borrower does not have an "accession to wealth" from the receipt of loan proceeds because there is an offsetting liability to repay the amount borrowed.

b. **No**—If no, then continue in this Part C.

6. **Deposits**—Is the taxpayer under an obligation to repay the amount received upon the occurrence of a contingency that is outside the taxpayer's control?

a. **Yes**—If yes, the taxpayer has received a deposit and there is no inclusion in gross income until such time as the contingency lapses and the taxpayer is entitled to keep the amount received. *Commissioner v. Indianapolis Power & Light Company*, 493 U.S. 203 (1990). Thus, for example, a damage deposit received by a landlord from a new tenant is not gross income to the landlord at the time of receipt because the tenant retains the power to reclaim the deposit upon surrendering an undamaged and clean premises to the landlord upon termination of the lease. If the premises is damaged to the point that the lease agreement permits the landlord to retain the damage deposit, the landlord then has gross income.

b. **No**—If no, then the item is not excepted out from the definition of income. If you concluded under Part A or Part B of this checklist that the item is income, then the item must be included in the taxpayer's gross income.

**D. ATTRIBUTING INCOME TO THE PROPER TAXPAYER**

Having determined that an item is gross income unless a specific exclusion provision applies (see Chapter 3), it is often important to consider to whom the income should be taxed. Most of the time, this will be obvious. But where it appears that the person whose efforts or assets created the income attempts to assign that income to another person (often a related person in a lower tax bracket), the issues in this Part D are triggered.

1. **Income from Services**—Does the income represent compensation for services, or is the income item attributable to services performed by a person?

a. **Yes**—If yes, then the income is generally taxed to the person who performed the services, not necessarily the person who receives the income. *Lucas v. Earl*, 281 U.S. 111 (1929).

   i. **Earner Has No Rights to Income**—If the person performing the services has no right to receive the income, the income cannot be taxed to that person even though he or she performed the services that generated the income. For example, in *Teschner v. Commissioner*, 38 T.C. 1003 (1962), a father entered a contest that would award an education annuity to an individual who was under a stipulated age. The father named his daughter as the beneficiary on the contest entry form. The taxpayer's entry form was selected as the winner, and the prize was awarded to the daughter. The Tax Court held that the daughter should be taxed on the value of the prize and not the father, for although he performed the services necessary to generate the income, he was never entitled to have the income and had no claim to it under the contest rules.

   ii. **Direction and Control**—If the service provider has the final say as to who receives the income, the service provider will be the one who is taxed. If the service provider disclaims all rights to the income and such income passes to person related to the service provider, the service provider likely would not be taxed on the income because the service provider had no control over the recipient of the income. See *Commissioner v. Giannini*, 129 F.2d 638 (9th Cir. 1942). If, however, the service provider knows that a disclaimer will cause the income to be paid to the related person, the Internal Revenue Service might succeed in claiming that the service provider indirectly controlled the payment of the income and therefore should still be taxed on it.

b. **No**—If no, then continue in this Part D.

2. **Income from Property**—Is the income attributable to property? Examples include rents from an apartment complex, royalties on a copyright, interest on a promissory note, damages on a cause of action, and dividends on stock.

    a. **Yes**—If yes, the income will generally be taxed to the person who owns the property. *Helvering v. Horst*, 311 U.S. 112 (1940). The income is said to be the "fruit" of the property "tree," and the fruit must be taxed to the person who owns the tree when the fruit is realized.

        i. **Transfer the Property to Assign the Income**—Accordingly, if a taxpayer wants to assign income from property to another person, the taxpayer must generally assign the entire property to the desired person. In *Horst*, a father attempted to assign interest income from a coupon bond to his son by giving the interest coupons to the son. Because the father retained the bond, however, the Court held that the father was the person to be taxed on the interest income and not the son. A different result may have occurred if the father had transferred the entire bond to the son.

        ii. **Exception for Transfers of Property with Vested Income**—If the taxpayer assigns property that already has vested income associated with it (a tree with ripe fruit?), the taxpayer may still be the person taxed on such vested income. In *Salvatore v. Commissioner*, T.C. Memo. 1970–30, for example, the taxpayer conveyed a one-half interest in a gas station to her children after accepting an offer from Texaco to sell the entire property. The court held that the entire gain from the sale to Texaco should be taxed to the taxpayer because her conveyance to the children was merely a single step in an overall plan to sell the entire property to Texaco. It was no different, said the court, than if the taxpayer sold the entire property to Texaco herself and then gave half of the cash to her children.

        iii. **Exception to Exception**—Even if property has vested income associated with it, a taxpayer can effectively shift such income by *selling* the property to the transferee instead of gifting it. In *Estate of Stranahan v.*

*Commissioner*, 472 F.2d 867 (6th Cir. 1973), for instance, the taxpayer wanted to recognize some income to offset a substantial interest expense deduction for the year at issue. So the taxpayer sold his rights to $123,000 in future dividends on stock to his son for $115,000 (the present value of the $123,000 that would be paid over time). The Tax Court held that the dividends ultimately paid to the son should be taxed to the son because the prior sale of the property interest (the right to dividends) was not a gratuitous transfer to any extent.

b. **No**—If no, then you have concluded that the income is attributable neither to services nor to property. In such a case, the income will be taxed to the person who receives it. Thus, for example, punitive damages (which, recall, represents neither gain from capital nor from labor) are taxed to the party who receives them.

## ILLUSTRATIVE PROBLEMS

Here are two problems designed to show how the checklist helps in analyzing a question involving gross income.

---

### ■ PROBLEM 2.1 ■

---

T, the parent of Child, obtained a divorce three years ago. Under the divorce decree, T is entitled to $1,000 each month from T's ex-spouse until T dies or remarries. Once Child reaches age 18, the monthly payments will drop to $700. In the most recent taxable year, T received $12,000 from the ex-spouse.

In June of that same year, T received notice that T's entry at a local contest had been selected the winner by a random draw. T asked that the $500 prize be paid directly to Child, and the contest sponsor heeded this wish.

In January of that same year, T borrowed $10,000 from Bank. T agreed to repay the loan by the end of the year. Near the end of the year, T's employment was terminated, and T (though solvent) was unable to repay Bank on time. Bank was frustrated by this turn of events, but after becoming convinced that T could not repay the loan and that T had no assets of interest or use to Bank, Bank forgave the loan at the end of the year.

What are the federal income tax consequences of these events to T?

## Analysis

The payments T receives from the ex-spouse qualify as "alimony" under IRC § 71(b) because they were payments in cash received by T under a divorce or separation instrument that apparently did not designate the payment as non-alimony, T and the ex-spouse were apparently not members of the same household at any time during the year, and the ex-spouse had no liability to continue making payments or any substitute for payments after the T's death. However, it appears that $300 of each $1,000 monthly payment represents disguised child support, for the amount of the monthly payments will drop by $300 once Child reaches age 18. Accordingly, only $700 of each payment ($8,400 total for the year) will be treated as alimony that T must include in gross income under IRC § 71(a). T is not required to include the disguised child support in gross income.

The $500 prize T won through the contest is gross income. IRC § 74 states that prizes and awards are included in gross income. The exception in IRC § 74(b) does not apply because T entered the contest and the prize was paid to Child and not a charitable organization. Furthermore, there is nothing to suggest that the prize was in recognition of religious, charitable, scientific, educational, artistic, literary, or civic achievement.

The $500 prize will be included in T's gross income and will not be taxed to Child, even though Child received the prize and T never touched it. Generally, income from services is taxed to the person who performed the services. T was the person whose efforts (submitting the entry) generated the income, so T will be the person taxed on the value of the prize.

The Bank loan is not gross income at the time of the loan in January because at that time the transaction was a consensual arrangement under which T had an obligation to repay Bank. There are no facts to suggest T knew the loan would not be repaid or that Bank did not expect repayment, so there was no gross income from the loan at its inception in January.

Bank's forgiveness of the loan in December, however, results in gross income. IRC § 61(a)(12) provides that a taxpayer has gross income from the discharge of indebtedness. There are no facts to indicate that any exclusion could apply here, so T will have to include the $10,000 borrowed in gross income even though T may lack the funds to pay the tax associated with this inclusion.

---

## ■ PROBLEM 2.2 ■

---

T is a lawyer. T contracts with C, an artist, to provide counsel for C's proposed acquisition of an art studio. T will provide legal advice and will assist in the negotiation and drafting of the documents effecting the acquisition. In exchange, C will transfer to T three works of art created by C.

The acquisition goes smoothly, and the deal is completed. Afterward, C contacts T to arrange for delivery of the three works of art. T asks C to deliver one of the pieces to E, one of T's employees. T wanted to reward E with a bonus for E's assistance during the acquisition transaction, and T knew E would treasure one of C's works. Accordingly, C delivered one piece to E and two pieces to T. The value of each piece was $10,000.

What are the federal income tax consequences of these events to T, C, and E?

### Analysis

---

T has gross income from the barter exchange with C. Barter exchanges are taxable, *Revenue Ruling 79–24*, so T will have gross income equal to the value of the pieces T receives. In this regard, C's transfer of one piece to E will be treated for tax purposes as though C transferred the piece to T. Under *Old Colony Trust Company v. Commissioner*, a third party's satisfaction of the taxpayer's legal obligation is treated as a transfer to the taxpayer. Here, C's transfer to E allows T to pay extra compensation to E. It is the same as if C had delivered all three pieces to T and then T gave one of them to E as compensation. Accordingly, T has gross income of $30,000 on these facts (the fair market value of the three works of art). T will also have a deduction for the bonus compensation paid to E. (See Chapter 4.)

C also has gross income from the barter exchange. Assuming the parties acted at arm's-length, C received $30,000 worth of legal services. C might be able to prove that T's services were worth less than this amount, but we have no facts to sustain such an assertion here. Consequently, C will have gross income of $30,000. C will not be able to claim a deduction for the value of the works transferred to T and E because these costs are part of the cost to acquire the studio. The cost will therefore be capitalized and added to the basis of the acquired asset(s). (See Chapter 4.)

E will have gross income of $10,000, the value of the work E receives as bonus compensation. Compensation for services can come in the form of property, so E has gross income here under IRC § 61(a)(1). By including $10,000 in gross income, E will take a basis of $10,000 in the work of art. (See Chapter 6.)

## POINTS TO REMEMBER

- The *Glenshaw Glass* test for income requires an accession to wealth that is clearly realized and over which the taxpayer has complete dominion.

- If an item is "income" under *Glenshaw Glass*, it is part of gross income unless the item is specifically excluded by another Code provision.

- A taxpayer need not receive an item directly to have income; for instance, a taxpayer has income if a third party satisfies an obligation of the taxpayer.

- Income from services is generally taxed to the person who performed the services, and income from property is generally taxed to the person who owns the property.

# CHAPTER 3

# Exclusions from Gross Income

This Chapter concerns several of the exclusion provisions that are frequently discussed in basic federal income tax courses. Some exclusions are discussed in other Chapters because they relate more to the concepts at issue there. See Chapter 7 for the IRC § 121 exclusion related to gain from the sale of a residence and see Chapter 10 for the IRC § 111 exclusion related to the recovery of an item previously deducted.

## EXCLUSIONS FROM GROSS INCOME REVIEW

Recall that under *Glenshaw Glass*, the general test is whether a taxpayer has an *accession to wealth, clearly realized, and over which the taxpayer has complete dominion and control*. Although lots of receipts fall within this very broad definition, Congress has specifically identified receipts that should not be subject to federal income tax even if they meet the *Glenshaw Glass* test for inclusion. Most of the exclusion provisions are grouped together in the Code (IRC §§ 101–140), so it is fairly easy to determine whether an exclusion is available for any given item of income.

*Life Insurance.* IRC § 101(a)(1) excludes amounts received under a life insurance contract if such amounts are paid because of the death of the insured. There are two general exceptions to this exclusion. The first is the "transfer-for value rule" set forth in IRC § 101(a)(2). If the owner-beneficiary of a policy acquired it for "valuable consideration," the exclusion is limited to the sum of the consideration paid and any amounts (including premiums) paid after the transfer by the owner-beneficiary. The other exception applies to installment payments of death benefits. Under IRC § 101(d), to the extent any such installment payment represents interest, such portion must be included in gross income.

*Gifts and Bequests.* The exclusion in IRC § 102(a) for gifts and bequests is one of the centerpieces of the Internal Revenue Code. The exclusion has been justified on the grounds of administrative convenience, that it softens the burden imposed on transferors by federal estate and gift taxes, and that it encourages generosity and wealth transfers. None of these justifications has been universally embraced, however. In any case, IRC § 102(a) ensures that donees do not have to include the value of gifted or inherited property in gross income. Gifts of income, however, are not eligible for the exclusion, as IRC § 102(b) makes clear. In addition, IRC § 102(c) declares that an employee can never receive a "gift" from an employer. As a result, any property transferred to an employee will likely be treated as compensation income unless a different exclusion provision applies.

*Interest on State and Local Bonds.* The exclusion in IRC § 103 for interest received on state and local bonds effectively represents a federal subsidy to state and local governments. Because the interest is tax-free, state and local governments can sell their bonds at a lower interest rate, making the bonds less expensive for the governmental units to issue. There are several limitations to the exclusion, most attributable to perceived abuses by local governments. For example, a city might issue bonds to finance the development of private businesses, an activity that may be of marginal public benefit. The interest on these "private activity bonds" generally is ineligible for the exclusion.

*Damages Received on Account of Physical Injury or Physical Sickness.* IRC § 104(a)(2) excludes from gross income most damages received "on account of personal physical injuries or physical sickness." Punitive damages are not excludable under this rule. The exclusion used to apply to damages received for "personal injury or sickness," but Congress added the word "physical" (twice, no less) in 1996 after courts interpreted the term "personal injury" to authorize exclusion for any tort recovery. Now it is clear that the taxpayer must receive damages on account of a physical injury or physical sickness to qualify for the exclusion. Congress also added language to IRC § 104(a) to make it clear that emotional distress, by itself, was not a physical injury or physical sickness. Accordingly, taxpayers suing only for emotional distress will recover taxable damages, while taxpayers suing for physical injuries will recover tax-free damages, even if some of those damages compensate for emotional distress.

*Certain Income from Discharge of Indebtedness.* The Supreme Court held that when a corporation was able to repurchase its own bonds for an amount less than it borrowed from investors, the corporation had gross income equal to the difference. Congress codified that result in IRC § 61(a)(12), which provides that gross income includes income from the discharge of indebtedness. The premise is simple: if a taxpayer borrows money from a lender, there is no gross income because the taxpayer's additional wealth is offset by the contemporaneous obligation to repay that amount to the lender in the future. If the lender cancels, forgives, or discharges the repayment obligation, then, the rationale for excluding the amount received by the taxpayer has likewise disappeared. Consequently, the amount of the discharged debt is included in gross income. Where the taxpayer is insolvent or bankrupt, however, there is little sense in requiring the taxpayer to include the amount of canceled debt in gross income because there is hardly an accession to the taxpayer's wealth in these instances. IRC § 108(a) lists five events (bankruptcy, insolvency, and three others) where the canceled debt is excluded from gross income. This exclusion comes at a cost, however; generally, the amount excluded must be applied to reduce the taxpayer's "tax attributes," features like loss and credit carryovers and the basis in property that would normally be of benefit to the taxpayer in later years. Thus, one should view IRC § 108(a) not as a permanent exclusion of income but instead as a deferral of income until a later date.

*Lessee Improvements.* IRC § 109 was expressly enacted to overrule the Supreme Court's holding that a landlord had gross income upon reclaiming possession of real property from a tenant where the tenant had made permanent improvements to the property. IRC § 109 provides that the value of the improvements is excluded from gross income, but IRC § 1019 then provides that the taxpayer's basis in the property cannot be adjusted to reflect the value of such improvements. This means that while the landlord will not have gross income upon repossession of the property, the landlord very likely will have gross income in the form of additional gain when the taxpayer later sells the property.

*Qualified Scholarships.* IRC § 117 contains a limited exclusion for certain scholarship and fellowship grants. Recall that prizes and awards are generally included in gross income under IRC § 74(a) (see Chapter 2), so this exclusion provision ensures that two types of scholarships are not subject to tax. The first is a "qualified scholarship," generally defined as a payment used for tuition and related expenses (but not room and board) by a degree candidate at a nonprofit educational institution. The second is a "qualified tuition reduction" extended to employees of certain education organizations generally for the undergraduate education of the employee, the employee's spouse, or the employee's children.

*Meals and Lodging on Employer's Premises.* Compensation can come in many forms, and free meals and lodging provided by an employer to an employee (or the employee's spouse or dependents) would normally qualify as compensation to the employee. But IRC § 119 generally provides that if the meals and lodging are furnished for the convenience of the employer and on the employer's business premises, the employee can exclude the value of these benefits from gross income. The thinking here is that the primary benefit of the meal or lodging inures to the employer and not the employee.

*Certain Fringe Benefits.* There are other forms of compensation that arguably benefit the employer more than the employee or which come at little or no cost to the employer. Congress has identified a number of other "fringe benefits" that can be excluded from an employee's gross income and crammed all of them into IRC § 132. IRC § 132 is a veritable cornucopia of exclusions, including no-additional-cost services, qualified employee discounts, working condition fringes, de minimis fringes, qualified moving expense reimbursements, and much more. It is important to note that all of these excludable benefits apply only to employees and not to self-employed individuals or independent contractors.

## EXCLUSIONS FROM GROSS INCOME CHECKLIST

This checklist will assist in determining whether an item otherwise includible in gross income may be excluded under a specific Code provision. It considers in detail nine of the more significant statutory exclusions set forth in IRC §§ 101–140.

**A. LIFE INSURANCE (IRC § 101)**

Use this Part A of the checklist if the taxpayer receives an amount under a life insurance contract.

    **1. Payable by Reason of Insured's Death**—Was the amount received because of the death of the insured?

        a.  **Yes**—If yes, continue in this Part A.

        b.  **No**—If no, the IRC § 101(a)(1) exclusion does not apply. Unless some other exclusion provision applies, the taxpayer likely has gross income.

    **2. Installment Payments After Death**—Is the amount received by the taxpayer one of several installments received or to be received under the life insurance contract?

        a.  **Yes**—If yes, then the amount received by the taxpayer is excluded from gross income but only to the extent the amount does not represent interest. IRC §§ 101(a)(1); 101(d). To determine whether any portion of an installment payment represents interest, take the lump sum death benefit that would have been payable under the contract if installment payments were not made and divide that number by the total number of installment payments to be made. The result is the excludable portion of the payment; any balance represents interest that must be included in gross income.

b. **No**—If no, continue in this Part A.

3. **No Transfer for Value**—Was the life insurance policy acquired by the taxpayer in exchange for "valuable consideration?"

a. **Yes**—If yes, then unless the "transfer for value" rule does not apply, the amount excluded from gross income is limited to the sum of the value of such consideration plus subsequent premiums paid by the taxpayer. IRC § 101(a)(2). The "transfer for value" rule does not apply to transfers where the taxpayer's basis in the policy is determined in whole or in part with reference to the transferor's basis in the policy (like certain part-gift, part-sale transactions, for example). It also does not apply where the taxpayer is the insured, a partner of the insured in a partnership activity, a partnership in which the insured is a partner, or a corporation in which the insured is a shareholder or officer. IRC § 101(a)(2)(A)–(B).

b. **No**—If no, then the entire amount of the death benefit is excluded from the taxpayer's gross income. IRC § 101(a)(1).

### B. GIFTS AND BEQUESTS (IRC § 102)

Use this Part B if the taxpayer acquires property by gift, bequest, devise, or inheritance.

1. **Employee Gifts**—Did the taxpayer receive (or benefit from) property transferred by (or on behalf of) the taxpayer's employer?

a. **Yes**—If yes, then the value of the property cannot qualify as a gift and will not be excluded from gross income under IRC § 102(a). IRC § 102(c)(1). The value of the property likely represents compensation that will be included in the taxpayer's gross income unless another exclusion provision applies. Consider, for example, whether the property represents a non-taxable "employee achievement award" (see Chapter 2) or a "de-minimis fringe benefit" (see Part I of this checklist). IRC § 102(c)(2).

b. **No**—If no, continue in this Part B.

2. **Gifts of Income**—Did the taxpayer receive only an income interest in property?

a. **Yes**—If yes, then the taxpayer must include the amounts received under this income interest in the year of receipt. Such amounts cannot be excluded as gifts because the gift exclusion does not apply to gifts of income. IRC § 102(b)(2).

b. **No**—If no, continue in this Part B.

3. **Detached and Disinterested Generosity**—Did the transferor exhibit "detached and disinterested generosity" in making the transfer to the taxpayer "out of affection, respect, admiration, charity or like impulses?"

a. **Yes**—If yes, then the taxpayer received the property as a gift or bequest. *Commissioner v. Duberstein,* 363 U.S. 278 (1960). Accordingly, the value of the property is excluded from gross income. IRC § 102(a). Note that the taxpayer's basis in the acquired property depends upon whether the taxpayer receives a gift from living person or a decedent. See the discussion of basis in Chapter 6. Also, note that any subsequent income earned on the gifted property is not excluded from gross income under IRC § 102(a). IRC § 102(b)(1).

b. **No**—If no, then the value of the property is not excluded under IRC § 102(a). If the motive of the transferor was to compensate the taxpayer for services rendered, the taxpayer has received compensation income. IRC § 61(a)(1). Otherwise, unless another exclusion provision applies, the taxpayer likely has to include the value of the property in gross income.

## C. INTEREST ON BONDS, STATE AND LOCAL BONDS (IRC § 103)

The exclusion for interest on state and local bonds in IRC § 103 is very complex; the details are very likely to be beyond the scope of an introductory course on federal income tax. When the exclusion comes up in most courses, if at all, professors often prefer to focus on the policy aspects of the federal government offering an indirect subsidy to state and local governments. Accordingly, this Part C of the checklist treads very lightly into the mechanics of the exclusion. Use this Part C when a taxpayer receives interest on a bond issued by a state or local government.

1.  **Arbitrage Bonds**—Has the state or local government placed the proceeds from the bond financing in investments that earn a rate of return in excess of interest payable on the bond?

    a.  **Yes**—If yes, the bond is considered an "arbitrage bond." IRC § 148(a). The interest received by the taxpayer on an arbitrage bond is not excluded from gross income. IRC § 103(b)(2).

    b.  **No**—If no, then continue in this Part C.

2.  **Private Activity Bonds**—Did the state or local government issue the bond to finance the development of private businesses or other activities that are only somewhat public in nature (like a stadium for a private professional sports franchise or the rehabilitation of a business district that has become dilapidated)?

    a.  **Yes**—If yes, the interest received by the taxpayer will be included in gross income unless the bond is a "qualified" private activity bond. IRC § 103(b)(1). As you might expect, there are literally dozens of examples of "qualified" private activity bonds. Some of these include bonds where at least 95 percent of the proceeds are to be used to provide airports, mass commuting facilities, and certain residential rental properties. IRC §§ 141–147 are devoted to identifying and limiting the types of bonds that are eligible to be "qualified" private activity bonds. Consult these provisions if you face the specific task of determining whether a bond is a qualified private activity bond.

    b.  **No**—If no, then it means the state or local government issued the bond to finance general governmental operations like roads, governmental buildings, schools, and utilities. Accordingly, the interest received by the taxpayer may be excluded from gross income. IRC § 103(a).

### D. DAMAGES RECEIVED ON ACCOUNT OF PHYSICAL INJURY OR SICKNESS (IRC § 104(a)(2))

Use this Part D if the taxpayer receives damages, no matter whether through a lawsuit or a settlement agreement, and no matter whether as a lump sum or in installment payments.

1. **Punitive Damages**—Does the taxpayer receive punitive damages?

    a. **Yes**—If yes, the amount of punitive damages received is included in gross income. *Commissioner v. Glenshaw Glass Company*, 348 U.S. 426 (1955). This is true even if the punitive damages are received on account of the taxpayer's physical injury or physical sickness. IRC § 104(a)(2), first parenthetical.

    b. **No**—If no, then continue in this Part D.

2. **Compensation for Medical Care Expenses**—Does the taxpayer receive reimbursement for medical expenses that were deducted in a prior taxable year?

    a. **Yes**—If yes, the amount of such reimbursement is included in gross income. This is consistent with the inclusionary arm of the common law tax benefit rule, which provides that the recovery of an item previously deducted must be included in the taxpayer's gross income. It is also required by the Code. IRC § 104(a), prologue.

    b. **No**—If no, then continue in this Part D.

3. **Emotional Distress Alone**—Does the taxpayer receive compensatory damages for emotional distress but not for physical injury or physical sickness?

    a. **Yes**—If yes, the amount of such compensatory damages received is included in gross income except to the extent of any medical expenses not previously deducted and attributable to emotional distress. IRC § 104(a), flush language. This is because emotional distress, by itself, cannot qualify as a physical injury or physical sickness even though there may be physical manifestations of the emotional distress.

    b. **No**—If no, then continue in this Part D.

4. **Physical Injury or Physical Sickness**—Did the taxpayer receive the damages on account of personal physical injury or physical sickness?

   a. **Yes**—If yes, the amount of such damages is excluded from gross income. IRC § 104(a)(2). This includes all forms of damages other than punitive damages disqualified above, even lost wages. The exclusion can also apply to that portion of the damages provided for attorney fees. If the damages are fully excludable, any award for attorney fees is likewise excluded. If a portion of the total damages is includible in gross income, however (because the award consists of punitive damages or reimbursement of previously deducted medical expenses, for instance), a proportionate share of an award for attorney fees is included in gross income. Thus, for example, if the taxpayer in a personal injury lawsuit receives punitive damages of $10,000, compensatory damages of $20,000, and a $6,000 award of attorney fees, the taxpayer excludes all of the compensatory damages and $4,000 of the attorney fee award (two-thirds, because two-thirds of the total damages is excluded). *Fite v. Commissioner*, T.C. Memo. 1993–594.

   b. **No**—If no, then the exclusion in IRC § 104(a)(2) does not apply. The damages will be included in gross income except to the extent they compensate for the loss of an asset. Any damages compensating for the loss of an asset are included in gross income to the extent they exceed the taxpayer's basis in the asset. *Raytheon Production Corporation v. Commissioner*, 144 F.2d 110 (1st Cir. 1944).

**E.  CERTAIN FORMS OF INCOME FROM DISCHARGE OF DEBT (IRC § 108)**

Use this Part E whenever a debt or liability of the taxpayer has been canceled, forgiven, or otherwise discharged to any extent. Recall the general rule is that gross income includes income from the discharge of indebtedness. IRC § 61(a)(12). The question here is whether such cancellation-of-debt (COD) income is excluded under IRC § 108.

1. **Bankruptcy**—Does the discharge of debt occur in a title 11 (bankruptcy) case?

a. **Yes**—If yes, then the COD income is excluded from the taxpayer's gross income. IRC § 108(a)(1)(A). But the amount excluded from gross income must be applied to reduce the taxpayer's "tax attributes." IRC § 108(b)(1). Go to E(7) in this checklist to apply such reduction correctly.

b. **No**—If no, then continue in this Part E.

2. **Insolvency**—Does the discharge occur when the taxpayer is insolvent? The taxpayer is insolvent to the extent the taxpayer's liabilities exceed the fair market value of the taxpayer's assets. IRC § 108(a)(3).

a. **Yes**—If yes, then the COD income is excluded from the taxpayer's gross income, IRC § 108(a)(1)(B), but only to the extent the taxpayer is insolvent. IRC § 108(a)(3). Thus, for example, if the taxpayer's liabilities exceed assets by $10,000 immediately before the discharge but the amount of COD income is $12,000, the taxpayer may exclude $10,000 of the debt forgiveness but must include the remaining $2,000 in gross income. Any amount excluded from gross income under this insolvency exception must be applied to reduce the taxpayer's "tax attributes." IRC § 108(b)(1). Go to E(7) in this checklist to apply such reduction correctly.

b. **No**—If no, then continue in this Part E.

3. **Purchase Price Reduction**—Does the discharge result from a reduction in the amount of debt owed by the taxpayer to the seller of property that arose from the purchase of such property?

a. **Yes**—If yes, then the amount of the reduction shall be treated as tax-free purchase price adjustment and not as COD income. IRC § 108(e)(5). Because there is no COD income to exclude, there is no need to make any adjustment to the taxpayer's tax attributes.

b. **No**—If no, then continue in this Part E.

4. **Qualified Farm Indebtedness**—Is the debt discharged "qualified farm indebtedness?" Qualified farm indebtedness means

debt from an unrelated bank or a governmental agency that is incurred directly in connection with a farming business, but only if at least half of the taxpayer's gross receipts for the three prior taxable years is attributable to the farming business. IRC § 108(g)(1)–(2).

    a. **Yes**—If yes, then the COD income is excluded from the taxpayer's gross income. IRC § 108(a)(1)(C). But the amount excluded from gross income must be applied to reduce the taxpayer's "tax attributes." IRC § 108(b)(1). Go to E(7) in this checklist to apply such reduction correctly. Generally, the total amount excludable under IRC § 108(a)(1)(C) cannot exceed the taxpayer's "adjusted tax attributes" plus his or her aggregate bases in farming assets. See IRC § 108(g)(3) if this becomes an issue.

    b. **No**—If no, then continue in this Part E.

5. **Qualified Real Property Business Indebtedness**—Is the debt discharged "qualified real property business indebtedness?" Generally, qualified real property business indebtedness is any debt incurred or assumed by the taxpayer in connection with the acquisition or improvement of real property used in the taxpayer's business and which is secured by such property. IRC § 108(c)(3).

    a. **Yes**—If yes, then the taxpayer may elect to exclude the COD income from the taxpayer's gross income, IRC § 108(a)(1)(D), but only to the extent that the outstanding principal amount of such debt immediately before the discharge exceeded the fair market value of such real property reduced by any other qualified real property business indebtedness secured by the same property as of that time. IRC § 108(c)(2)(A). Furthermore, the total amount excluded under IRC § 108(a)(1)(D) cannot exceed the aggregate bases of depreciable real property held by the taxpayer. IRC § 108(c)(2)(B). Any amount excluded shall be applied to reduce the basis of the taxpayer's depreciable real property. IRC § 108(c)(1)(A). See IRC § 1017 for the rules of how to make this basis reduction.

    b. **No**—If no, then continue in this Part E.

6. **Qualified Principal Residence Indebtedness**—Is the discharged debt "qualified principal residence indebtedness" that was discharged in 2007, 2008, or 2009? Qualified principal residence indebtedness means up to $2 million in debt incurred to buy, build, or improve the taxpayer's principal residence, provided the debt is secured by the principal residence. IRC § 108(h)(2).

    a. **Yes**—If yes, then the COD income is excluded from the taxpayer's gross income, IRC § 108(a)(1)(E), provided the discharge does not result from services performed for the lender or any other reason not directly related to a decline in the value of the residence or the taxpayer's financial condition. IRC § 108(h)(3). But the amount excluded from gross income must be applied to reduce the taxpayer's basis in the principal residence, but not below zero. IRC § 108(h)(1).

    b. **No**—If no, then the COD income must be included in the taxpayer's gross income because no exclusion in IRC § 108(a) applies.

7. **Reduction in Tax Attributes**—The method for reducing a taxpayer's tax attributes is generally set forth in IRC § 108(b)(2). Absent an election by the taxpayer, the taxpayer must generally reduce the following tax attributes in this order until the entire amount excluded has been accounted for: the net operating loss deduction and carryover; the general business credit; the minimum tax credit; net capital loss and capital loss carryovers; the basis of the taxpayer's property; any passive activity loss or credit carryover; and finally any foreign tax credit carryover. A taxpayer may elect to make any reduction first to the basis of depreciable property. IRC § 108(b)(5).

**F. LESSEE IMPROVEMENTS TO LESSOR'S PROPERTY (IRC § 109)**

Use this Part F if the taxpayer is the lessor of real property and the lessee has constructed buildings or made other permanent improvements to the property.

1. **Not Disguised Rent**—Did the lessee make the improvements in order to fulfill its obligation to pay rent under the lease?

   a. **Yes**—If yes, then IRC § 109 does not apply and the taxpayer must include the value of the improvements in gross income in the year in which the lease terminates. Continue in this Part F for additional consequences.

   b. **No**—If no, then the taxpayer does not have gross income because the exclusion in IRC § 109 applies. Continue in this Part F for additional consequences.

2. **No Adjustment to Basis**—Did the IRC § 109 exclusion apply?

   a. **Yes**—If yes, then the taxpayer may not increase his or her basis in the real property by any amount. IRC § 1019.

   b. **No**—If no, then the value of the lessee's improvements may be added to the taxpayer's basis in the real property. This is because such value will be included in the taxpayer's gross income and thus represents a "tax cost" associated with the property.

### G. QUALIFIED SCHOLARSHIPS (IRC § 117)

Use this Part G if the taxpayer receives an award to cover all or a portion of the taxpayer's education expenses for the taxable year.

1. **Qualified Scholarship**—Did the taxpayer receive a scholarship or fellowship grant during the taxable year? Scholarships and fellowship grants are "relatively disinterested, 'no-strings' educational grants, with no requirement of any substantial *quid pro quo* from the recipients." *Bingler v. Johnson*, 394 U.S. 741 (1969). In *Bingler*, the taxpayers could not exclude the value of a purported fellowship because it required the taxpayers to work for the sponsor as a condition to receiving the award.

   a. **Yes**—If yes, proceed to G(2).

   b. **No**—If no, proceed to G(3).

2. **Qualified Tuition and Related Expenses**—Does the taxpayer use the scholarship or grant for "qualified tuition and related expenses?" This means tuition and fees paid by a student for enrollment or attendance (as well as fees, books, supplies, and

equipment required for courses of instruction) at a normal educational institution with resident faculty and students. IRC § 117(b)(1)–(2).

a. **Yes**—If yes, then the scholarship or grant is excluded from the taxpayer's gross income, IRC § 117(a), except to the extent the scholarship or grant represents compensation for teaching, research, or other services performed by the taxpayer required as a condition to receiving the scholarship or grant. IRC § 117(c)(1).

b. **No**—If no, then the scholarship or fellowship must be included in the taxpayer's gross income unless some other exclusion provision applies.

c. **Yes and No**—If the taxpayer uses only a portion of the scholarship or grant for qualified tuition and related expenses, that portion of the scholarship or fellowship may be excluded. The balance must be included in the gross income unless another exclusion provision applies.

2. **Qualified Tuition Reduction**—Did the taxpayer receive a "qualified tuition reduction?" This means a tuition reduction provided to an employee of an educational organization for the education of the employee, the employee's spouse, or the employee's children. IRC § 117(d)(2).

a. **Yes**—If yes, then the amount of the tuition reduction is excluded from the taxpayer's gross income, provided the reduction relates either to education below the graduate level or to a graduate student who is engaged in teaching or research activities for the school. IRC § 117(d)(1), (4). If such the reduction is only available to highly-compensated employees (as defined in IRC § 414(q)) of the educational organization, however, the exclusion is not available. IRC § 117(d)(3).

b. **No**—If no, then the amount of the award or reduction must be included in the taxpayer's gross income unless some other exclusion provision applies.

**H. MEALS AND LODGING FOR THE CONVENIENCE OF THE EMPLOYER (IRC § 119)**

Use this Part H if the taxpayer receives meals or lodging from his or her employer.

1. **Required to Accept Lodging**—In the case of lodging, is the taxpayer required to accept the lodging as condition of the taxpayer's employment? This means that the employee must accept the lodging in order to be able to perform the duties of employment properly. Treas. Reg. § 1.119–1(b). (This requirement does not apply to meals; if meals are at issue, proceed to H(2).)

    a. **Yes**—If yes, then continue in this Part H.

    b. **No**—If no, then the value of the lodging cannot be excluded under IRC § 119(a). Unless another exclusion provision applies, the taxpayer must include the value of the lodging in gross income as compensation for services. IRC § 61(a)(1). Check out H(5) to see if the lodging can be excluded under IRC § 119(d).

2. **Furnished by Employer**—Was the meal or lodging furnished to the taxpayer by or on behalf of the taxpayer's employer? Note that the exclusion in IRC § 119 is limited to meals and lodging furnished in kind; it does not apply to cash payments from an employer intended to be used for meals or lodging. *Commissioner v. Kowalski*, 434 U.S. 77 (1977).

    a. **Yes**—If yes, then continue in this Part H.

    b. **No**—If no, then the value of the meal or lodging cannot be excluded under IRC § 119(a). Unless another exclusion provision applies, the taxpayer must include the value of the meal or lodging in gross income as compensation for services. IRC § 61(a)(1). In the case of lodging, check out H(5) to see if the lodging can be excluded under IRC § 119(d).

3. **Convenience of Employer**—Was the meal or lodging furnished for the convenience of the employer?

    a. **Meals**—Meals are furnished for the convenience of the employer if there is a "substantial noncompensatory business reason" for providing the meal. Treas. Reg. § 1.119–1(a)(2)(i). Although this a fact-intensive inquiry, the regulations list six safe harbors where a substantial noncompensatory business reason is deemed to exist. Treas. Reg. § 1.119–1(a)(2)(ii).

b. **Lodging**—Lodging is generally furnished for the convenience of an employer if there is a direct nexus between the meals and lodging furnished to the employee and the business interests of the employer. *Adams v. United States*, 585 F.2d 1060 (Ct. Cl. 1978).

c. **Yes**—If yes, then continue in this Part H.

d. **No**—If no, then the value of the meal or lodging cannot be excluded under IRC § 119(a). Unless another exclusion provision applies, the taxpayer must include the value of the meal or lodging in gross income as compensation for services. IRC § 61(a)(1). In the case of lodging, check out H(5) to see if the lodging can be excluded under IRC § 119(d).

4. **On Employer's Business Premises**—Was the meal or lodging furnished on the business premises of the employer? An employer's business premises consists of any location where the taxpayer performs his or her duties as an employee. Treas. Reg. § 1.119–1(c)(1); *Adams v. United States*, 585 F.2d 1060 (Ct. Cl. 1978).

a. **Yes**—If yes, then the value of the meal or lodging is excluded from gross income under IRC § 119(a).

b. **No**—If no, then the value of the meal or lodging cannot be excluded under IRC § 119(a). Unless another exclusion provision applies, the taxpayer must include the value of the meal or lodging in gross income as compensation for services. IRC § 61(a)(1). In the case of lodging, check out H(5) to see if the lodging can be excluded under IRC § 119(d).

5. **Qualified Campus Lodging**—Did the taxpayer receive "qualified campus lodging?" This means lodging furnished to an employee of an educational organization (and/or the employee's spouse and/or dependents) that is not already excluded under IRC § 119(a), which is located on or near campus, and which is furnished for use as a home. IRC § 119(d)(3).

a. **Yes**—If yes, then the value of the lodging is excluded from gross income under IRC § 119(d)(1), but not to the extent that the annual fair rental value of equivalent lodging exceeds the amount of rent paid by the taxpayer during the year. IRC § 117(d)(2). The annual fair rental value of equivalent lodging is the lesser of the average rentals paid by non-employees to the same educational organization for comparable lodging and five percent of the appraised value of the qualified campus lodging. IRC § 117(d)(2)(A).

b. **No**—If no, then the value of the lodging cannot be excluded under IRC § 119(d). Unless another exclusion provision applies, the taxpayer must include the value of the lodging in gross income as compensation for services. IRC § 61(a)(1).

## I. CERTAIN FRINGE BENEFITS (IRC § 132)

Use this Part I for any non-cash compensation received by the taxpayer as an employee. Keep in mind that most forms of compensation are included in gross income under IRC § 61(a)(1). IRC § 132, the provision at issue here in this Part I of the checklist, offers several exceptions.

1. **No–Additional–Cost Service**—Does the taxpayer, the taxpayer's spouse, or the taxpayer's dependent child receive a "no-additional-cost service?" A no-additional-cost service is any service provided by the taxpayer's employer if such service is offered for sale to customers in the same line of the employer's business in which the taxpayer works and for which the employer incurs no substantial additional cost (including foregone revenue). IRC § 132(b).

a. **Yes**—If yes, then the value of the service is excluded from the taxpayer's gross income under IRC § 132(a)(1). If the taxpayer is a highly-compensated employee, however, the exclusion applies only if the same benefit is also available to the rank and file employees of the employer. IRC § 132(j)(1). Note that the exclusion applies to no-additional-cost services used by the taxpayer as well as the taxpayer's spouse and/or dependent children. IRC

§ 132(h)(2). Any use of air transportation by the taxpayer's parent also qualifies for the exclusion. IRC § 132(h)(3).

b. **No**—If no, continue in this Part I.

2. **Qualified Employee Discount**—Does the taxpayer, the taxpayer's spouse, or the taxpayer's dependent child receive a "qualified employee discount?" A qualified employee discount is any discount related to "qualified property or services" that does not exceed the "gross profit percentage" (in the case of property) or 20 percent of the price charged to customers (in the case of services). IRC § 132(c)(1).

   a. **Qualified Property or Services**—Qualified property or services means any services and any personal property not held for investment purposes that is sold to customers in the same line of the employer's business in which the taxpayer works. IRC § 132(c)(4).

   b. **Gross Profit Percentage**—The gross profit percentage is generally determined by dividing the employer's profit from the sale of all property sold to customers in the same line of the employer's business in which the taxpayer works by the aggregate sales price of such property. IRC § 132(c)(2).

   c. **Yes**—If yes, then the amount of the discount is excluded from gross income under IRC § 132(a)(2). If the taxpayer is a highly-compensated employee, however, the exclusion applies only if the same benefit is also available to the rank and file employees of the employer. IRC § 132(j)(1). Note that if the taxpayer receives a discount that is greater than the qualified employee discount limitation, the qualified employee discount portion remains excludable but any excess discount is not excludable under IRC § 132(a)(2). Note here, too, that any discount given to the taxpayer's spouse and dependent children also qualifies for the exclusion. IRC § 132(h)(2).

   d. **No**—If no, continue in this Part I.

3. **Working Condition Fringe**—Does the taxpayer receive property or services from the employer which the employee would

have been able to deduct as a business expense or depreciation expense if the taxpayer himself or herself paid for such item?

    a.  **Yes**—If yes, then the value of the property or services received is excluded from gross income as a "working condition fringe" under IRC § 132(a)(3). IRC § 132(d).

    b.  **No**—If no, continue in this Part I.

4.  **De Minimis Fringe**—Does the taxpayer receive property or services from the employer the value of which (considering the frequency with which similar benefits are provided to all of the employer's employees) is so small as to make accounting for such property or services unreasonable or administratively impracticable?

    a.  **Yes**—If yes, then the value of the property or service received is excluded from gross income under IRC § 132(a)(4) as a "de minimis fringe." IRC § 132(e)(1).

    b.  **No**—If no, continue in this Part I.

5.  **Certain Eating Facilities**—Does the taxpayer receive discounted meals from an eating facility operated by the employer and located on or near the employer's business premises?

    a.  **Yes**—If yes, then the amount of such discount is deemed to be a "de minimis fringe" (and thus excluded from gross income under IRC § 132(a)(4)) if the revenue derived by the employer from such facility normally equals or exceeds the direct operating costs of the facility. IRC § 132(e)(2). This exclusion is not available, however, if the taxpayer is a highly-compensated employee and the same benefit is not also provided to the rank and file employees of the employer.

    b.  **No**—If no, continue in this Part I.

6.  **Qualified Transportation Fringe**—Does the taxpayer receive a "qualified transportation fringe?"

    a.  **Three Types of Qualified Transportation Fringes**—A qualified transportation fringe is any of the following three benefits provided by the employer to the taxpayer-employee: (i) transportation between the taxpayer's home and job site in a "commuter highway vehicle" (one that seats at least six and that is used at least 80 percent of the time to make trips between homes and work during which the vehicle is at least half-full); (ii) a transit pass; or (iii) "qualified parking" (parking on or near the employer's business premises or at a location where the taxpayer can access transportation on a commuter highway vehicle). IRC § 132(f)(1), (5).

b. **Yes**—If yes, then the value of the qualified transportation fringe is excluded from gross income under IRC § 132(a)(5). Note, however, that there is a maximum amount that is excludable as a qualified transportation fringe. IRC § 132(f)(2). The dollar amounts set forth in these limitations are adjusted annually for inflation, so one should always be sure to verify the correct limitations in effect for the taxable year(s) at issue. IRC § 132(f)(6).

c. **No**—If no, continue in this Part I.

7. **Qualified Moving Expense Reimbursement**—Does the taxpayer receive payment for (or reimbursement of) expenses that would have been deductible by the taxpayer as moving expenses under IRC § 217 if there had been no payment or reimbursement? See Chapter 5 for a discussion of the deduction for moving expenses under IRC § 217.

a. **Yes**—If yes, then the payment qualifies as a "qualified moving expense reimbursement," IRC § 132(g), meaning the payment is excluded from gross income. IRC § 132(a)(6).

b. **No**—If no, continue in this Part I.

8. **Qualified Retirement Planning Services**—Does the taxpayer or the taxpayer's spouse receive any retirement planning advice or information from an employer maintaining a "qualified employer plan?"

a. **Qualified Employer Plan**—A qualified employer plan generally means any employee benefit plan under IRC §§ 401(a), 403(a), 403(b), 408(k), or 408(p), as well as any retirement plan for government employees. IRC §§ 132(m)(3); 219(g)(5).

b. **Yes**—If yes, then the taxpayer can exclude the value of such advice from gross income under IRC § 132(a)(7) as "qualified retirement planning services." IRC § 132(m)(1).

c. **No**—If no, continue in this Part I.

9. **Qualified Military Base Realignment and Closure Fringe**— Does the taxpayer receive any payment under 42 U.S.C. § 3374 to offset the adverse effects on housing values as a result of a military base realignment or closure?

a. **Yes**—If yes, then such payment is excluded from gross income under IRC § 132(a)(8) as a "qualified military base realignment and closure fringe," IRC § 132(n)(1), provided the total amount of such payments with respect to any one property does not exceed the maximum limitations set forth in 42 U.S.C. § 3374. IRC § 132(n)(2).

b. **No**—If no, continue in this Part I.

10. **On–Premises Athletic Facility**—Does the taxpayer receive the use of a gymnasium or other athletic facility operated by the employer on the employer's business premises, and is substantially all of the use of such facility by the employer's employees, their spouses, or their dependent children?

a. **Yes**—If yes, then the taxpayer may exclude the value of this benefit from gross income. IRC § 132(j)(4).

b. **No**—If no, then the benefit received by the taxpayer is not excludable under any of the provisions in IRC § 132. Unless another exclusion applies, the value of the benefit must be included in gross income as compensation for services. IRC § 61(a)(1).

## ILLUSTRATIVE PROBLEMS

Here are two problems illustrating the application of this checklist.

---

### ■ PROBLEM 3.1 ■

---

T is an employee of Corporation. During the winter holidays, T receives a tofu turkey from Corporation. A card attached to the tofu turkey thanks T for another year of loyal service and wishes T a "happy and healthy holiday season."

As an employee T receives free lunches every weekday at Corporation's cafeteria located in Corporation's main office building in a downtown metropolitan setting.

T borrowed $10,000 from Corporation to pay for various expenses. When T became insolvent (T owed about $50,000 more in liabilities than T had in assets), Corporation, at T's request, forgave the loan.

What are the federal income tax consequences of these events to T?

## Analysis

The turkey might be excludable from gross income as a de minimis fringe benefit. IRC § 132(e)(1) defines a de minimis fringe as property or services from the employer the value of which (considering the frequency with which similar benefits are provided to all of the employer's employees) is so small as to make accounting for such property or services unreasonable or administratively impracticable. If Corporation sent similar turkeys to all employees, accounting for the cost might not be so unreasonable after all, meaning T could not use this exclusion to cover the value of the turkey. Treas. Reg. § 1.132–6(e)(1) provides that "traditional birthday or holiday gifts of property . . . with a low fair market value" can qualify as a de minimis fringe, however, so T has a strong case for exclusion. If the de minimis fringe exclusion does not apply, T likely has gross income. T cannot exclude the value of the turkey as a gift because IRC § 102(c) provides that transfers to employees from employers cannot qualify as gifts.

T might seek to exclude the value of the free meals under IRC § 119 but this likely will not work. Although the meals are furnished on the employer's business premises, meals must be furnished for the convenience of the employer if they are to qualify for IRC § 119 exclusion. Meals are furnished for the convenience of the employer if there is a "substantial noncompensatory business reason" for providing the meal. Treas. Reg. § 1.119–1(a)(2)(i). The regulations list six safe harbors where a substantial noncompensatory business reason is deemed to exist, Treas. Reg. § 1.119–1(a)(2)(ii), but the facts here do not fit within any of these safe harbors. Accordingly, IRC § 119 will not apply. There appears to be no other authority for an exclusion, either, so T will have to include the value of the meals in gross income as compensation for services.

T had no gross income at the time of the loan because of the obligation to repay the loan to Corporation. When Corporation forgave the loan, however, T had cancellation of debt (COD) income under IRC § 61(a)(12). T cannot argue that the COD income should be excluded as a gift, again because IRC § 102(c) precludes gift treatment of transfers from employers to employees. Fortunately (?), T here was insolvent at the time of the discharge because T's liabilities exceeded T's assets by more than the amount of the discharged debt. Consequently, T can exclude the $10,000 of COD income under IRC § 108(a)(1)(B). However, T will be required to reduce T's tax attributes by $10,000. We have no facts here to indicate whether T has any tax attributes and, if so, the amount of these benefits.

## ■ PROBLEM 3.2 ■

T is a college sophomore at University. In the current year, T was selected by a nonprofit organization to receive one of its "merit scholarships." Under the terms of this award, T received $25,000 for use in paying tuition and fees. In fact, T used $20,000 of the award for tuition and fees and $5,000 for room and board.

To make ends meet, T had a part-time job working at a convenience store near campus. One evening, T was assaulted by a masked gunman seeking to rob the store. T prevented the robbery but was injured during a struggle that ensued. T eventually received a $1,000 reward from a local civic group that wanted to honor T's bravery. T also sued the gunman for the injuries sustained in the incident and recovered $25,000 in a settlement.

What are the federal income tax consequences of these events to T?

## Analysis

T can exclude $20,000 of the merit scholarship under IRC § 117(a) because that portion of the award was used for "qualified tuition and related expenses." Housing is not included within the definition of that term, so the $5,000 used for room and board costs is not eligible for the IRC § 117(a) exclusion. But the payment from the nonprofit organization might be classified as a "gift" under IRC § 102(a) if it is determined that the organization acted with "detached and disinterested generosity." After all, the transfer might be from "charity or like impulses." *Commissioner v. Duberstein.* If it is a gift, then T can exclude the entire payment from gross income.

T can probably exclude the $1,000 reward from the civic organization as a gift under IRC § 102(a). The group does not appear to be compensating T for services; instead, based on the facts it appears to be acting out of "detached and disinterested generosity" (here, out of "admiration" and "respect"). Thus there is a good argument for excluding the award.

The $25,000 settlement from the gunman can be excluded under IRC § 104(a)(2) because the payment represents damages received on account of physical injury. It does not matter that the payment came from a settlement agreement, as IRC § 104(a)(2) specifically mentions this as qualifying for the exclusion.

## POINTS TO REMEMBER

- Because any item of income is excludible only if specifically authorized by a provision of the Code, it is a good idea to get in the habit of citing an applicable exclusion when discussing it in the answer to a problem.

- If the first exclusion provision that comes to mind for a particular problem proves not to apply, don't give up. Consider whether another exclusion provision might apply. All you need is for one exclusion provision to apply!

- The gift exclusion turns on the intention of the transferor, not on the understanding of the transferee.

- Many exclusions come with a "string attached;" the exclusion might apply, but there may be collateral tax consequences that effectively defer the recognition of income. For instance, the IRC § 102(a) gift exclusion appears to be a complete forgiveness of income, but as seen in Chapter 6, donees generally take the donor's basis in gifted property, meaning any gain lurking in the asset at the time of the gift will be taxed to the donee upon a sale or other disposition of the gifted property. See also the reduction of tax attributes required when IRC § 108 applies and the prohibition against adding the value of improvements to the basis of real property when IRC § 109 applies. Be sure to consider whether any applicable exclusion has a "string attached," and if it does be sure to address that in your answer.

**CHAPTER 4**

# Deductions Generally

In computing taxable income, taxpayers are allowed a variety of deductions for costs paid or incurred during the taxable year. When a taxpayer pays or incurs a cost, the taxpayer would prefer that the cost give rise to a deduction. Not all taxpayer costs are deductible, however. In fact, IRC § 161 provides that costs are deductible only to the extent a specific Code provision authorizes a deduction. There is, therefore, no general rule of deduction. The general rule is that a cost is not deductible unless a specific provision of the Code authorizes one. Accordingly, you should get in the habit of citing authority whenever you conclude that a particular cost is deductible.

Whether a taxpayer can deduct any given cost is a function of two variables: the nature of the cost and the activity to which the cost relates. This Chapter helps you identify the proper federal income tax treatment of taxpayer costs.

## DEDUCTIONS REVIEW

*Nature of the Cost.* There are only two types of taxpayer costs: capital expenditures and expenses. Capital expenditures are those that produce a substantial future benefit, while expenses represent costs for benefits that are enjoyed or consumed in the short term. Capital expenditures are generally not deductible; rather, a "capitalized" cost creates or adds to the taxpayer's basis in property. For example, the cost to acquire a building is a capital expenditure because the taxpayer reasonable expects that the benefit of the building will extend substantially beyond the end of the year of purchase. Instead of deducting the cost of the building in the year of purchase, the taxpayer takes a basis in the building equal to the purchase price.

Expenses, on the other hand, do not create or add to the basis of any property. Expenses are either currently deductible or they are not—period. Obviously, a taxpayer would generally prefer that a particular cost be a deductible expense. If a cost is not a deductible expense, a taxpayer would then prefer that it be a capital expenditure, for at least in that case the cost will give rise to basis that will benefit the taxpayer in some later year. If the asset to which the increase in basis relates is sold in a later taxable year, for instance, the addition to basis from the taxpayer's capital expenditure will reduce the amount of gain (or increase the amount of loss) the taxpayer would otherwise realize. If the cost is an expense but not deductible, the taxpayer will receive no tax benefit at all from the cost.

*Activity to Which Cost Relates.* Assuming a taxpayer's cost is an expense, the taxpayer wants to know if it is deductible. Although there are a great many exceptions, deductibility generally hinges on the activity to which the cost relates. If the cost relates to the taxpayer's trade or business activity, the expense will very likely be deductible under IRC § 162(a). If the cost relates to a for-profit activity of the taxpayer that does not rise to the level of a trade or business (generally referred to as an "investment activity"), the expense is also likely to be deductible, but the authority for the deduction changes to IRC § 212. This is significant, because most business expenses deductible under IRC § 162(a) are "above-the-line" deductions available to any taxpayer regardless of whether the taxpayer itemizes deductions or claims the standard deduction. Most investment expenses under IRC § 212, however, are "miscellaneous itemized deductions," and that has four potentially negative consequences: (1) the deductions are only available if the taxpayer itemizes instead of claiming the standard deduction; (2)

the deductions are only taken to the extent that, in the aggregate, they exceed two percent of the taxpayer's adjusted gross income; (3) like all itemized deductions, they will be disallowed in part if the taxpayer's adjusted gross income exceeds a certain threshold; and (4) the deductions are generally disallowed for purposes of the alternative minimum tax, thus increasing the taxpayer's risk of exposure to this additional tax.

Expenses unrelated to a taxpayer's business or investment activities are considered personal expenses. The general rule is that personal expenses are not deductible. IRC § 262. But there are a number of personal expenses that are specifically made deductible, so many that they are set forth in a separate Chapter. See Chapter 5.

## DEDUCTIONS CHECKLIST

This checklist will assist in determining whether a particular cost is deductible.

### A.  CAPITAL EXPENDITURES

Capital expenditures are not deductible. IRC § 263(a). If a taxpayer pays or incurs a capital expenditure, the cost is "capitalized," meaning it creates or adds to basis.

1.  **Cost to Acquire New Tangible Asset**—Does the cost result in the acquisition of a separate and distinct tangible asset that will have a useful life substantially beyond the taxable year in which the cost is paid or incurred?

    a.  **Yes**—If yes, then the cost must be capitalized. Treas. Reg. § 1.263(a)–2(a). The cost becomes the taxpayer's basis in the new asset. To determine whether this cost can be depreciated or amortized, proceed to Part D of this checklist.

    b.  **No**—If no, continue in this Part A.

    c.  **12–Month Rule**—In determining whether an asset or other economic benefit has a useful life substantially beyond the taxable year, the so-called "12–month rule" provides that if the benefit of the cost will last no more than 12 months and not beyond the end of the year following the year in which the cost is paid, the cost need not be capitalized. Prop. Reg. § 1.263(a)–2(d)(4)(i). In that case, the cost is an expense, and analysis shifts to Part B of this checklist.

2. **Cost to Construct or Produce New Tangible Asset**—Does the cost relate to the creation or production of real property or tangible personal property?

   a. **Yes**—If yes, then the cost must be capitalized. IRC § 263A generally requires all direct and indirect costs allocable to the construction or production of real property and tangible personal property be capitalized. Direct costs include raw materials and wages paid to employees. Treas. Reg. § 1.263A–1(e)(2). Indirect costs include repairs, depreciation on equipment used in the construction or production process, utilities, taxes, insurance, and storage. Treas. Reg. § 1.263A–1(e)(3). Such costs are added to the taxpayer's basis in the constructed or produced property. These costs may be eligible for cost recovery deductions if the constructed or produced property meets the requirements for depreciation, so proceed to Part D of this checklist.

   b. **No**—If no, continue in this Part A.

   c. **Exceptions**—The rule of capitalization in IRC § 263A does not apply to the construction or production of personal-use property. IRC § 263A(c)(1). Accordingly, such costs must be analyzed individually to determine whether they are capitalized or expensed. Likewise, IRC § 263A does not apply to certain animals and plants produced by farmers and ranchers. IRC § 263A(d). It also does not apply to free-lance photographers, writers, and artists. IRC § 263A(h).

3. **Tangible Property Held for Resale**—Does the cost result in the acquisition or creation of tangible property that the taxpayer intends to sell to another party?

a. **Yes**—If yes, then the cost must be capitalized even if the taxpayer intends to sell the asset in the very near future. Prop. Reg. § 1.263(a)–2(d)(1)(i). The cost becomes the taxpayer's basis in the new asset. To determine whether this cost can be depreciated, proceed to Part D of this checklist, although generally such property will not be subject to deductions for cost recovery.

b. **No**—If no, continue in this Part A.

4. **Improvements to Tangible Property**—Does the cost materially add to the value of tangible property owned by the taxpayer or restore such property to a like-new condition?

a. **Yes**—If yes, then the cost must be capitalized. Treas. Reg. § 1.263(a)–1(b)(1). The cost is added to the taxpayer's basis in the new asset. If the asset is subject to depreciation, the cost of the improvement will likewise be eligible for cost recovery deductions. In that case, proceed to Part D of this checklist.

b. **No**—If no, continue in this Part A.

c. **Distinguish from Repairs**—Mere repairs are usually treated as expenses and do not have to be capitalized. There is a fine line between deductible repairs and improvements that have to be capitalized. Generally, repairs represent costs that neither materially add to the value of an asset nor substantially prolong its useful life.

5. **Pre–Existing Defect Related to Tangible Property**—Does the cost relate to repairing or fixing a defect of tangible property that existed before the taxpayer acquired such property?

a. **Yes**—If yes, then the cost must be capitalized. Prop. Reg. § 1.263(a)–3(e)(1). The cost is considered to be part of the purchase price of the asset because the taxpayer knew or reasonably should have known that he or she would have to pay this cost at the time the taxpayer acquired the property, so the cost is added to the taxpayer's basis in the property. If the asset is subject to depreciation, the cost of the improvement will likewise be eligible for cost recovery deductions. In that case, proceed to Part D of this checklist.

b. **No**—If no, continue in this Part A.

6. **Pre–Use Costs Related to Tangible Property**—Does the taxpayer incur the cost prior to taking possession of tangible property in order to make it suitable for the taxpayer's intended use?

   a. **Yes**—If yes, then the cost must be capitalized. Prop. Reg. § 1.263(a)–3(e)(1). The cost is considered to be part of the cost to acquire the property, so it is added to the basis of the acquired property. If the asset is subject to depreciation or amortization, the cost of the improvement will likewise be eligible for cost recovery deductions. In that case, proceed to Part D of this checklist.

   b. **No**—If no, continue in this Part A.

7. **Adaptations to Tangible Property**—Does the cost adapt the taxpayer's tangible property to a new or different use?

   a. **Yes**—If yes, then the cost must be capitalized. Treas. Reg. § 1.263(a)–1(b)(2). The cost is added to the taxpayer's basis in the subject property. If the asset is subject to depreciation or amortization, the cost of the improvement will likewise be eligible for cost recovery deductions. In that case, proceed to Part D of this checklist.

   b. **No**—If no, continue in this Part A.

8. **Betterments and Increased Productivity**—Does the cost extend or expand the taxpayer's tangible property or otherwise serve to increase the tangible property's productivity?

   a. **Yes**—If yes, then the cost must be capitalized. Prop. Reg. § 1.263(a)–3(e)(1). The cost is added to the taxpayer's basis in the subject property. If the asset is subject to depreciation or amortization, the cost of the improvement will likewise be eligible for cost recovery deductions. In that case, proceed to Part D of this checklist.

   b. **No**—If no, continue in this Part A.

9. **Substantial Future Intangible Benefit**—Does the cost provide the taxpayer with a substantial future benefit?

   a. **Yes**—If yes, then the cost must be capitalized even though it does not result in the creation of a separate and distinct asset. *INDOPCO, Inc. v. Commissioner*, 503 U.S. 79 (1992). Such cost adds to the basis of the tangible and intangible assets to which such benefit relates. For instance, if the taxpayer pays attorney fees to defend against a hostile takeover of the taxpayer's business, the cost should be added to the basis of the taxpayer's business assets. To the extent those assets are eligible for cost recovery deductions, then Part D or Part E of this checklist applies.

b. **No**—If no, continue in this Part A.

10. **Amounts Paid to Acquire Intangible Asset**—Does the taxpayer incur the cost to acquire an intangible asset from another party?

    a. **Yes**—If yes, then the cost must be capitalized. Treas. Reg. §§ 1.263(a)–4(b)(1)(i) and–4(c). The cost becomes the taxpayer's basis in the acquired intangible asset. The basis may be eligible for the IRC § 197 amortization deduction, so proceed to Part E of this checklist.

    b. **No**—If no, continue in this Part A.

    c. **Facilitation Costs**—Costs to acquire an intangible asset include the costs paid to "facilitate" the acquisition. Treas. Reg. §§ 1.263(a)–4(b)(1)(v) and–4(e)(1). Facilitation costs include the costs paid to investigate or pursue the transaction, including attorney fees, accountant fees, inspections, and appraisals.

11. **Amounts Paid to Create Intangible Asset**—Does the taxpayer incur the cost to create an intangible asset that will last more than 12 months or beyond the year after the year payment?

    a. **Yes**—If yes, then the cost must be capitalized. Treas. Reg. §§ 1.263(a)–4(b) (1)(ii) and –4(d). The cost becomes the taxpayer's basis in the acquired intangible asset. The basis is usually not eligible for the IRC § 197 amortization deduction, but proceed to Part E of this checklist to make sure.

    b. **No**—If no, and if the cost has not been described elsewhere in this Part A, then the cost is an expense. Proceed to Part B of this checklist.

c. **Facilitation Costs**—Costs to create an intangible asset include the costs paid to "facilitate" the creation. Treas. Reg. §§ 1.263(a)–4(b)(1)(v) and–4(e)(1). Facilitation costs include the costs paid to investigate or pursue the creation of the asset, including attorney fees, accountant fees, inspections, and appraisals.

d. **12–Month Rule**—Costs paid to create (or facilitate creation of) any intangible benefit that does not last more than 12 months or beyond the end of the year after the year of payment need not be capitalized. Treas. Reg. § 1.263(a)–4(f)(1).

## B. BUSINESS EXPENSES

This Part B applies to a cost paid or incurred by a taxpayer that is not capitalized under Part A of this checklist. Such a cost is an expense, and the deductibility of the expense turns on the activity or activities to which the expense relates. Start by considering whether the expense is a business expense deductible under IRC § 162(a). This is the usually the best result because the IRC § 162(a) deduction is generally an above-the-line deduction available to the taxpayer regardless of whether the taxpayer chooses to itemize deductions or claim the standard deduction.

1. **Trade or Business**—Does the expense bear a proximate relationship to a trade or business activity?

   a. **Yes**—If yes, proceed in this Part B.

   b. **No**—If no, then the expense is not a business expense. Proceed to Part C of this checklist.

   c. **Full-Time Effort and Profit Motive**—The Supreme Court has said that "to be engaged in a trade or business, the taxpayer must be involved in the activity with continuity and regularity and . . . the taxpayer's primary purpose for engaging in the activity must be for income or profit." *Commissioner v. Groetzinger*, 480 U.S. 23 (1987). Accordingly, a taxpayer must both have a profit motive and regularly participate in the activity in order for it to rise to the level of a trade or business. If a taxpayer has a profit motive but is not regularly involved in the activity, it is an investment activity and not a trade or business. If the taxpayer is regularly involved but lacks a profit motive, it is a hobby activity and not a trade or business.

2. **Ordinary and Necessary Expense**—Is the expense ordinary and necessary to the taxpayer's business?

   a. **Yes**—If yes, proceed in this Part B.

   b. **No**—If no, then the expense is not a deductible business expense because IRC § 162(a) only permits a deduction for "ordinary and necessary" business expenses. Unless there is some other authority for a deduction, the taxpayer cannot deduct the expense.

   c. **Ordinary**—An expense is ordinary if its "common and accepted" within that industry. *Welch v. Helvering*, 290 U.S. 111 (1933). The focus is not on whether the taxpayer himself or herself regularly incurs such an expense but whether the cost is not uncommon within the community of which the taxpayer's business is part. There is no magic set of factors to apply in determining whether an expense is ordinary. Indeed, Justice Cardozo in *Welch* said that "life in all its fullness" is to supply the answer.

   d. **Necessary**—*Welch* says that an expense is necessary to the taxpayer's business if it is "appropriate and helpful" to the business. Courts give significant deference to the business judgment of taxpayers in this regard, so it is rare for a business expense to be rendered non-deductible because of the necessity requirement.

3. **Carrying On**—Is the taxpayer already carrying on the trade or business activity when the business expense is paid or incurred?

   a. **Yes**—If yes, then the business expense is deductible under IRC § 162(a).

   b. **No**—If no, then proceed in this Part B.

4. **Start–Up Expenditures**—Is the expense incurred in starting the trade or business activity?

   a. **Yes**—If yes, then the expense is classified as a "start-up expenditure." Under IRC § 195(a), start-up expenditures are generally capitalized and added to the basis of the business assets. But under IRC § 195(b)(1) a taxpayer may elect to amortize start-up expenditures once the business activity begins, generally over the first 15 years of the business.

    i. **Up-Front Deduction**—If the taxpayer makes an election under IRC § 195(b)(1), the taxpayer can deduct up to $5,000 of start-up expenditures in the year in which the business begins unless the total start-up expenditures exceed $50,000. IRC § 195(b)(1)(A). If such expenses exceed $50,000, then the $5,000 up-front deduction is reduced dollar-for-dollar by the amount by which the start-up expenditures exceed $50,000. So once start-up expenditures exceed $55,000, there is no up-front-deduction at all.

    ii. **Amortize Balance Over 15 Years**—If the taxpayer makes an election under IRC § 195(b)(1), then any start-up expenditures not deducted in the year in which the business begins are amortized (deducted on a straight-line, proportionate basis) over the first 15 years of the business beginning in the month in which the business formally launches. IRC § 195(b)(1)(B). If the business does not last for 15 years, the taxpayer may treat any unrecovered start-up expenditures as a loss in the last year of the business. IRC § 195(b)(2).

  b. **No**—If no, then the expense is not deductible unless there is specific authority elsewhere for the deduction.

## C. INVESTMENT EXPENSES

This Part C applies to expenses that do not bear a proximate relationship to a trade or business activity.

  **1. Production or Collection of Income**—Is this an ordinary and necessary expense paid or incurred in the production or collection of income (an investment activity)?

    a. **Yes**—If yes, then the expense is deductible under IRC § 212(1).

    b. **No**—If no, proceed in this Part C unless the taxpayer paid or incurred this expense in a hobby activity (one not engaged in for profit). If the expense is incurred in a hobby activity, see Chapter 5 to determine whether the expense may be deductible. In determining whether an activity is a hobby activity, keep two rules in mind. First, there is a presumption that the taxpayer has a profit motive if the activity has generated a net profit for three of the five most recent taxable years, including the year at issue (the test is two of the most recent seven years for most activities involving horses). IRC § 183(d). Second, the regulations offer nine factors for distinguishing for-profit business or investment activities on the one hand from hobby activities on the other. See Treas. Reg. § 1.183–2(b) for the list and a description of how to apply them.

c. **Ordinary and Necessary**—These terms have the same meaning as for business expenses, as explained in Part B(2) of this checklist.

2. **Maintenance of Property Held for Production or Collection of Income**—Is this an ordinary and necessary expense paid or incurred in managing, conserving, or maintaining property held for the production of income (an investment activity)?

a. **Yes**—If yes, then the expense is deductible under IRC § 212(2).

b. **No**—If no, proceed in this Part C.

3. **Tax Matters**—Is this an ordinary and necessary expense paid or incurred in connection with the determination, collection, or refund of any tax?

a. **Yes**—If yes, then the expense is deductible under IRC § 212(3).

b. **No**—If no, then the expense is neither a business expense nor an investment expense. It is therefore a personal expense. Personal expenses are not generally deductible. IRC § 262. But there are many exceptions to this general rule. To determine whether the personal expense is deductible, see Chapter 5.

### D. DEPRECIATION DEDUCTIONS

As previously explained, a capitalized cost creates or adds to basis in property. If the property is not subject to depreciation or amortization deductions, the taxpayer will get the benefit of this basis upon a sale or other disposition of the property. Although the taxpayer can control when such a disposition will occur, the taxpayer must dispose of the asset in order to claim the benefit of the extra basis. Most taxpayers would prefer to recover the capitalized cost throughout the useful life of the property to which the cost relates. Depreciation deductions under IRC § 168 and amortization deductions under IRC § 197 provide the rules for claiming these deductions. This Part D concerns the depreciation deductions under IRC § 168.

1. **Tangible Property Subject to Wear and Tear**—Is the property to which a capitalized cost relates tangible property subject to wear and tear?

   a. **Yes**—If yes, continue in this Part D of the checklist.

   b. **No**—If no, then the property is not eligible for depreciation deductions. If the problem is that the property is not tangible property, proceed to Part E of this checklist. If the problem is that the property is not subject to wear and tear in the taxpayer's hands, no form of cost recovery deductions applies, so the taxpayer must wait until a sale or other disposition of the asset in order to claim the benefit of the added basis.

   c. **Wear and Tear**—A taxpayer need not prove the estimated useful life of a tangible asset in order to claim depreciation deductions. Indeed, there is not even a requirement that the value of the asset decline over time. It is sufficient that the asset is subject to wear and tear given the taxpayer's use of the asset. *Simon v. Commissioner*, 68 F.3d 41 (2d Cir. 1995).

2. **Used for Business or Investment**—Does the taxpayer use the property in a business activity or hold it for the production of income?

   a. **Yes**—If yes, then the asset is eligible for depreciation deductions. The method for computing depreciation deductions is described generally in Part D(3).

   b. **No**—If no, then the tangible property is not eligible for depreciation deductions or any other form of cost recovery. The taxpayer simply sits on the capitalized cost and waits for a sale or other disposition of the property.

c.  **Mixed Personal Use**—If the asset is held both for business and personal purposes (or both for investment and personal use), then only a portion of the asset may be depreciable. For instance, if a taxpayer owns a vehicle that is used 80 percent of the time in the taxpayer's business and 20 percent of time for the taxpayer's personal pursuits, then the taxpayer can depreciation 80 percent of the cost of the vehicle.

3.  **Mechanics of Depreciation**—This Part D(3) only explains how depreciation deductions are computed. It does not provide a checklist for computing the depreciation deductions with respect to any particular asset. If your instructor expects you to be able to perform these computations, be sure to work out your own flow chart or checklist for this purpose.

a.  **Depreciation Base**—The taxpayer is entitled to depreciate his or her entire cost basis in the asset; there is no reduction for the asset's "salvage value" (what the asset can be sold for at the end of its estimated useful life). IRC § 167(c)(1).

b.  **IRC § 179 Election**—Under IRC § 179, a taxpayer can elect to treat the cost of any "IRC § 179 property" as an expense and not a capital expenditure. IRC § 179(a). "IRC § 179 property" is any depreciable personal property (not buildings or other items of depreciable real property) acquired by purchase for use in the active conduct of the taxpayer's business. IRC § 179(d). There is a limit to the amount that a taxpayer can elect to expense under IRC § 179. Under current law, the maximum dollar amount that can be expensed by an election under IRC § 179 is $250,000 for 2008, $125,000 for 2009 and 2010, and $25,000 as of 2011. IRC § 179(b)(1). Be careful, however, because Congress seems to enjoy playing around with this limitation every few years. An additional limitation under IRC § 179(b)(2) provides that the dollar limitation in IRC § 179(b)(1) is reduced dollar-for-dollar to the extent the total amount of IRC § 179 property placed in service during the year exceeds a certain threshold. Under current law, the threshold is $800,000 for 2008, $500,000 for 2009 and 2010, and $200,000 as of 2011. Here too, Congress loves to play with the dollar amounts, so it is always wise to double-check these dollar amounts in the latest version of the Code. A final limitation in IRC § 179 ensures that the amount elected as a current expense does not exceed the taxpayer's taxable income from all of the taxpayer's actively conducted business activities.

c. **Depreciation Method**—Assuming there is still some basis left to recover after the application of the IRC § 179 election, the taxpayer must determine the "applicable depreciation method." IRC § 168(b). Generally, unless the taxpayer elects or is required to use the "straight-line method" (where the cost is recovered ratably over the asset's recovery period), the applicable depreciation method is the "double-declining balance method." Under this method, a taxpayer each year deducts a portion of the asset's adjusted basis equal to twice the percentage that would apply to the original cost if the straight-line method were used. IRC § 168(b)(1)(A). For example, a taxpayer using the double-declining balance method to depreciate an asset with a five-year recovery period would deduct 40 percent of the asset's adjusted basis each year (40 percent is double the 20 percent that would be used if the taxpayer depreciated the original cost of the asset over its five-year recovery period). Importantly, the double-declining balance method switches over to the straight-line method in the first year in which the taxpayer would have a larger deduction if he or she used the straight-line method for the adjusted basis over the asset's remaining recovery period. IRC § 168(b)(1)(B). This conversion to the straight-line method enables the taxpayer to recover the entirety of the asset's basis. Note that the double-declining balance method is not available for depreciable real property; these assets must be depreciated on a straight-line basis. IRC § 168(b)(3).

d. **Recovery Period**—The recovery period is the number of years over which depreciation deductions with respect to the property will be claimed. While it is intended to be a rough approximation of the asset's estimated useful life, the applicable recovery period is determined by reference to a table that generally provides for accelerated recovery periods. Property is assigned to a recovery period under IRC § 168(c) based on its classification in IRC § 168(e). Classification, in turn, often depends on the asset's "class life," another arbitrary estimation of an asset's estimated useful life provided in official pronouncements of the Internal Revenue Service.

e. **Convention**—Most property is depreciated using the "half-year convention." IRC § 168(d)(1). The half-year convention is an assumption that the asset is first placed in service at the midpoint of the taxable year. IRC § 168(d)(4)(A). In other words, the first year's depreciation deduction with respect to any asset placed in service during the taxable year is equal to half of a full-year's deduction amount. The half-year convention relieves the taxpayer from having to compute a more complicated fraction based on the exact number of days the property was in service during its first year. The same convention applies if the depreciable asset is sold before the end of the recovery period; regardless of when a taxpayer disposes of the asset, he or she may claim a deduction equal to half of the amount that would be allowed if the asset were held for the entire year. A mid-month convention applies in the case of depreciable real property. IRC § 168(d)(2). If the taxpayer acquires more than 40 percent of his or her depreciable property during the last three months of the year, a special mid-quarter convention applies instead of the half-year convention. IRC § 168(d)(3)(A).

## E. AMORTIZATION DEDUCTIONS

Just as IRC § 168 depreciation is the general cost recovery regime for tangible assets subject to wear and tear, IRC § 197 amortization is the general cost recovery regime for intangible assets. This Part E helps you consider whether the taxpayer can amortize the basis of an intangible asset.

1. **IRC § 197 Intangible**—Is the property to which a capitalized cost relates a "IRC § 197 intangible?"

   a. **Definition**—IRC § 197(d)(1) provides that a "IRC § 197 intangible" means any of the following: (1) goodwill; (2) going concern value; (3) workforce in place (including its composition and the terms of any employment agreements); (4) business books and records and other information bases; (5) a patent, copyright, formula, process, design, pattern, knowhow, format or similar item of intellectual property; (6) a customer-based intangible (market share, market makeup, and similar value from providing future goods or services to customers in the ordinary course of business); (7) a supplier-based intangible (value from certain relationships with suppliers); (8) a license, permit or other right granted by a governmental unit or agency; (9) a covenant not to compete entered into in connection with the acquisition of a trade or business or an interest in a trade or business; and (10) any franchise, trademark, or trade name.

   b. **Yes**—If yes, continue in this Part E of the checklist.

   c. **No**—If no, then the asset is not subject to IRC § 197 amortization. Unless the asset is an intangible asset eligible for depreciation under IRC § 167(f) or Treas. Reg. § 1.167–3, there is no cost recovery for the asset. Instead, the taxpayer will claim the benefit of the capitalized cost when the intangible asset is sold or otherwise disposed of by the taxpayer.

2. **Not Excepted Out**—Is the property expressly excluded from the definition of a "IRC § 197 intangible?"

   a. **Exceptions**—IRC § 197(e) provides that the term "IRC § 197 intangible" does not include any of the following (this is not a complete list, but it covers most of the exceptions): (1) interests in corporations, partnerships, estates, or trusts; (2) interests under existing futures contracts, foreign currency contracts, notional principal contracts, or similar financial contracts; (3) any interests in land; (4) any readily available computer software (although such software is eligible for depreciation under IRC § 167(f)); (5) any other software not acquired as part of the acquisition of a trade or business; (5) interests in films, sound recordings, video tapes, books, or similar property not acquired as part of the acquisition of a trade or business; (6) rights to tangible property or services under a government contract not acquired as part of the acquisition of a trade or business; (7) interests in patents or copyrights not acquired as part of the acquisition of a trade or business; (8) rights in certain government contracts lasting less than 15 years and not acquired as part of the acquisition of a trade or business; (9) interests under existing leases of tangible property; (10) interests under any existing debt instrument; and (11) professional sports franchises.

b. **Yes**—If yes, then the asset is not subject to IRC § 197 amortization. Unless the asset is an intangible asset eligible for depreciation under IRC § 167(f) or Treas. Reg. § 1.167–3, there is no cost recovery for the asset. Instead, the taxpayer will claim the benefit of the capitalized cost when the intangible asset is sold or otherwise disposed of by the taxpayer.

c. **No**—If no, continue in this Part E of the checklist.

3. **Amortizable IRC § 197 Intangible**—Is the IRC § 197 intangible held for use in the taxpayer's business or investment activity, and was it acquired by the taxpayer after August 10, 1993?

a. **Yes**—If yes to both, then continue in this Part E of the checklist.

b. **No**—If no to either, then the asset is not subject to IRC § 197 amortization. Unless the asset is an intangible asset eligible for depreciation under IRC § 167(f) or Treas. Reg. § 1.167–3, there is no cost recovery for the asset. Instead, the taxpayer will claim the benefit of the capitalized cost when the intangible asset is sold or otherwise disposed of by the taxpayer.

4. **Not Self–Created**—Is the IRC § 197 intangible any of the following: self-created goodwill; self-created going concern value; self-created workforce in place (including its composition and the terms of any employment agreements); self-created business books and records and other information bases; self-created patents, copyrights, formulas, processes, designs, patterns, knowhow, formats or similar items of intellectual property; self-created customer-based intangibles (market share, market makeup, and similar value from providing future goods or services to customers in the ordinary course of business); or self-created supplier-based intangibles (value from certain relationships with suppliers)?

   a. **Yes**—If yes, then the asset is not subject to IRC § 197 amortization unless it was created in connection with an asset acquisition transaction (one involving the acquisition of assets constituting a trade or business). Unless the asset is an intangible asset eligible for depreciation under IRC § 167(f) or Treas. Reg. § 1.167–3, there is no cost recovery for the asset. Instead, the taxpayer will claim the benefit of the capitalized cost when the intangible asset is sold or otherwise disposed of by the taxpayer.

   b. **No**—If no, then the asset is an "amortizable IRC § 197 intangible." IRC § 197(c). IRC § 197 will apply to this asset; in fact, it represents the exclusive form of cost recovery for this asset. IRC § 197(b). Continue in this Part E of the checklist.

5. **15–Year Amortization**—The taxpayer can amortize an amortizable IRC § 197 intangible over a 15–year period beginning with the month in which the asset is acquired. IRC § 197(a). The taxpayer therefore divides the asset's adjusted basis by 180 to determine the monthly amortization deduction amount. Treas. Reg. § 1.197–2(f)(1).

## ILLUSTRATIVE PROBLEMS

These two problems show how the checklist can be used to determine the federal income tax treatment of various taxpayer costs.

---

## ■ PROBLEM 4.1 ■

---

T operates a bakery as T's trade or business. T's gross income from the bakery business is $100,000. In February of the current year, T paid the following costs:

- $5,000 for flour, sugar, and other supplies used in T's business;

- $10,000 for a new oven to replace the old oven used in T's business;

- $2,000 to repair ceiling tiles damaged in a kitchen fire at T's business;

- $10,000 to acquire the secret recipe for a special high-protein donut from an unrelated party; and

- $300 to an accountant to prepare T's federal income tax return.

What are the federal income tax consequences of these events to T?

### Analysis

---

Each of the costs will be examined separately. The $5,000 paid for flour, sugar, and other supplies used in T's business is an expense because such supplies are generally used or consumed within a short period of time. The facts stipulate that T incurred these costs while carrying on a trade or business activity. These supplies are ordinary and necessary expenses to operating a bakery. Therefore, T can deduct the $5,000 as a business expense under IRC § 162(a).

The $10,000 paid for a new oven is a capital expenditure. The cost serves to create a separate and distinct asset, so the cost must be capitalized. T's cost basis in the oven will be its $10,000 cost. T might argue that the cost represents a deductible repair expense because T is replacing an old oven that may no longer be sufficient for T's bakery business, but because the cost serves to acquire a whole new asset instead of bringing the old oven to a pre-damage condition, T's argument would not be persuasive. Because the oven will be used in T's business and will be subject to wear and tear in T's hands, T can depreciate the $10,000 cost over the applicable recovery period set forth in IRC § 168. Alternatively, T can elect to treat the entire cost of the oven as an expense under IRC § 179. The oven is depreciable personal property used in the active conduct of T's business, and the cost of the oven does not exceed the applicable dollar limitation in IRC § 179(b)(1). If T makes the IRC § 179 election, T can deduct the entire cost of the oven in the current year. If T does not make the election, T will instead claim depreciation deductions under IRC § 168. T will be allowed to use the double-declining balance method of depreciation, under which T can claim as a deduction in each year of the recovery period a percentage of T's adjusted basis equal to twice the percentage amount of the original cost that would be permitted if T used the straight-line method of depreciation. This will generate larger depreciation deductions in the early years of ownership. T will limited to one-half of the deduction amount for the first year because of the half-year convention, which assumes the asset is placed in service at the mid-point of the year even though T purchased this oven in February.

The $2,000 spent to repair T's ceiling tiles is a deductible repair expense. The cost does not materially add to the value of T's bakery premises or substantially prolong its useful life. Instead, the cost merely returns the premises to its pre-damage condition. Accordingly, the cost should be treated as a repair and not as an improvement. Because this repair is an ordinary and necessary expense incurred in T's business, T can deduct the cost as a business expense under IRC §§ 62(a).

The $10,000 spent for the secret recipe is a capital expenditure. The payment serves either to create a separate and distinct asset (the formula) or, alternatively, to create a substantial long-term future benefit for T. In either case, the cost must be capitalized. The formula is an intangible asset, so T would want to amortize the cost of the formula under IRC § 197. The formula is a IRC § 197 intangible under IRC § 197(d)(1)(C)(iii), and it is not excepted out of the definition of IRC § 197 intangibles under IRC § 197(e). T acquired the formula after 1993, the formula was not created by T, and T uses the formula in T's business. Accordingly, the formula is an amortizable IRC § 197 intangible. This means T can amortize the cost of the formula over a 15–year period that begins in February of the current year. In other words, T's deduction for the current year will be computed by dividing the $10,000 cost by 180 months (15 years) and then multiplying that result by the 11 months during which T owned the asset in the current year.

The $300 paid to the accountant to prepare T's federal income tax return is an expense and not a capital expenditure. The cost does not serve to create any long-term future benefit for T, nor does the cost create or add to the value of some tangible asset. Although T operates a business and this business affects T's tax return, the expense is not a business expense because the return relates to T's personal liability for federal income tax. Under IRC § 212(3), however, T can deduct this expense because it is an ordinary and necessary expense paid in the determination of a tax. This will be a miscellaneous itemized deduction, so it is deductible only to the extent it and T's other miscellaneous itemized deductions, in the aggregate, exceed two percent of T's adjusted gross income.

---

## ■ PROBLEM 4.2 ■

---

T operates a winery as T's trade or business activity. In the current year, T paid $40,000 to construct wine barrels for use in T's business. T stores wine in the barrels before bottling the wine for shipment to retailers and consumers. The $40,000 price for the barrels consisted of $25,000 in wood, metal rings, and nails and $15,000 in wages paid to T's employees who assisted in construction.

In the current year, T also paid $20,000 to an attorney for legal advice in connection with T's possible acquisition of a tavern in a nearby metropolitan area. T is contemplating the purchase of a tavern, not only because of his long-standing interest in the restaurant industry but also as an outlet for featuring T's wines. T has not yet purchased a tavern or even decided for certain that T will do so.

      What are the federal income tax consequences of these events to T?

## Analysis

As before, each of the costs will be considered separately. The amounts paid in the construction of the wine barrels must be capitalized. These are costs paid in the construction of a new asset, and the Uniform Capitalization Rules in IRC § 263A require taxpayers to capitalize all costs paid in the construction or production of personal property. Even though supplies and wages are normally deductible expenses if incurred in a trade or business activity, such costs must be capitalized if they go toward construction or production of some new asset. Consequently, T will have a $40,000 basis in the barrels. The barrels are used in T's winery business and are subject to wear and tear in T's hands, so T can depreciate this cost under IRC § 168. Alternatively, T can elect to treat the entire cost of the barrels as an expense under IRC § 179. The barrels are depreciable personal property used in the active conduct of T's business, and the cost of the barrels does not exceed the applicable dollar limitation in IRC § 179(b)(1). If T makes the IRC § 179 election, T can deduct the entire $40,000 cost in the current year. If T does not make the election, T will instead claim depreciation deductions under IRC § 168. T will be allowed to use the double-declining balance method of depreciation, under which T can claim as a deduction in each year of the recovery period a percentage of T's adjusted basis equal to twice the percentage amount of the original cost that would be permitted if T used the straight-line method of depreciation. This will generate larger depreciation deductions in the early years of ownership. T will limited to one-half of the deduction amount for the first year because of the half-year convention, which assumes the barrels are placed in service at the mid-point of the year. If the barrels are T's only depreciable asset for the year, the mid-quarter convention will apply instead of the half-year convention if the barrels are first placed in service during the last three months of the current year; we need more facts to determine whether this special rule applies.

The $20,000 in legal fees is likely an expense and not a capital expenditure. The fees have not resulted in the creation of a new asset and have not yet yielded any substantial future benefit for T. Although the cost is an expense, it is not currently deductible because T is not yet "carrying on" the business of operating a tavern. The tavern is probably a separate business activity from the winery even though T hopes to sell T's wines in the tavern. Thus there is no deduction under IRC § 162(a). Instead, the cost will be treated as a start-up expenditure under IRC § 195. Once T launches the tavern business, T can amortize the legal fees and all other start-up costs over the first 15 years of the tavern business. T will be able to deduct $5,000 of the start-up expenditures in the first year of the new business, assuming the total start-up expenditures do not exceed $50,000.

## POINTS TO REMEMBER

- There must be authority for every deduction claimed by a taxpayer.

- Capital expenditures represent long-term benefits from a cost. Capital expenditures are generally not deductible in full in the year of payment, but such payments do serve to create or add to basis.

- Once a taxpayer has basis in an asset, the analysis shifts to whether the taxpayer can depreciate or amortize that basis over some number of years. If not, the taxpayer must wait until a sale or other disposition of the asset to claim the benefit of the capital expenditure.

- Any cost that is not a capital expenditure is an expense. Expenses paid in connection with business or investment activities are generally deductible, while expenses paid in connection with personal activities are generally not deductible.

*

# CHAPTER 5

# Personal Expenses

This Chapter considers several deduction provisions that relate to personal matters, activities unrelated to a taxpayer's business or investment activities. IRC § 262(a) generally disallows deductions for "personal, living, or family expenses," but most of the provisions at issue in this Chapter deviate from that general rule. The general rule is based mainly on the theory that income is measured in part by *consumption*, which represents (again, in part) expenditures made for a taxpayer's personal use. If consumption is part of income, therefore, it is inconsistent to permit deductions for personal expenses. The deductions discussed in this Chapter are thus inconsistent with a "pure" income tax measured in part by consumption and are viewed by some as improper. Nonetheless, Congress recognized that other economic or public policy concerns may justify departure from the pure income tax model.

## PERSONAL EXPENSES REVIEW

*Interest Expense.* IRC § 163(a) generally permits a deduction for interest paid or accrued during the taxable year. Prior to 1986, most any payment of interest generated a deduction. But the Tax Reform Act of 1986 sharply curtailed the scope of the interest deduction. While the general rule in IRC § 163(a) remains, IRC § 163(h) renders all but six forms of interest non-deductible. In effect, then, the real general rule is one of non-deduction with six discreet exceptions. Four of these exceptions (active business interest, taxable investment interest, education loan interest, and qualified residence interest) are significant, especially the last one. The deduction for home mortgage interest enables many taxpayers to transition from renters to homeowners. Some studies estimate that in 2008 alone Congress will forego $80.7 billion in tax revenues by allowing the deduction for qualified residence interest, but the home mortgage interest is politically sacred, so hopefully the economic benefits of the deduction outweigh the cost of this forgone revenue.

*Taxes.* Paying federal income tax on dollars used to pay other taxes may seem on its face to be a harsh rule, but an ideal income tax would not allow a deduction for such expenses to the extent they relate to personal consumption or personal-use activities. Yet IRC § 164(a) generally permits a deduction for various tax expenses, most likely because exempting from the federal income tax the dollars used to pay taxes to other governmental bodies acts as an indirect subsidy to such bodies. Notice that IRC § 164 generally makes no distinction between taxes related to business matters, investment activities, or personal activities—all are deductible if listed in IRC § 164(a). IRC § 275 specifically disallows a deduction for most federal taxes paid—a sensible provision given there is no need for the federal government to subsidize itself. With respect to foreign taxes paid, one should also consider the availability of the foreign tax credit under IRC § 901. Taxpayers who pay taxes to foreign governments generally have a choice between deducting such payments under IRC § 164(a) or claiming the credit under IRC § 901. In most cases, the credit is the better option, for it reduces tax liability dollar-for-dollar, while a deduction reduces tax liability only by that proportion equal to the taxpayer's marginal tax rate. The deduction is the better option in those cases where the various limitations on the credit (most notably in IRC § 904) reduce the amount of the credit to a point below the tax savings from the deduction.

*Bad Debts.* If the taxpayer is unable to collect on a debt owed by another person, the taxpayer has suffered a loss in the colloquial sense. Because losses from these "bad debts" are real economic losses to a taxpayer, IRC § 166 permits a deduction for bad debts, and the deduction is made available to debts arising from business, investment, *and personal* activities. Under IRC § 166, there are two types of bad debts: business bad debts (those connected to the taxpayer's trade or business) and nonbusiness bad debts (all other debts). Both can be deducted in the year in which they become worthless, but there are two significant limitations with respect to nonbusiness bad debts. First, individual taxpayers can only deduct nonbusiness bad debts where they have become entirely (as opposed to partially) worthless. Second, individual taxpayers must treat losses from entirely worthless nonbusiness bad debts as short-term capital losses. As explained in Chapter 9, capital losses are less favorable than ordinary losses because capital losses are currently deductible only to the extent of a taxpayer's capital gains plus up to $3,000 of ordinary income. See IRC § 1211(b). In all cases where a deduction is available for a bad debt, IRC § 166(b) limits the deduction to the taxpayer's basis in the debt. In most cases, that means the deduction is limited to the outstanding amount of the loan.

*Charitable Contributions.* Perhaps it is a sad reflection of our society, but Congress provides the deduction in IRC § 170 to encourage us to do what we might not do otherwise: give to charity. There are strict limits on the charitable contribution deduction, however. First, only gifts to certain charitable organizations will qualify for the deduction. A handout given to a street peddler will not be deductible. Second, the transfer must be a "gift" and not a bargained-for exchange. So when you give $100 to National Public Radio and receive a $10 mug as a token of the charity's appreciation, the amount of the deduction is limited to the $90 gift portion. Third, in the case of charitable contributions of property there are several situations where the deduction will be limited to the donor's basis in the contributed property (for more on basis, see Chapter 6). And finally, there is an overall cap on the total amount of charitable contributions a taxpayer may claim in any single year. The cap is always a function of the taxpayer's adjusted gross income, but the exact cap depends on the type of property contributed and the nature of the recipient organization.

*Hobby Expenses.* Chapter 4 explained that expenses incurred in business and investment activities are generally deductible. Hobbies often generate expenses too, but because the taxpayer lacks a profit motive when engaging in a hobby, those expenses cannot be classified as business or investment expenses. Accordingly, the general rule in IRC § 183(a) prohibits any deductions attributable to an activity "not engaged in for profit." But IRC § 183(b) then *allows* two types of deductions attributable to a hobby: those deductions that would be allowable to the taxpayer no matter whether they relate to a hobby activity (like taxes deductible under IRC § 164) (the "independently deductible expenses"); and those deductions that would be allowable to the taxpayer if the hobby was instead a for-profit activity, but only to the extent that the income from the hobby exceeds the independently deductible expenses attributable to the hobby. In effect, losses and expenses attributable to a hobby activity that otherwise may not be deductible can be used to offset income from the hobby, but only to that extent.

*Medical Expenses.* Expenses paid for medical care are clearly personal in nature and thus would not be deductible in a "pure" tax system. The lack of a deduction is not a hardship for people who are insured since they incur little or no out-of-pocket expenses for medical care in the first place. Uninsured persons, however, may incur substantial medical costs with no hope of reimbursement. Where an uninsured taxpayer pays extraordinarily high costs for medical care in a single year, IRC § 213 allows a deduction for uncompensated medical expenses. However, the deduction is allowed only to the extent such costs exceed 7.5 percent of the taxpayer's adjusted gross income. The 7.5 percent threshold is a substantial limitation. Because of the high "co-payment," most taxpayers do not get any benefit from IRC § 213; instead, the deduction is helpful only to those who pay excessive health care costs in the taxable year.

*Alimony.* Just as the receipt of alimony is gross income under IRC § 71(a) (see Chapter 2), the payment of alimony can give rise to a deduction under IRC § 215. The deduction is taken above the line. IRC § 62(a)(10). The taxpayer seeking a deduction for alimony must provide the social security number of the recipient spouse on the taxpayer's return, and if the recipient spouse is a nonresident alien individual, the taxpayer must even withhold a percentage of the payment for federal income taxes. As discussed in Chapter 2, the payment must qualify as "alimony" in order to be deductible.

*Moving Expenses.* IRC § 217(a) authorizes a deduction for moving expenses "in connection with the commencement of work. . . at a new principal place of work." Beyond the fact that the taxpayer must be starting a new job, there are two conditions for the deduction. The first condition is that the distance between his or her old residence and the new job location must be at least 50 miles further than the distance between the old residence and the old job location. IRC § 217(c)(1). The second condition is that the taxpayer must be employed at the new work location (though not necessarily in the same job or even with same employer) for at least 39 weeks of the 12–month period following the move. If the taxpayer cannot meet this test, there is an alternate test using 78 weeks over 24 months. Notice that self-employed taxpayers may only use this second test to meet the time condition. IRC § 217(c)(2). If both conditions are present, the taxpayer gets to deduct the "reasonable" expenses of moving items from the old residence to the new residence, along with the expenses of traveling from the old residence to the new residence. IRC § 217(b)(1). The moving and traveling expenses of the taxpayer's spouse and dependents are also deductible if the spouse and dependents lived in the old residence before the move and will live with the taxpayer in the new residence following the move.

*Education Expenses.* Education expenses can serve both business and personal objectives. They can help improve skills required for use in a trade or business, and they can broaden personal horizons. Service professionals (including attorneys) are required to take continuing education courses to maintain their licenses or certifications. There is no doubt that those expenses should be deductible. But if the educational expenses qualify a taxpayer for a new occupation, there is less justification for a deduction. The regulations impose a two-tiered test for deducting education expenses as business expenses under IRC § 162(a). In order to be deductible, education expenses must *either*: (1) maintain or improve skills required in the taxpayer's trade or business; or (2) be incurred by the taxpayer's employer as a condition to maintaining employment. Treas. Reg. § 1.162–5(c). Furthermore, if the expenses fall into one of these two categories, they must *neither*: (1) constitute the minimum educational requirements for qualifying the taxpayer for his or her current trade or business; nor (2) be related to a course of study that will qualify the taxpayer for a new trade or business. Treas. Reg. § 1.162–5(b). If education expenses are not deductible as business expenses, the taxpayer may be able to claim a deduction instead under IRC § 222 if the costs are for "qualified tuition and related expenses."

*Clothing Expenses.* As one of life's necessities, costs for clothing are quintessential personal expenses. Nonetheless, the Internal Revenue Service and the courts have allowed taxpayers to deduct the costs of clothing used in a taxpayer's business under IRC § 162(a), provided such clothing is not suitable for ordinary wear. Accordingly, the professional rodeo clown can likely deduct amounts paid for wigs and oversize overalls, but not the cost of regular shirts or boots as those would suitable for ordinary wear. The test is objective, so a slacker who seeks a deduction for a business suit on the grounds that he or she would never, ever wear such a garment outside of the office will fail.

*Travel Costs.* IRC § 162(a)(2) permits a deduction for "traveling expenses" so long as the taxpayer is "away from home" and "in the pursuit of a trade or business." Traveling expenses typically include costs for transportation, lodging and meals. Thus, in seeking to deduct these costs, taxpayers must first determine whether they were incurred "away from home." If so, then IRC § 162(a)(2) provides specific authority for the deduction. If not, then a deduction is unlikely. To be "away from home," the taxpayer must be gone overnight from his or her principal place of business. Commuting expenses, the cost to travel from home to work and back again, are not deductible because the taxpayer is not away from home. Even if the taxpayer lives very far from work, that is viewed as a personal choice of the taxpayer that undermines any claim for a deduction.

*Entertainment Expenses and Business Meals.* To close an important business deal, for example, a taxpayer might take a client out for dinner and a show. Even if the expenses of the meal and entertainment qualify as ordinary and necessary business expenses, to claim a deduction the expenses must also survive the limitations set forth in IRC § 274. IRC § 274(a)(1)(A) disallows a deduction for entertainment expenses unless the entertainment is "directly related" to a trade or business or, in the case of entertainment before or after a business discussion, "associated with" a trade or business. Both meals and entertainment expenses are subject to strict substantiation requirements in IRC § 274(d). And IRC § 274(n) limits the deduction for meals and entertainment to 50 percent of the cost. In the case of meals, there are two additional limitations. First, the meals must not be "lavish or extravagant under the circumstances." Second, the taxpayer who claims the deduction must be present when the meals are served.

## PERSONAL EXPENSES CHECKLIST

This checklist will assist in determining whether a particular cost is deductible.

### A. INTEREST EXPENSE (IRC §§ 163; 221)

Use this Part A if the taxpayer pays or accrues interest expense during the taxable year. IRC § 163(h)(1) precludes a deduction for "personal interest," so this checklist focuses on whether the interest expense at issue is non-deductible personal interest.

1. **Active Business Interest**—Is the interest attributable to debt related to a trade or business of the taxpayer in which he or she materially participates other than performing services as an employee?

   a. **Yes**—If yes, the interest expense is deductible. IRC § 163(a), (h)(2)(A).

   b. **No**—If no, continue in this Part A.

2. **Passive Activity Business Interest**—Is the interest attributable to debt related to a trade or business of the taxpayer in which he or she does not materially participate?

a. **Yes**—If yes, the interest expense is deductible, IRC § 163(a), (h)(2)(C), but only to the extent the deduction is permitted by IRC § 469. See Chapter 8.

b. **No**—If no, continue in this Part A.

3. **Taxable Investment Interest**—Is the interest attributable to debt used to finance investment activities that will yield income subject to federal income tax?

a. **Yes**—If yes, the interest expense is classified as "investment interest," IRC § 163(d)(3)(A), and is deductible to the extent of the taxpayer's "net investment income." IRC § 163(a), (d)(1), (h)(2)(B). Net investment income, generally, is the excess of the taxpayer's income and gains from investment activities over the deductible expenses directly connected to such activities. IRC § 163(d)(4).

b. **No**—If no, continue in this Part A.

4. **Qualified Residence Interest**—Is the interest attributable to either "acquisition indebtedness" with respect to a "qualified residence" or "home equity indebtedness" with respect to a "qualified residence?"

a. **Qualified Residence**—A qualified residence means the taxpayer's principal residence and one other personal residence selected by the taxpayer for purposes of this rule. IRC § 163(h)(4)(A)(i). To be a "principal residence," the taxpayer generally needs to live in the home for the majority of the taxable year, although other factors will be considered in making this determination. Treas. Reg. § 1.121–1(b)(2). To be a "personal residence," the taxpayer generally needs to live in the home for at least 14 days during the taxable year (even more if the taxpayer rents the home to others for more than 140 days during the year). IRC § 280A(d)(1).

b. **Acquisition Indebtedness**—Acquisition indebtedness is any debt incurred to buy, build, or improve a qualified residence that is secured by such residence. IRC § 163(h)(3)(B)(i). It also includes any debt that represents the refinancing of any acquisition indebtedness, but only to the extent of such prior acquisition indebtedness. Note that there is a $1,000,000 ceiling ($500,000 in the case of a married person filing a separate return) on the total amount of acquisition indebtedness. IRC § 163(h)(3)(B)(ii). Thus, for example, if the taxpayer incurs a $1,200,000 mortgage to purchase his or her personal residence, only the interest paid on the first $1,000,000 of the mortgage can qualify as interest on acquisition indebtedness.

c.  **Home Equity Indebtedness**—Generally, home equity indebtedness is any debt (other than acquisition indebtedness) secured by a qualified residence, but only to the extent of the taxpayer's "equity" in the residence (measured by subtracting any acquisition indebtedness from the fair market value of the residence). IRC § 163(h)(3)(C)(i). The amount of home equity indebtedness cannot exceed $100,000, however, even if the taxpayer has more than $100,000 of equity in the residence. IRC § 163(h)(3)(C)(ii).

d.  **Yes**—If yes, the interest expense is deductible. IRC § 163(a), (h)(2)(D).

e.  **No**—If no, continue in this Part A.

5.  **Estate Tax Interest**—Is the interest attributable to debt arising from the deferred payment of federal estate taxes under IRC §§ 6163 and 6601?

a.  **Yes**—If yes, the interest expense is deductible. IRC § 163(a), (h)(2)(E).

b.  **No**—If no, continue in this Part A.

6.  **Education Loan Interest**—Is the interest attributable to a "qualified education loan?"

a.  **Qualified Education Loan**—Generally, a qualified education loan is one that meets the following four requirements: (i) it was incurred solely to pay "qualified higher education expenses" (meaning the costs of attending most post-secondary educational institutions, including tuition, fees, books, supplies, transportation, and room and board); (ii) it was incurred for the benefit of the taxpayer, the taxpayer's spouse, or anyone who was the taxpayer's dependent when the loan was incurred; (iii) its proceeds were used within a reasonable time to pay the qualified higher education expenses; and (iv) the qualified higher education expenses are attributable to education furnished to the person described in (ii) above during the period in which such person was in attendance as a degree candidate on at least a half-time basis. IRC § 221(d).

b. **Yes**—If yes, then as long as the taxpayer cannot be claimed as a dependent on another taxpayer's return, the taxpayer can deduct the interest expense paid. IRC §§ 163(a); 163(h)(2)(F); 221(a); 221(c). The taxpayer may claim the deduction even if the interest expense was actually paid by a third party on behalf of the taxpayer. Treas. Reg. § 1.221–1(b)(4). Note that if the taxpayer is married, a deduction is permitted only if the taxpayer files a joint return with his or her spouse. IRC § 221(e)(2). The maximum amount of the deduction is limited under IRC § 221(b)(1) as follows:

| Taxpayer's modified adjusted gross income | Maximum deduction amount |
|---|---|
| $0–$100,000 for married couples filing jointly; $0–$50,000 for all others (these brackets are adjusted annually for inflation) | **$2,500** |
| $100,001–$130,000 for married couples filing jointly; $50,001–$65,000 for all others (these brackets are adjusted annually for inflation) | **$2,500** *minus* **the "reduction amount."** The reduction amount is determined by multiplying $2,500 by a fraction, the numerator of which is the excess of the taxpayer's modified adjusted gross income over $100,000 (married filing jointly) or $50,000 (all others), and the denominator of which is $30,000 (married filing |

| Taxpayer's modified adjusted gross income | Maximum deduction amount |
|---|---|
| | jointly) or $15,000 (all others). [The $50,000 and $100,000 numbers are adjusted annually for inflation, but not the other numbers.] |
| $130,001+ for married couples filing jointly; $65,001 for all others (these numbers are adjusted annually for inflation) | **Zero** |

    c. **No**—If no, then the interest expense is "personal interest" and, therefore, not deductible. IRC § 163(h)(1).

## B. TAXES (IRC § 164)

Use this Part B to determine whether any tax paid or accrued by the taxpayer during the taxable year is deductible.

    1. **Federal Income Taxes**—Is the tax a federal income tax, including not only the federal income tax of which we are now so fond but also social security tax and federal tax withheld from wages?

        a. **Yes**—If yes, then no deduction is allowed. IRC § 275(a)(1). The only exception is that a self-employed taxpayer may deduct one-half of the self-employment taxes he or she pays during the taxable year. IRC §§ 164(f); 275(a).

        b. **No**—If no, continue in this Part A.

    2. **Wealth Transfer Taxes**—Is the tax an estate, inheritance, legacy, succession, or gift tax imposed by the federal, state, or local government?

        a. **Yes**—If yes, then no deduction is allowed. IRC § 275(a)(3).

        b. **No**—If no, continue in this Part A.

    3. **Special Assessments**—Is the tax an assessment against local benefits of a kind that tends to increase the value of the

assessed property (like a special assessment imposed on homes in a neighborhood to pay for installation of street lighting in the neighborhood)?

   a.  **Yes**—If yes, then no deduction is allowed. IRC § 164(c)(1). Instead, the amount of the tax paid by the taxpayer should be added to the taxpayer's basis in the property subject to the assessment, as the tax represents a cost that permanently improves the property.

   b.  **No**—If no, continue in this Part A.

4. **Real Property Taxes Where Property Not Sold**—Is the tax a state, local, or foreign tax on real property that was not sold by the taxpayer during the taxable year?

   a.  **Yes**—If yes, then the taxpayer may deduct the tax expense. IRC § 164(a)(1).

   b.  **No**—If no, continue in this Part A.

5. **Real Property Taxes Where Property Sold During Year**—Is the tax a state, local, or foreign tax on real property assessed on property that was sold by or to the taxpayer during the taxable year?

   a.  **Yes**—If yes, then the taxpayer is generally deemed to have paid a share of the tax that accrued during the taxable year proportionate to the number of days during the year that the taxpayer owned the property. IRC § 164(d). Accordingly, a deduction is allowed for that share of the taxes. IRC § 164(a)(1). The taxpayer cannot deduct any tax beyond that which is allocable to the taxpayer under IRC § 164(d), even if the taxpayer actually paid such amount. IRC § 164(c)(2).

   b.  **No**—If no, continue in this Part A.

6. **Personal Property Taxes**—Is the tax an ad valorem tax imposed by a state or local government on an annual basis in respect of personal property? (An ad valorem tax is a tax based on the value of property.)

   a.  **Yes**—If yes, then the taxpayer may deduct the tax expense. IRC § 164(a)(2).

   b.  **No**—If no, continue in this Part A.

7. **Foreign Income Taxes**—Is the tax an income, war profits, or excess profits tax imposed by a foreign country?

   a. **Yes**—If yes, then the taxpayer has two options. First, the taxpayer can claim the foreign tax credit under IRC § 901 and, generally, credit the amount of foreign tax paid dollar-for-dollar against his or her United States tax liability. Second, the taxpayer can deduct the amount of foreign tax paid under IRC § 164(a)(3). If the taxpayer claims the foreign tax credit, the taxpayer cannot also claim the deduction. IRC § 275(a)(4). In most cases, taxpayers will prefer the foreign tax credit because it will result in a greater tax savings.

   b. **No**—If no, continue in this Part A.

8. **State and Local General Sales Taxes**—Is the tax a sales tax imposed by a state or local government? A "sales tax" is one imposed at one rate with respect to the retail sale of a broad range of items. IRC § 164(b)(5)(B).

   a. **Yes**—If yes, then the taxpayer may deduct the tax expense, IRC § 164(b)(5)(A), or, alternatively, deduct state and local income taxes, as discussed in B(9) below. To save the headache of saving all receipts indicating sales tax paid, a taxpayer may use tables prescribed by the Internal Revenue Service to compute the amount of the deduction. The tables assume no major expenditures for the year, so sales tax paid on any big-ticket items like cars, boats, and other assets identified by the Internal Revenue Service are deductible in addition to the amounts specified in the tables. IRC § 164(b)(5)(H). Note that the deduction for state and local general sales taxes may not be in effect for the taxable year at issue; be sure to consult the version of the Code in effect at that time to determine if the deduction for state and local general sales taxes is available.

   b. **No**—If no, continue in this Part B.

9. **State and Local Income Taxes**—Is the tax an income tax imposed by a state or local government?

   a. **Yes**—If yes, then the taxpayer may deduct the tax expense, IRC § 164(a)(3), or, alternatively, deduct state and local general sales taxes, as discussed in B(8) above. A taxpayer may not deduct both income taxes and general sales taxes imposed by state and local governments. Note that the deduction for state and local general sales taxes may not be in effect for the taxable year at issue; be sure to consult the version of the Code in effect at that time to determine if the deduction for state and local general sales taxes is available.

b. **No**—If no, continue in this Part B.

10. **Generation–Skipping Transfer Taxes on Income Distributions**—Is the tax a generation-skipping transfer tax imposed on an income distribution received by the taxpayer?

a. **Yes**—If yes, then the taxpayer may deduct the tax expense. IRC § 164(a)(4).

b. **No**—If no, continue in this Part B.

11. **Taxes Paid Upon Purchase or Sale**—Is the tax paid or incurred in connection with the acquisition or disposition of property?

a. **Yes**—If yes, then the tax expense is not deductible. IRC § 164(a), last sentence. In the case of a tax imposed upon the acquisition of property, the tax expense is added to the taxpayer's basis in the acquired property. In the case of a tax imposed upon the disposition of property, the tax expense is subtracted from the amount realized in the disposition. See Chapter 6.

b. **No**—If no, then continue in this Part B.

12. **Other Taxes Incurred in Business or Investment Activity**—Is the tax paid or accrued in carrying on a trade or business or an investment activity?

a. **Yes**—If yes, then the taxpayer may deduct the tax expense. IRC § 164(a). In the case of taxes incurred for business purposes, the appropriate authority is IRC § 162. For taxed incurred with respect to an investment activity, the authority for the deduction is IRC § 212.

b. **No**—If no, then the tax expense is not deductible.

## C. BAD DEBTS (IRC § 166)

Use this Part C when the taxpayer is unable to collect repayment of an amount loaned to another party.

1. **Bona Fide Debt**—Was the taxpayer owed a bona fide debt?

    a. **Definition**—A bona fide debt is a debt arising from a debtor-creditor relationship based upon a valid and enforceable obligation to pay a fixed sum of money. Treas. Reg. § 1.166–1(c). There must have been a contemporaneous intent by both the taxpayer and the borrower at the time of the loan to create an enforceable obligation of repayment. *Delta Plastics Corporation v. Commissioner*, 54 T.C. 1287 (1970).

    b. **Yes**—If yes, then continue in this Part C.

    c. **No**—If no, then there is no deduction under IRC § 166.

2. **Debt Gone Bad**—Has the debt become worthless, in whole or in part?

    a. **Worthlessness**—All pertinent evidence must be considered to determine whether a debt is entirely or partially worthless. Treas. Reg. § 1.166–2(a). The debtor's bankruptcy "is an indication of the worthlessness of at least a part of an unsecured and unpreferred debt." Treas. Reg. § 1.166–2(c)(1). The taxpayer is not required to take legal action in order to establish that a debt is worthless; it is sufficient if the taxpayer can prove that any such action would be futile because the debt is uncollectible. Treas. Reg. § 1.166–2(b).

    b. **Yes**—If yes, then continue in this Part C.

    c. **No**—If no, then there is not yet any deduction under IRC § 166. The debt must become worthless to some extent before IRC § 166 is triggered.

3. **Business Bad Debt or Nonbusiness Bad Debt**—Was the debt created or acquired in connection with the taxpayer's trade or business, or does the loss from this debt becoming worthless arise in the taxpayer's trade or business?

    a. **Yes**—If the answer to either of these questions is yes, then this is a business bad debt. IRC § 166(d)(2). Consequently, if the debt has become entirely worthless, the taxpayer can deduct his or her entire basis in the debt (which is generally equal to the amount loaned less any repayments that were made before the debt became worthless). IRC § 166(a)(1), (b). If the debt has become partially worthless, the taxpayer may deduct such portion of the debt that the taxpayer has actually charged off during the year. IRC § 166(a)(2); Treas. Reg. § 1.166–3(a)(2).

b.  **No**—If the answer to both of these questions is no, then this is a nonbusiness bad debt. IRC § 166(d)(2). Consequently, if the debt has become entirely worthless, the taxpayer can deduct his or her entire basis in the debt (which is generally equal to the amount loaned less any repayments that were made before the debt became worthless), IRC § 166(b), but the deduction will be characterized as a short-term capital loss. IRC § 166(d)(1)(B). If the debt has become partially worthless, there is no deduction at all. IRC § 166(d)(1)(A); Treas. Reg. § 1.166–5(a)(2).

## D.  CHARITABLE CONTRIBUTIONS (IRC § 170)

Use this Part D whenever the taxpayer contributes cash or property to a charitable organization.

1.  **Qualified Recipient**—Did the taxpayer transfer cash or property to an organization described in IRC § 170(c)?

a.  **Yes**—If yes, then continue in this Part D.

b.  **No**—If no, then no deduction under IRC § 170 is allowed.

2.  **No Quid Pro Quo**—Did the taxpayer receive or expect to receive property or services from the charity in exchange for the cash or property transferred?

a.  **Yes**—If yes, then no deduction is allowed unless (and only to the extent that) the value of the cash or property transferred to the charity exceeds the value of the property or services received from the charity. Treas. Reg. § 1.170A–1(h)(2)(i). If the taxpayer receives full consideration for an amount transferred to charity, there is no deduction because there has been no charitable contribution. *Hernandez v. Commissioner*, 490 U.S. 680 (1989).

   b. **No**—If no, continue in this Part A.

3. **Deduction Amount**—How much of the contribution may the taxpayer deduct? The answer to this question depends on the type of property contributed to the charity. Use the following table to determine the amount of the deduction:

| Type of Contribution | Deduction Amount |
|---|---|
| **Cash** | Amount of cash contributed |
| **Loss property** (basis exceeds value) | Value of property [Treas. Reg. § 1.170A–1(c)(1)] |
| **Ordinary income property** (value exceeds basis, but it's not a capital asset) | Basis of property [IRC § 170(e)(1)(A)] |
| **Short-term capital gain property** (value exceeds basis in capital asset held for not more than one year) | Basis of property [IRC § 170(e)(1)(A)] |
| **Long-term capital gain real property** (value exceeds basis in real property that is a capital asset and held more than one year) | Value of property [Treas. Reg. § 1.170A–1(c)(1)], but basis of property if contributed to private foundation [IRC § 170(e)(1)(B)(ii)] |
| **Long-term capital gain intellectual property** (value exceeds basis in certain intellectual property that is a capital asset and held for more than one year) | Basis of property [IRC § 170(e)(1)(B)(iii)] |
| **Other intangible long-term capital gain property** (value exceeds basis in an intangible capital asset and held for more than one year) | Value of property [Treas. Reg. § 1.170A–1(c)(1)], but basis of property if contributed to private foundation [IRC § 170(e)(1)(B)(ii)] unless it's "qualified appreciated stock" [IRC § 170(e)(5)] |

| Type of Contribution | Deduction Amount |
|---|---|
| **Long-term capital gain re-lated tangible property** (value exceeds basis in a tangible capital asset held more than one year and related to the charity's purpose) | Value of property [Treas. Reg. § 1.170A–1(c)(1)], but basis of property if contributed to private foundation [IRC § 170(e)(1)(B)(ii)] |
| **Long-term capital gain un-related tangible property** (value exceeds basis in a tangible capital asset held more than one year and unrelated to charity's purpose) | Basis of property [IRC § 170(e)(1)(B)(i)] |

4. **Annual Deduction Limitation and Carryover**—How much of the deduction amount may the taxpayer claim in the year of contribution? The answer to this question depends both on the type of contribution and the nature of the organization receiving the contribution. Generally speaking, a taxpayer cannot claim total charitable contributions in excess of 50 percent of the taxpayer's "contribution base." The taxpayer's contribution base, generally, is his or her adjusted gross income (the only difference is that any net operating loss carryback to the year at issue is ignored in computing the contribution base). IRC § 170(b)(1)(F). In some cases, however, there is a more limited ceiling on the total amount deductible for any one taxable year. Use the table below to determine the maximum amount the taxpayer can deduct in the year of contribution. Note that any amount not deductible in the year of contribution carries over for up to five succeeding taxable years. IRC § 170(d)(1).

| Type of Contribution | % Limit if Contributed to Public Charity [one described in IRC § 170(b)(1)(A)] | % Limit if Contributed to Private Charity [one not described in IRC § 170(b)(1)(A)] |
|---|---|---|
| **Cash** | 50% of adjusted gross income [IRC § 170(b)(1)(A)] | 30% of adjusted gross income [IRC § 170(b)(1)(B)] |
| **Loss property** (basis exceeds value) | 50% of adjusted gross income [IRC § 170(b)(1)(A)] | 30% of adjusted gross income [IRC § 170(b)(1)(B)] |
| **Ordinary income property** (value exceeds basis, but it's not a capital asset) | 50% of adjusted gross income [IRC § 170(b)(1)(A)] | 30% of adjusted gross income [IRC § 170(b)(1)(B)] |
| **Short-term capital gain property** (value exceeds basis in capital asset held for not more than one year) | 50% of adjusted gross income [IRC § 170(b)(1)(A)] | 20% of adjusted gross income [IRC § 170(b)(1)(D)(i)] |
| **Long-term capital gain real property** (value exceeds basis in real property that is a capital asset and held more than one year) | 30% of adjusted gross income [IRC § 170(b)(1)(C)(i)] | 20% of adjusted gross income [IRC § 170(b)(1)(D)(i)] |
| **Long-term capital gain intellectual property** (value exceeds basis in certain intellectual property that is a capital asset and held for more than one year) | 50% of adjusted gross income [IRC § 170(b)(1)(A)] | 20% of adjusted gross income [IRC § 170(b)(1)(D)(i)] |

| Type of Contribution | % Limit if Contributed to Public Charity [one described in IRC § 170(b)(1)(A)] | % Limit if Contributed to Private Charity [one not described in IRC § 170(b)(1)(A)] |
|---|---|---|
| **Other intangible long-term capital gain property** (value exceeds basis in an intangible capital asset and held for more than one year) | 30% of adjusted gross income [IRC § 170(b)(1)(C)(i)] | 20% of adjusted gross income [IRC § 170(b)(1)(D)(i)] |
| **Long-term capital gain related tangible property** (value exceeds basis in a tangible capital asset held more than one year and related to the charity's purpose) | 30% of adjusted gross income [IRC § 170(b)(1)(C)(i)], but 50% of adjusted gross income if to a private foundation [IRC § 170(b)(1)(A)] | 20% of adjusted gross income [IRC § 170(b)(1)(D)(i)] |
| **Long-term capital gain unrelated tangible property** (value exceeds basis in a tangible capital asset held more than one year and unrelated to charity's purpose) | 50% of adjusted gross income [IRC § 170(b)(1)(A)] | 20% of adjusted gross income [IRC § 170(b)(1)(D)(i)] |

### E. HOBBY EXPENSES (IRC § 183)

Use this Part E if the taxpayer has expenses attributable to a hobby activity. Recall from Chapter 4 that a hobby activity is generally one not engaged in for profit.

1. **Expenses Deductible Under Other Authority**—Is the expense deductible another Code provision even though the taxpayer lacks a profit motive? Examples of these already-deductible expenses might include tax expense under IRC

§ 164 (see Part B of this checklist) and interest expense under IRC § 163 (see Part A of this checklist).

   a. **Yes**—If yes, then the expense remains deductible. For purposes of applying IRC § 183 to other expenses, these already-deductible expenses are called "Type (1) expenses." The deduction for a Type (1) expense is not lost simply because the taxpayer lacks a profit motive, and the deduction is permitted even if the taxpayer has no income from the hobby activity. IRC § 183(b)(1).

   b. **No**—If no, then continue in this Part E.

**2. Other Expenses Not Affecting Basis**—Will a deduction for the expense affect the basis of property used in the hobby activity because it is attributable to such property? Examples of deductions affecting basis include depreciation and amortization under IRC §§ 167 and 197, respectively (see Chapter 4), and partially worthless bad debts (see Part C of this checklist).

   a. **Yes**—If yes, then such expense is a "Type (3) expense." Type (3) expenses are deductible only to the extent that the taxpayer's gross income from the hobby activity exceeds both the taxpayer's Type (1) expenses from the activity and the taxpayer's Type (2) expenses from the activity. IRC § 183(b)(2); Treas. Reg. § 1.183–1(b)(1)(iii).

   b. **No**—If no, then such expense is a "Type (2) expense." Type (2) expenses are deductible to the extent that the taxpayer's gross income from the hobby activity exceeds the taxpayer's Type (1) expenses from the activity. IRC § 183(b)(2); Treas. Reg. § 1.183–1(b)(1)(ii).

**F. MEDICAL EXPENSES (IRC § 213)**

Use this Part F to determine whether and to what extent a taxpayer may deduct medical expenses paid during the year.

**1. Expense Paid for Medical Care**—Was the expense paid for the "medical care" of the taxpayer, the taxpayer's spouse, or the taxpayer's dependent?

   a. **Medical Care**—Medical care generally means amounts paid for the diagnosis, cure, mitigation, treatment, or prevention of disease, or for the purpose of affecting any structure or function of the body. IRC § 213(d)(1)(A). The term also includes transportation costs primarily for (and essential to) such care, IRC § 213(d)(1)(B), qualified long-term care services as defined in IRC § 7702B(c), IRC § 213(d)(1)(C), and insurance covering such care, IRC § 213(d)(1)(D). The term even includes expenses paid for reasonable lodging (up to $50 per night) while away from home primarily for (and essential to) medical care, as long as such care is provided by a physician at a licensed hospital or similar medical care facility and as long as there is no significant element of personal pleasure or recreation in such travel. IRC § 213(d)(2). Note that expenses for the medical care of the decedent paid by the taxpayer's estate within one year of death are considered to have been paid by the decedent unless the estate claims such expenses as a deduction for purposes of computing federal estate tax liability. IRC § 213(c).

b. **No Cosmetic Surgery**—The term "medical care" expressly does not include "cosmetic surgery" or similar procedures unless they are necessary to ameliorate a deformity arising from a congenital abnormality or injury resulting from an accident, trauma, or disfiguring disease. IRC § 213(d)(9)(A). Cosmetic surgery is defined as a procedure directed at improving appearance and not promoting the proper function of the body or preventing disease. IRC § 213(d)(9)(B).

c. **Yes**—If yes, then continue in this Part F.

d. **No**—If no, the expense is not deductible under IRC § 213.

2. **Not Compensated For**—Has the taxpayer received reimbursement for the medical care expense, whether by insurance or otherwise?

a. **Yes**—If yes, then the expense is not deductible under IRC § 213.

b. **No**—If no, then continue in this Part F.

3. **No Over-the-Counter Drugs**—Was the expense paid for over-the-counter drugs or medicine other than insulin?

    a. **Yes**—If yes, then the expense is not deductible under IRC § 213. Expenses for medicines and drugs are deductible only if they are prescribed drugs or insulin.

    b. **No**—If no, then continue in this Part F.

**4. 7.5% Floor**—Does the total amount of medical expenses paid by the taxpayer during the taxable year exceed 7.5 percent of the taxpayer's adjusted gross income?

    a. **Yes**—If yes, then the taxpayer may claim a deduction equal to the amount of such excess. IRC § 213(a). The deduction will be an itemized deduction, but it will not be subject either to the IRC § 67 limitation or the IRC § 68 limitation. IRC §§ 67(b)(5); 68(c)(1).

    b. **No**—If no, then no portion of the medical expenses are deductible.

## G. ALIMONY PAYMENTS (IRC § 215)

Use this Part G if the taxpayer pays any amounts to the taxpayer's ex-spouse during the taxable year.

**1. Payment of Alimony**—Did the taxpayer pay "alimony" during the taxable year?

    a. **Alimony Defined**—IRC § 215(b) defines alimony as payments meeting the requirements of IRC § 71(b) which are included in the gross income of the recipient. As explained in Chapter 2, IRC § 71(b)(1) provides that alimony is a payment in cash that meets these three requirements: (i) the payment is received by (or on behalf of) the ex-spouse under a divorce or separation instrument (specially defined in IRC § 71(b)(2)) that does not designate the payment as non-alimony; (ii) if the taxpayer and the ex-spouse are legally separated, they are not members of the same household at the time of payment; and (iii) the taxpayer has no liability to continue making payments or any substitute for payments after the ex-spouse's death.

    b. **Child Support**—Payments for child support are not considered to be payments of alimony. IRC § 71(c)(1). Therefore, such amounts are not deductible. To the extent the amount of any cash payment to the ex-spouse will be reduced upon the occurrence of a contingency related to a child, such amount will be considered child support and not alimony. IRC § 71(c)(2). If the taxpayer pays an amount for alimony and child support that is less than the amount required to be paid under the divorce or separation instrument, the taxpayer is deemed to have paid all of the required child support before paying any portion of the alimony. IRC § 71(c)(3).

   c.   **Yes**—If yes, then the taxpayer may deduct the amount of alimony paid. IRC § 215(a). But continue to Part G(2) below to consider whether the alimony recapture rule applies or will apply.

   d.   **No**—If no, then continue in this Part B.

**2.**   **Watch Out for Alimony Recapture**—If the amount of alimony paid by the taxpayer in the first two years of alimony payments substantially exceeds the payments made in later years, the taxpayer may have gross income under IRC § 71(f) for the "excess front-loading" of payments in the first two years. Here are formulas for determining whether this "alimony recapture" applies and, if so, the amount of the taxpayer's gross income:

---

<u>STEP ONE</u>: Compute the excess payments for the second calendar year in which alimony payments are made.

  1. Alimony in the second post-
      separation year:                       1. _____
  2. Alimony in third post-separation
      year:                                 2. _____
  3. Add $15,000 to line 2:           3. _____
  4. Subtract line 3 from line 1:      4. _____

*The amount in line 4 is the excess payment for the second post-separation year; the taxpayer paying the alimony must include this amount in gross income for the third post-separation year.*

<u>STEP TWO</u>: Compute the excess payments for the first calendar year in which alimony payments are made.
  5. Alimony in the first post-separation
      year:                                 5. _____
  6. Enter the amount in line 1 here:    6. _____

---

> 7. Enter the amount in line 4 here: 7. _____
> 8. Subtract line 7 from line 6: 8. _____
> 9. Enter the amount in line 2 here: 9. _____
> 10. Enter the average of the amounts in
>      lines 8 and 9: 10. _____
> 11. Add $15,000 to line 10: 11. _____
> 12. Subtract line 11 from line 5: 12. _____
>
> *The amount in line 12 is the excess payment for the first post-separation year; the taxpayer paying the alimony must include this amount in gross income for the third post-separation year.*

## H. MOVING EXPENSES (IRC § 217)

Use this Part H if the taxpayer pays moving expenses during the taxable year. This Part H does not include the special rules in IRC § 217(g) for members of the United States armed forces or the special rules in IRC § 217(h) for foreign moves. Be sure to consult those provisions when they apply.

1. **Moving Expenses**—Did the taxpayer pay or incur moving expenses during the taxable year?

   a. **Definition**—Moving expenses means the reasonable expenses of moving household goods and personal effects from the taxpayer's old residence to the new residence. IRC § 217(b)(1)(A). It includes the cost of transportation and lodging, but not the cost of any meals. IRC § 217(b)(1)(B). It also includes the moving expenses of all members of the taxpayer's old household provided they will live with the taxpayer at the new residence. IRC § 217(b)(2).

   b. **Yes**—If yes, then continue in this Part H.

   c. **No**—If no, then the costs are not deductible under IRC § 217.

2. **New Job**—Did the taxpayer move in connection with the commencement of work at a new principal place of work?

   a. **Yes**—If yes, then continue in this Part H.

b.   **No**—If no, then the moving expenses are not deductible under IRC § 217. IRC § 217(a).

3.   **Time Requirement for Employees**—Is the taxpayer working as a full-time employee in the general location of the new job (though not necessarily at the same job or even with the same employer) for at least 39 weeks during the 12–month period following the move? (If 12 months have not passed since the taxpayer's move, the answer can still be "yes" as long as the taxpayer expects to be able to meet this test, IRC § 217(e)(2), but if this test is not ultimately met the taxpayer will have to include the amount of deducted moving expenses in gross income. IRC § 217(e)(3).)

a.   **Yes**—If yes, then the taxpayer has met the IRC § 217(c)(2) requirement that the taxpayer work at the new location for a certain period of time. Go to Part H(5).

b.   **No**—If no, then go to Part H(4).

4.   **Alternate Time Requirement**—Is the taxpayer working either as a full-time employee or as a full-time self-employed individual in the general location of the new job for at least 78 weeks during the 24–month period following the move, of which at least 39 weeks are during the 12–month period following the move? (If 24 months have not passed since the taxpayer's move, the answer can still be "yes" as long as the taxpayer expects to be able to meet this test, IRC § 217(e)(2), but if this test is not ultimately met the taxpayer will have to include the amount of deducted moving expenses in gross income. IRC § 217(e)(3).)

a.   **Yes**—If yes, then the taxpayer has met the IRC § 217(c)(2) requirement that the taxpayer work at the new location for a certain period of time. Go to Part H(5).

b.   **No**—If no, then the moving expenses are not deductible under IRC § 217 unless the taxpayer could not satisfy this condition because of death, disability, or the involuntary termination of employment that the taxpayer reasonably expected would continue. If one of those conditions applies, then the IRC § 217(c)(2) requirement that the taxpayer work at the new location for a certain period of time is waived. IRC § 217(e)(1). In that case, go to Part H(5).

5. **Geographical Test**—Did the taxpayer leave a job to make the move?

    a. **Yes**—If yes, then the taxpayer may deduct the moving expenses if the distance between the taxpayer's old residence and the new job location at least 50 miles further than the distance between the taxpayer's old residence and the old job location. IRC § 217(a), (c)(1). Otherwise, the moving expenses are not deductible.

    b. **No**—If no, then the taxpayer may deduct the moving expenses if the new job location is at least 50 miles away from the taxpayer's old residence. IRC § 217(a), (c)(1). Otherwise, the moving expenses are not deductible.

## I. EDUCATION EXPENSES

Use this Part I if the taxpayer pays or incurs costs for education.

1. **Travel as Education**—Does the taxpayer pay or incur expenses for travel as form of education? This occurs when, for example, a high school social studies teacher travels to Egypt in the summer to learn more about the pyramids for a unit he or she will teach to students.

    a. **Yes**—If yes, then the expenses are not deductible. IRC § 274(m)(2).

    b. **No**—If no, continue in this Part I.

2. **Minimum Educational Requirement**—Does the taxpayer pay or incur costs for education required in order to meet the minimum educational requirements for qualification in the taxpayer's employment or other trade or business?

    a. **Yes**—If yes, then the costs cannot be deducted as business expenses. Treas. Reg. § 1.162–5(b)(1), (2). But go to Part I(6) to see if there is other authority for a deduction.

    b. **No**—If no, then continue in this Part I.

3. **Qualification for New Business**—Does the taxpayer pay or incur costs for education which is part of a program of study

being pursued by the taxpayer which will lead to qualifying the taxpayer for a new trade or business?

a. **Yes**—If yes, then the costs cannot be deducted as business expenses. Treas. Reg. § 1.162–5(b)(1), (3). But go to Part I(6) to see if there is other authority for a deduction.

b. **No**—If no, then continue in this Part I.

4. **Skill Improvement**—Does the taxpayer pay or incur costs for education that maintains or improves skills required by the taxpayer in his or her business activity?

a. **Yes**—If yes, then the costs can be deducted as business expenses under IRC § 162(a). Treas. Reg. § 1.162–5(a)(1), (c)(1).

b. **No**—If no, then continue in this Part I.

5. **Required for Job Preservation**—Does the taxpayer pay or incur costs for education that meets the requirements of the taxpayer's employer (or the requirements of applicable law) imposed as a condition to the taxpayer's retention of an established employment relationship, status, or rate of compensation?

a. **Yes**—If yes, then the costs can be deducted as business expenses under IRC § 162(a). Treas. Reg. § 1.162–5(a)(2), (c)(2).

b. **No**—If no, then the costs cannot be deducted as business expenses. Continue in this Part I, however, to see if there is other authority for a deduction.

6. **Qualified Tuition and Related Expenses**—Does the taxpayer pay "qualified tuition and related expenses" during the taxable year?

a. **Definition**—Qualified tuition and related expenses means the tuition and fees paid at most colleges and universities for the enrollment or attendance of the taxpayer, the taxpayer's spouse, or the taxpayer's dependent for courses of instruction at such institution. IRC § 25A(f)(1)(A). It does not include student activity fees, athletic fees, insurance costs, or room and board expenses. IRC § 25A(f)(1)(B), (C).

b. **Yes**—If yes, then the taxpayer generally has a choice of deducting such costs under IRC § 222 or claiming a credit for the amount of such costs under IRC § 25A. A taxpayer cannot claim both the deduction and the credit in the same taxable year. IRC § 222(c)(2)(A). If the taxpayer chooses the IRC § 222 deduction, there is a limit on the amount deductible that varies according to the taxpayer's adjusted gross income. IRC § 222(b). Use the following table to determine the maximum amount deductible:

| Adjusted gross income | Maximum IRC § 222 deduction |
| --- | --- |
| $0–$65,000 ($0–$130,000 for married filing jointly) | $4,000 |
| $65,001–$80,000 ($130,001–$160,000 for married filing jointly) | $2,000 |
| $80,001+ ($160,001+ for married filing jointly) | Zero |

If, instead, the taxpayer claims the credit under IRC § 25A, the taxpayer again faces a choice, this time between the Hope Scholarship Credit and the Lifetime Learning Credit. These credits are also subject to income-based phase-outs: very generally, the total IRC § 25A credit amount is reduced if the taxpayer's adjusted gross income exceeds $40,000 ($80,000 for married couples filing jointly). The credits are phased-out entirely if the taxpayer's adjusted gross income exceeds $50,000 ($100,000 for married couples filing jointly). All of these threshold amounts are adjusted annually for inflation.

i. **Hope Scholarship Credit**—The Hope Scholarship Credit covers qualified tuition and related expenses incurred during the first two years of college education. IRC § 25A(b). The student must attend school on at least a half-time basis, and the credit is lost if the student is convicted of a felony drug offense.

The first $1,000 of qualified tuition and related expenses is fully creditable, as are half of such expenses in excess of $1,000.

ii. **Lifetime Learning Credit**—The Lifetime Learning Credit covers qualified tuition and related expenses incurred to develop or improve the student's job skills. This credit is limited to 20 percent of the first $10,000 in qualified tuition and related expenses, making the maximum creditable amount equal to $2,000 for all taxpayers.

c. **No**—If no, then continue in this Part I.

7. **Interest on Education Loans**—Does the cost represent interest on a loan incurred to finance education costs?

a. **Yes**—If yes, then go to Part A(6) of this checklist to determine if such interest expense is deductible.

b. **No**—If no, then the education cost is not deductible to any extent.

## J. CLOTHING EXPENSES

Use this Part J if the taxpayer pays for clothing to be worn in the taxpayer's business.

1. **Suitable for Ordinary Wear**—Is the clothing suitable for ordinary wear outside of the taxpayer's business activity? This is an objective test that does not turn on whether the taxpayer actually makes use of the clothing outside of his or her business activity. *Pevsner v. Commissioner*, 628 F.2d 467 (5th Cir. 1980).

a. **Yes**—If yes, then the clothing cost is not deductible. It is seen as a personal expense. IRC § 262.

b. **No**—If no, continue in this Part J.

2. **Distinctive to the Related Business Activity**—Is the clothing distinctive to the taxpayer's business activity? This has been true, for example, of uniforms for police officers, firefighters, postal carriers, bus drivers, and railroad workers. *Revenue Ruling 70–474*. It is also true of military uniforms purchased by reservists. Treas. Reg. § 1.262–1(b)(8).

a. **Yes**—If yes, then the clothing cost is deductible.

b. **No**—If no, then the clothing cost is not deductible. It is seen as a personal expense. IRC § 262.

## K. TRAVEL COSTS

Use this Part K if the taxpayer pays or incurs costs for transportation, meals, or lodging in connection with the taxpayer's business.

1. **Commuting**—Does the cost relate to travel between the taxpayer's home and business?

   a. **Yes**—If yes, no deduction is allowed. *Commissioner v. Flowers*, 326 U.S. 465 (1946); Treas. Reg. § 1.162–2(e).

   b. **No**—If no, continue in this Part K.

2. **Travel Between Work Locations**—Does the cost relate to transportation from one place of work to another place of work?

   a. **Yes**—If yes, the expense is deductible under the general rule of IRC § 162(a) assuming the expense is ordinary and necessary. *Revenue Ruling 55–109.*

   b. **No**—If no, continue in this Part K.

3. **Travel to Temporary Work Locations**—Does the cost relate to transportation between the taxpayer's residence and a temporary work location outside the metropolitan area where the taxpayer lives and normally works?

   a. **Temporary Work Location**—A temporary work location is one where the taxpayer reasonably expects to work (and in fact does work) for one year or less. If the taxpayer reasonably expects to work for more than one year at the location, or there is no realistic chance that the job will last for one year or less, the location is not temporary regardless of whether it actually exceeds one year. *Revenue Ruling 99–7.*

   b. **Yes**—If yes, the expense is deductible under the general rule of IRC § 162(a) assuming the expense is ordinary and necessary. *Revenue Ruling 99–7.*

   c. **No**—If no, continue in this Part K.

4. **Travel Away from Home**—Does the cost relate to transportation or lodging while "away from home?"

    a. **Away**—To be "away" from home, the travel must require sleep or rest. *United States v. Correll*, 389 U.S. 299 (1967). It does not matter how far the taxpayer travels or how many cities the taxpayer visits.

    b. **Home**—A taxpayer's home is his or her principal place of work, not necessarily the location of the taxpayer's residence. *Hantzis v. Commissioner*, 638 F.2d 248 (1st Cir. 1981).

    c. **Yes**—If yes, then a deduction is allowed for the transportation costs under IRC § 162(a)(2). If the trip involves business and pleasure, transportation costs are deductible if the primary purpose of the trip is for business, usually based on the number of days spent on business versus the number of pleasure days. Treas. Reg. § 1.162–2(b)(1). Likewise, lodging costs will be deductible under IRC § 162(a)(2), although any lodging attributable to pleasure days will not. In any case, the taxpayer must be able to substantiate the deduction with proper records. IRC § 274(d). Also, travel expenses paid by the taxpayer attributable to persons accompanying the taxpayer on the trip are not deductible unless such other persons are employees of the taxpayer making the trip for a bona fide business purpose such that they could deduct the expenses themselves if they were not paid by the taxpayer. IRC § 274(m)(3).

    d. **No**—If no, then the travel expense is not deductible under IRC § 162(a).

## L. ENTERTAINMENT EXPENSES

Use this Part L if the taxpayer pays or incurs costs for entertainment.

1. **Expectation of Specific Benefit**—Did the taxpayer incur the expense with more than a general expectation of some future benefit?

    a. **Yes**—If yes, then continue in this Part L.

    b. **No**—If no, then the entertainment expense is not "directly related to the active conduct of a trade or business." Treas.

Reg. § 1.274–2(c)(3)(i). But proceed to L(5) to see if there is another avenue for deduction.

2. **Active Business During the Entertainment**—Did the taxpayer actively engage in a business meeting, negotiation, or other business transaction during the entertainment period to which the expense relates?

   a. **Yes**—If yes, then continue in this Part L.

   b. **No**—If no, then the entertainment expense is not "directly related to the active conduct of a trade or business." Treas. Reg. § 1.274–2(c)(3)(ii). But proceed to L(5) to see if there is another avenue for deduction.

3. **Principal Character of Business**—Was the principal character or aspect of the combined business and entertainment the active conduct of the taxpayer's business? This is judged not solely on the amount of time on business versus entertainment but from all facts and circumstances.

   a. **Yes**—If yes, then continue in this Part L.

   b. **No**—If no, then the entertainment expense is not "directly related to the active conduct of a trade or business." Treas. Reg. § 1.274–2(c)(3)(iii). But proceed to L(5) to see if there is another avenue for deduction.

4. **Expense Covers Taxpayer and Persons Engaged in Business Activity**—Is the expense allocable to the taxpayer and a person or persons with whom the taxpayer engaged in the active trade or business during the entertainment?

   a. **Yes**—If yes, then the entertainment expense is "directly related to the active conduct of a trade or business" and therefore deductible under IRC § 162(a). IRC § 274(a)(1)(A). The taxpayer must have adequate substantiation for the expense in order to claim the deduction. IRC § 274(d).

   b. **No**—If no, then the entertainment expense is not "directly related to the active conduct of a trade or business." Treas. Reg. § 1.274–2(c)(3)(iv). But proceed to L(5) to see if there is another avenue for deduction.

5. **Clear Business Purpose**—Did the taxpayer have a clear business purpose in incurring the entertainment expense (like

obtaining new business or encouraging the continuation of an existing business relationship)?

a. **Yes**—If yes, then continue in this Part L.

b. **No**—If no, then the entertainment expense is not "associated with the active conduct of a trade or business." Treas. Reg. § 1.274–2(d)(2). Accordingly, there is no deduction for the entertainment expense. IRC § 274(a)(1)(A).

6. **Substantial Business Discussion**—Did the entertainment immediately precede or follow a substantial, bona fide business discussion in which the taxpayer participated with the hope of deriving some specific future benefit?

a. **Immediately Preceding or Following**—Note that entertainment provided anytime during the same day as the substantial and bona fide business discussion meets this standard. Treas. Reg. § 1.274–2(d)(3)(ii). If the entertainment is not on the same day, all facts and circumstances should be considered. *Id.* Usually, entertainment the night before or the morning after the business discussion will be sufficient.

b. **Yes**—If yes, then the entertainment expenses attributable to those who participate in the business discussion and those "closely connected" with such persons are "associated with the active conduct of a trade or business" and therefore deductible. IRC § 274(a)(1)(A); Treas. Reg. § 1.274–2(d)(2), (3). The taxpayer must have adequate substantiation for the expense in order to claim the deduction. IRC § 274(d).

c. **No**—If no, then the entertainment expense is not "associated with the active conduct of a trade or business." Treas. Reg. § 1.274–2(d)(3). Accordingly, there is no deduction for the entertainment expense. IRC § 274(a)(1)(A).

## M. BUSINESS MEALS

Use this Part M if the taxpayer pays for meals in connection with the taxpayer's business.

1. **Paying for Meals of Others**—Does the taxpayer pay for someone else's meal in connection with the taxpayer's business?

    a. **Yes**—If yes, then the taxpayer may deduct one-half of the cost of the meal, IRC § 274(n), as a business expense under IRC § 162(a) provided four requirements are met:

    (i) **Meal as Entertainment**—The meal constitutes entertainment or part of the entertainment provided to such person by the taxpayer and such entertainment expense is otherwise deductible under Part L of this checklist. This means that the meal must be "directly related" to the conduct of the taxpayer's business or "associated with" such business. IRC § 274(a)(1)(A).

    (ii) **Substantiation**—The taxpayer has adequate substantiation for the expense, which usually would come in the form of a receipt showing the amount, the time and place, the business purpose for the meal, and a summary of the business discussion. IRC § 274(d).

    (iii) **Not Lavish**—The meal is not "lavish or extravagant under the circumstances." IRC § 274(k)(1).

    (iv) **Taxpayer's Presence**—The taxpayer is present when such meal is provided. IRC § 274(k)(2).

    b. **No**—If no, then the taxpayer cannot deduct the cost of the meal as a business expense.

2. **Taxpayer's Own Entertainment Meal**—If the taxpayer also had a meal, did the cost of the taxpayer's own meal during the business exceed the amount the taxpayer would otherwise pay?

    a. **Yes**—If yes, there is authority for deducting the cost of the meal. See *Sutter v. Commissioner*, 21 T.C. 170 (1953); *Moss v. Commissioner*, 758 F.2d 211 (7th Cir. 1985). Only one-half of the cost of the meal may be deductible. IRC § 274(n). No deduction will be permitted, however, to the extent the meal is "lavish or extravagant under the circumstances." IRC § 274(k). Here too, taxpayer must have adequate substantiation for the expense in order to claim the deduction, which usually would come in the form of a receipt showing the amount, the time and place, the business purpose for the meal, and a summary of the business discussion. IRC § 274(d).

b. **No**—If no, then the taxpayer cannot deduct the cost of the taxpayer's meal as an entertainment expense.

3. **Meals Away From Home**—Did the taxpayer pay for the meal while traveling "away from home" in pursuit of a trade or business (see Part K of this checklist)?

a. **Yes**—If yes, the taxpayer may claim a deduction, IRC § 162(a)(2), but only for one-half of the cost of the meal. IRC § 274(n). No deduction will be permitted, however, to the extent the meal is "lavish or extravagant under the circumstances." IRC § 274(k)(1). Again, taxpayer must have adequate substantiation for the expense in order to claim the deduction, which usually would come in the form of a receipt showing the amount, the time and place, the business purpose for the meal, and a summary of the business discussion. IRC § 274(d).

b. **No**—If no, then the taxpayer cannot deduct the cost of the taxpayer's meal as a business expense to any extent.

## ILLUSTRATIVE PROBLEMS

These problems show how the checklist can be used to discuss the deductibility of various personal expenses.

---

### ■ PROBLEM 5.1 ■

---

In the current year, T realized a dream by purchasing a new home. To pay the $300,000 purchase price, T paid $100,000 and borrowed $200,000 from Bank. Bank took a mortgage on T's home as security for T's repayment obligation. T paid a total of $12,000 interest on this loan to Bank. T also paid $3,000 in state real property taxes attributable to the residence. The city in which T lives imposed a special assessment on all homes in T's neighborhood to pay for the installation of a new drainage system in the neighborhood. T paid the $1,500 assessment to the city as required.

What are the federal income tax consequences of these events to T?

## Analysis

T does not have gross income from borrowing $200,000 from Bank because of T's obligation to repay the amount borrowed. T's basis in the home will be the $300,000 cost to acquire the property.

The interest paid by T to bank is deductible as qualified residence interest. The loan is "acquisition indebtedness" because it was incurred to purchase the home and the amount of the loan does not exceed the $1,000,000 ceiling amount. T's home is a "qualified residence" because the facts suggest it is T's only home and therefore T's principal residence. Therefore, the interest expense is deductible. This is a regular itemized deduction under IRC § 67(b)(1).

The $3,000 in state real property taxes is deductible under IRC § 164(a)(1). This too is a regular itemized deduction. See IRC § 67(b)(2). The $1,500 assessment, however, is one against local benefits that tends to improve the value of T's residence. Accordingly, no deduction is allowed for this cost. IRC § 164(c)(1). However, since the cost relates to the permanent improvement of the home, T may add this cost to T's basis in the home. IRC § 1016(a)(1). This will be helpful when T eventually sells the home.

## ■ PROBLEM 5.2 ■

T had gross income of $100,000 for the most recent taxable year. In that year, T paid $10,000 in alimony to T's former spouse. The terms of the divorce decree require such annual payments until the former spouse dies or remarries, whichever happens first (although T has a preference in this regard).

In that same year, T donated Blackacre, a parcel of real property T held for many years as an investment, to a charitable organization described in IRC § 170(b)(1)(A). T's adjusted basis in Blackacre was $20,000 but it was worth $35,000 at the time of the gift.

Finally, in that same year, T paid $2,000 for laser eye surgery to improve T's eyesight.

What are the federal income tax consequences of these events to T?

## Analysis

The alimony paid by T will be deductible under IRC § 215. The cash payment here appears to meet all of the required elements for the deduction: it was received by T's ex-spouse under a divorce or separation instrument that apparently did not designate the payment as non-alimony; T and the ex-spouse were not members of the same household at the time of payment; and T has no liability to continue making payments or any substitute for payments after the ex-spouse's death. The deduction for alimony is an above-the-line deduction, IRC § 62(a)(10), so T's adjusted gross income on these facts will be $90,000 ($100,000 gross income less the $10,000 alimony deduction).

The contribution of Blackacre to the charity will qualify for the IRC § 170 charitable contribution deduction. T does not appear to receive anything in exchange for the transfer, and the facts state that the organization qualifies as a charity for purposes of the deduction. T will be entitled to deduct the full value of Blackacre, as it is a capital asset held for more than one year but is not described in IRC § 170(e). Treas. Reg. § 1.170A–1(c)(1). This would appear to give T a $35,000 deduction for the year; however, IRC § 170(b)(1)(C)(i) limits the maximum amount of the deduction for the year to 30 percent of T's "contribution base." On these facts, T's contribution base is $90,000, T's adjusted gross income. Thus the maximum deduction for the year is $27,000 (30% x $90,000).

The remaining $8,000 deduction will carry over to the next taxable year as if it were donated then. IRC § 170(d)(1).

The $2,000 paid for laser eye surgery would be deductible as a medical expense because it relates to the medical care of the taxpayer and was not compensated for by insurance or otherwise. But this is T's only medical expense for the year, and medical expenses are deductible under IRC § 213 only to the extent they exceed 7.5 percent of adjusted gross income. Thus, only medical expenses in excess of $6,750 would be deductible. T's total medical expenses do not exceed this amount to any extent, so none of the expense is deductible.

## POINTS TO REMEMBER

- The general rule in IRC § 262(a) is that personal, living, and family expenses are not deductible. If a personal expense does not have other express authority for deduction, the general rule applies and the deduction is lost.

- If you conclude that a personal expense is deductible, be sure to explain where the deduction fits in the tax ladder. Above-the-line deductions are better than regular itemized deductions, which are better than miscellaneous itemized deductions.

*

# CHAPTER 6

# Property Transactions

Taxpayers buy and sell assets all the time, and federal income tax consequences lurk at every corner. For a very simple example, suppose a taxpayer acquires a small parcel of real estate as investment property by paying $50,000 for it. If the taxpayer later sells the property to a stranger for $60,000, what are the federal income tax consequences? To the extent the taxpayer now has $60,000 of cash, notions of *Glenshaw Glass* might suggest that the taxpayer has $60,000 of gross income. But from a transactional perspective, the additional wealth to the taxpayer is only the $10,000 difference between what the taxpayer got for the property upon sale and what the taxpayer originally paid for it. Put another way, a taxpayer should be entitled to recover his or her cost in an asset before having gross income from a sale.

Likewise, if the taxpayer in the prior example sells the property for only $45,000, the taxpayer has no gross income at all. In fact, the taxpayer only recovers $45,000 of the $50,000 cost of the asset. Such a transaction creates a loss, not a gain.

For all property dispositions, the framework in IRC § 1001(a) applies. If the disposition results in a realized gain, IRC §§ 61(a)(3) and 1001(c) generally provide that the taxpayer must include the amount of such gain in gross income. If the transaction creates a loss, the question is whether the loss is deductible. IRC § 1001(c) generally provides that all losses are deductible, but IRC § 165(c) limits the deduction to only three kinds of losses.

# PROPERTY TRANSACTIONS REVIEW

Upon any sale or other disposition of property, IRC § 1001(a) applies a formula to determine whether the taxpayer realizes a gain or loss. Under this formula, gain is the excess of the amount realized over the adjusted basis for determining gain, and loss is the excess of the adjusted basis for determining loss over the amount realized. IRC § 1001(a) can be expressed in formula form for convenience:

> Amount Realized
> -Adjusted Basis
> REALIZED GAIN
>
> Adjusted Basis
> -Amount Realized
> REALIZED LOSS

Although the statute does not use the terms "realized gain" and "realized loss," the regulations do. See Treas. Reg. § 1.1001–1(a).

The "amount realized" by a taxpayer is the sum of any money received plus the fair market value of property (other than money) received. IRC § 1001(b). The taxpayer's "adjusted basis" in the property disposed of is "the basis (determined under section 1012 or other applicable sections of this subchapter . . . ), adjusted as provided in section 1016." IRC § 1011. So one must determine the "basis" of property under IRC § 1012 and then determine whether that basis is subject to any of the adjustments listed in IRC § 1016.

IRC § 1012 generally defines basis as "cost." And IRC § 1016(a) lists no less than 28 possible adjustments to basis. Generally, a taxpayer increases basis by the cost of any improvements made to the property, and decreases basis by the amount of any depreciation deductions that are claimed with respect to the property.

Under IRC § 1001(c), "the entire amount of the gain or loss, determined under this section, on the sale or exchange of property shall be recognized." In the case of realized gains, this means the realized gain is included in gross income. In the case of realized losses, it means the realized loss is deductible. But IRC § 1001(c)'s rule of recognition expressly takes a back seat to other Code provisions that provide otherwise. Thus, for example, if another Code provision states that gain shall not be recognized upon a particular transaction, that Code provision outweighs IRC § 1001(c)'s general rule of recognition.

In the case of losses, IRC § 165(c) imposes such a significant exception to the rule of recognition that it is fair to conclude that the general rule is one of disallowance instead of recognition. IRC § 165(c) limits loss deductions for individuals to three types of losses: business losses, investment losses, and casualty or theft losses of personal-use assets.

## PROPERTY TRANSACTIONS CHECKLIST

This checklist will serve as a guide for any disposition of property by a taxpayer.

### A. REALIZATION EVENT

The framework set forth beginning in Part B of this checklist applies only if there has been a realization event. In many cases, it is easy to determine whether a realization event has occurred. Three common realization events are identified below. If there is a transaction involving the taxpayer's property that does not come within one of these three realization events, it may well be the case that no taxable event has occurred.

1. **Sale or Exchange**—Did the taxpayer sell or exchange an interest in property? This is the most common form of realization event and the easiest to identify. A sale or exchange involves a disposition whereby the taxpayer transfers the property interest to another party and receives back cash or some other property interest.

   a. **Yes**—If yes, the sale or exchange is a realization event, so proceed to Part B of this checklist.

b. **No**—If no, continue in this Part A.

2. **Other Non–Gift Disposition**—Did the taxpayer dispose of the property other than by a gift?

a. **Common Dispositions**—A sale or exchange is not required for realization to occur. Realization can occur through other dispositions of property interests, including the involuntary conversion of property (whether because of damage, theft, bankruptcy, requisition, or condemnation), or abandonment of the property, for example.

b. **Gifts are Not Realization Events**—Taxpayers often dispose of their property interests through inter-vivos gifts and testamentary bequests. Theoretically, perhaps, gifts of property should be realization events in the sense that the donor receives the benefit of the property's value by gifting it to his or her selected donee. A gift of raw land, for example, may bring the same satisfaction to the donor as if the donor sold the property for cash (a clear realization event) and then gifted the cash to the donee. Yet it is well accepted that a gift of property is not a realization event for federal income tax purposes. Instead, any lurking gain in the donor's hands (but generally not lurking loss) will pass to the donee.

c. **Yes**—If yes, a realization event has occurred even though the taxpayer may receive no benefit in exchange for the disposed property. Proceed to Part B of this checklist.

d. **No**—If no, continue in this Part A.

3. **Satisfaction of Obligation**—Did the taxpayer transfer the property in satisfaction of an enforceable obligation?

a. **Yes**—If yes, a realization event has occurred. The Supreme Court confirmed this result in *United States v. Davis*, 370 U.S. 65 (1962), holding that the transfer of appreciated stock to a taxpayer's former spouse pursuant to a property settlement agreement results in realized gain. The specific result in *Davis* (that property transfers incident to a divorce could be taxable) was overturned by Congress through the enactment of IRC § 1041(a), but the general principle—that the transfer of appreciated property in satisfaction of an enforceable obligation gives rise to gain—remains good law. Thus, for example, where an employer transfers appreciated property to an employee as compensation for services, the employer realizes gain.

b. **No**—If no, then most likely a realization event has not yet occurred and it would be premature to apply the remainder of this checklist. Wait until there is a realization event.

## B. AMOUNT REALIZED

Because IRC § 1001(b) defines the "amount realized" as the sum of any cash received and the fair market value of any property received, one must always take into account all of the cash and non-cash consideration received by the taxpayer.

1. **Cash**—Did the taxpayer receive cash in exchange for the disposed property?

   a. **Yes**—If yes, such cash is part of the taxpayer's "amount realized" from the transaction. Continue in this Part B to see if there is more to the amount realized.

   b. **No**—If no, continue in this Part B.

2. **Non–Cash Property**—Did the taxpayer received property other than cash in the exchange?

   a. **Yes**—If yes, then include the fair market value of such property in the taxpayer's amount realized. Continue in this Part B to see if there is more to the amount realized.

      i. **Fair Market Value**—The fair market value of any property is the price at which such property would trade between a willing buyer and a willing seller, both having knowledge of all material facts and neither acting under compulsion to buy or sell. Treas. Reg. § 20.2031–1(b). In many cases it is easy to determine the fair market value of an asset. The value of publicly-traded stock, for example, is the average of the stock's highest and lowest trading prices on the day of the sale (or on the day closest to the sale if the sale occurs on a day when the markets are closed). Other assets, like real estate, can often be valued by a professional appraiser.

ii. **Hard-to-Value Assets**—If the property received by the taxpayer is particularly hard to value for whatever reason, one can look to the value of the property *transferred* assuming the transaction occurs at arm's-length. *Philadelphia Park Amusement Company v. United States*, 126 F.Supp. 184 (Ct. Cl. 1954). In the *Philadelphia Park* case, for example, the court indicated that if the taxpayer could not value the property it received in the exchange (an extension of a railway franchise), it could assume that the value of the property received is equal to the value of the property the taxpayer gave up (a bridge) because the facts indicated that the transaction was at arm's-length (a negotiated transaction between unrelated parties, in this case).

b. **No**—If no, continue in this Part B.

3. **Debt Relief**—Did the taxpayer dispose of property encumbered by one or more liabilities for which the other party directly or indirectly became responsible?

a. **Yes**—If yes, then the amount realized by the taxpayer includes the outstanding balance of such liabilities as of the date of the transfer. Treas. Reg. § 1.1001–2(a)(1); *Commissioner v. Tufts*, 461 U.S. 300 (1983). For this purpose, it does not matter whether the other party formally assumes the debt encumbering the property transferred by the taxpayer (i.e., the other party becomes the obligor on the debt and the lender discharges the taxpayer from any further liability on the debt) or simply takes the property subject to the debt (i.e., the other party does not become the obligor and the taxpayer is not discharged, but the other party may still lose the property if the debt is not repaid because the property remains collateral for the debt). Add up all components of the taxpayer's amount realized in this Part B and proceed to Part C of this checklist.

i. **Assumption of Debt**—Where the other party formally assumes the debt, it is like the other party gives the taxpayer cash in an amount equal to the debt which the taxpayer uses to discharge the taxpayer's liability.

In this latter case, the receipt of additional cash would clearly add to the taxpayer's amount realized. Accordingly, the economic equivalent—the other part assuming liability for the debt—must be treated like additional cash received by the taxpayer.

ii. **Transfers Subject to Debt**—Likewise, when the other party takes the property subject to the liability there is a benefit to the taxpayer because the taxpayer no longer has the risk of losing that particular property if the debt is not repaid. Functionally that is the same as formally relieving the taxpayer of the liability, especially where the value of the transferred property exceed the outstanding balance of the debt.

b. **No**—If no, then there is no additional component to the taxpayer's amount realized. Add up the other components to the taxpayer's amount realized in this Part B and proceed to Part C of this checklist.

## C. ADJUSTED BASIS

IRC § 1001(a) defines gain or loss the difference between the taxpayer's amount realized and the taxpayer's adjusted basis in the property transferred. IRC § 1011(a), in turn, defines adjusted basis as the taxpayer's "basis" as "adjusted" under other Code provisions. Accordingly, one begins by computing the taxpayer's basis and then determining whether any adjustments are required.

1. **Cost**—What cost did the taxpayer incur to acquire the property?

a. **General Cost**—IRC § 1012 defines a taxpayer's basis as his or her "cost" to acquire the property. Thus, where a taxpayer pays $1,000 to purchase an asset, the taxpayer has a cost basis of $1,000.

b. **Tax Cost**—If the taxpayer realizes a gain in the course of acquiring property, such gain is considered part of the cost of acquiring the property. *Philadelphia Park Amusement Company v. United States*, 126 F.Supp. 184 (Ct. Cl. 1954). This "tax cost" (realization of gain) is thus added to the taxpayer's basis in the property. For example, if a taxpayer purchases a $10,000 piano by transferring $10,000 worth of Microsoft stock in which the taxpayer has a basis of $3,000, the taxpayer will realize and recognize a gain of $7,000. Thus, the taxpayer's cost basis in the piano is $10,000: in order to acquire the piano, the taxpayer transferred an asset that cost $3,000 and incurred a $7,000 gain.

c. **Impact of Debt**—If the taxpayer takes on debt to acquire the property, the amount of the debt is part of the taxpayer's cost basis. *Crane v. Commissioner*, 331 U.S. 1 (1947). This can occur in several different contexts:

   i. **Taxpayer Liable to Seller**—If the taxpayer pays for the property by giving a promissory note to the seller, the taxpayer's cost basis includes the principal amount of the note. This is because the taxpayer agrees to the obligation to pay the principal amount of the note to the seller, and is thus part of the cost to acquire the property.

   ii. **Taxpayer Assumes Seller's Liability**—If the taxpayer agrees to assume a debt of the seller that encumbers the property, the taxpayer certainly incurs an additional cost by agreeing to pay off the seller's debt.

   iii. **Taxpayer Takes Seller's Property Subject to Liability**—If the taxpayer takes the property subject to a debt of the seller, the taxpayer incurs the risk of losing the property if the debt is not repaid. As explained in Part B, this is the equivalent of paying additional cash to the seller, so necessarily it is likewise seen as an additional cost incurred by the taxpayer.

   iv. **Taxpayer Borrows to Purchase from Seller**—If the taxpayer borrows money from a third-party lender and uses the cash to pay the seller for the property, the taxpayer's obligation to repay the lender is a cost incurred to acquire the property so the loaned monies are considered part of the taxpayer's basis in the property.

d. **Gifted Property Generally**—A taxpayer acquiring property by gift by definition has incurred no cost. But IRC

§ 1015(a) provides that for purposes of computing realized gain, the taxpayer takes the donor's basis in the gifted property. If, at the time of the gift, the fair market value of the property was less than the donor's basis in the property, then the taxpayer's basis in the property is equal to such fair market value *but only for purposes of computing the amount of any realized loss*. Note that if the donor pays federal gift taxes as a result of the gift, the taxpayer is permitted to add a portion of such gift tax paid to the taxpayer's basis in the property. IRC § 1015(d)(1), (6). The addition to basis can be expressed in formula form as follows:

$$\frac{\text{value of gift minus donor's basis at time of gift}}{\text{value of gift}} \quad x \quad \begin{array}{c}\text{(gift tax}\\\text{paid)}\end{array} \quad = \quad \begin{array}{c}\text{addition to}\\\text{basis}\end{array}$$

e. **Property Acquired in Part–Gift, Part–Sale Transaction**—If the taxpayer acquired the property in a part-gift, part-sale transaction (the taxpayer purchased the property for less than its value at the time of the purchase and the reason for the discount was because of the seller's detached and disinterested generosity), then the taxpayer's basis in the property is either the amount paid for the property or the seller's basis in the property, whichever is greater. Treas. Reg. § 1.1015–4.

f. **Property Passing from a Decedent**—If the property passed to the taxpayer from a decedent, the taxpayer's basis in the property is its fair market value at the date of the decedent's death. IRC § 1014(a)(1). This is often referred to as a "stepped-up" basis, but that phrase is somewhat misleading because sometimes the value of property at a decedent's death is less than the decedent's basis. Property is considered to have passed from a decedent if it meets any of the conditions set forth in IRC § 1014(b). These include: acquiring the property by bequest, devise, or inheritance; receiving the property from a revocable living trust created by the decedent during the decedent's lifetime; acquiring the property through the decedent's exercise of a testamentary power of appointment; and any property included in the decedent's gross estate for federal estate tax purposes. Note, too, that surviving spouses in community property states enjoy a nice bonus: not only does the decedent's one-half share of community property get a stepped-up basis but so too does the surviving spouse's one-half share. IRC § 1014(b)(6).

2. **Adjustments to Basis**—Are there any adjustments to the taxpayer's cost basis? IRC § 1016(a) lists all of the adjustments to basis, but two such adjustments are especially common:

   a. **Increase Basis for Improvements**—Under IRC § 1016(a)(1), a taxpayer's basis is adjusted upward (increased) by the cost of permanent improvements made to the property. For example, if a taxpayer spends $10,000 for a station wagon and then spends another $7,000 to make the wagon suitable as an ambulance, the taxpayer's basis in the wagon-turned-ambulance is $17,000: the taxpayer's basis is increased by the $7,000 spent to make improvements to the property.

   b. **Decrease Basis for Depreciation Deductions**—Under § 1016(a)(2), the taxpayer's basis in property is adjusted downward (decreased) by depreciation deductions.

      i. **Property Must be Depreciable**—This adjustment only applies in the case of tangible property and buildings subject to wear and tear and used for business or investment purposes. See Chapter 4.

      ii. **Greater of Amount Allowed or Allowable**—The flush language to IRC § 1016(a)(2) requires that the reduction in basis for depreciation be the greater of the amount allowed as a deduction (i.e., the amount actually claimed on the taxpayer's return and unchallenged by the Internal Revenue Service) and the amount allowable as a deduction (i.e., the proper amount of depreciation to which the taxpayer was entitled to claim as a deduction). For example, assume a taxpayer with an asset costing $100,000 is entitled to claim a $10,000 depreciation deduction with respect to the asset in the first year of ownership but, for whatever reason, only claims a $2,000 deduction on the taxpayer's tax return that year. The taxpayer's adjusted basis in the asset is $90,000: the $100,000 original cost less the $10,000 amount *allowable* as a depreciation deduction. If instead, for whatever reason, the taxpayer claims a $13,000 deduction that year and the Service does not challenge the deduction within the applicable statute of limitations, then the taxpayer's asset as of the end of the first year would be $87,000: $100,000 less the $13,000 *allowed* as a deduction.

## D. REALIZED GAIN OR LOSS

**1. Realized Gain**—Does the amount realized (Part B) exceed the taxpayer's adjusted basis (Part C)?

    a. **Yes**—If yes, there is a realized gain. IRC § 1001(c) generally provides that all realized gains are "recognized," meaning they are included in gross income. Realized gains are not recognized only to the extent some other Code provision expressly provides for nonrecognition.

        i. **Examples of Gains Not Recognized**—Here are some examples of gains that are not recognized by individual taxpayers, together with cross-references to more detailed checklists on those nonrecognition provisions where applicable: (A) like-kind exchanges (see IRC § 1031 and Chapter 7); (B) involuntary conversions (see IRC § 1033 and Chapter 7); (C) gain from the sale of a principal residence (see IRC § 121 and Chapter 7); (D) transfers between spouses and former spouses incident to divorce (see IRC § 1041 and Chapter 7); (E) formation of a corporation (see IRC § 351) or partnership (see IRC § 721); and (F) a corporate reorganization whereby a shareholder receives stock in a new corporation in exchange for the shareholder's appreciated stock in the target corporation (see IRC § 354(a)(1)).

ii. **Character of Recognized Gain**—If all or any portion of the realized gain is recognized, the character or flavor of the gain becomes relevant. Items of ordinary income will be taxed at the progressive tax rates set forth in § 1(a)–(d), but a taxpayer's net capital gain will be taxed at a preferential rate as set forth in § 1(h). See Chapter 9.

b. **No**—If no, continue in this Part D.

2. **Realized Loss**—Does the taxpayer's adjusted basis (Part C) exceed the amount realized (Part B)?

a. **Yes**—If yes, there is a realized loss. IRC § 165(a) permits a deduction for losses that are "sustained" during the taxable year. This means that there has been a "closed and completed [transaction], fixed by identifiable events." Treas. Reg. § 1.165–1(b). The realization events described in Part A of this checklist typically fix the loss for purposes of IRC § 165(a) so it is not usually an issue in this context. The mere decline in value in an asset is not a realization event; likewise, no loss is "sustained" merely because of a reduction in value.

i. **Deductible Losses for Individuals**—IRC § 165(c) imposes an additional limitation on the deductibility of losses by individual taxpayers. It provides that an individual taxpayer can only deduct three kinds of realized losses. First, a taxpayer can deduct losses incurred in a **trade or business** activity. IRC § 165(c)(1). So when a taxpayer sells an item of inventory to a customer at a loss, the realized loss is deductible. Second, a taxpayer can deduct losses incurred in a **transaction entered into for profit** even if it is not related to the taxpayer's business. IRC § 165(c)(2). So when a taxpayer sells an asset held for investment purposes (like stocks and bonds, raw land, or a collectible) at a loss, the realized loss is deductible. Finally, an individual taxpayer can deduct losses not connected with a business activity or a transaction entered into for profit only if the losses result from "fire, storm, shipwreck, or other casualty, or from theft." IRC § 165(c)(3). See Chapter 8 for other rules related to **casualty and theft losses of personal-use property**. Any other realized loss is not deductible. Thus, for example, if a taxpayer sells his or her personal residence at a loss, the loss is not deductible because it is not described in IRC § 165(c).

ii. **Other Loss Limitations**—Assuming the realized loss fits within IRC § 165(c), the loss will be deductible unless some other Code provision disallows the deduction. Common examples of losses that are disallowed even though these pass muster under IRC § 165(c) are losses from transactions between related parties (IRC § 267), losses from so-called "wash sales," (IRC § 1091), and passive activity losses (IRC § 469). These and other limitations on the deductibility of losses are discussed in Chapter 8.

iii. **Special Rule for Worthless Securities**—IRC § 165(g)(1) permits a loss deduction when securities have become "worthless," meaning that they have completely lost value based on all the facts and circumstances. *Boehm v. Commissioner*, 326 U.S. 287 (1945). Such loss is deemed to arise from the sale or exchange of a capital asset, meaning the deductible loss will be either a short-term capital loss (if the securities were held for one year or less) or a long-term capital loss (if the securities were held for more than one year). For purposes of this special rule, "securities" generally consist of stocks and bonds; a complete definition is provided in IRC § 165(g)(2).

iv. **Character of Deductible Loss**—If a realized loss is recognized (i.e., it is described in IRC § 165(c) in the case of an individual taxpayer and it not otherwise disallowed), one must determine the character of the loss. As explained in Chapter 9, ordinary losses offset all forms of income but capital losses generally offset only capital gains plus up to $3,000 of ordinary income.

b. **No**—If no, then there is neither realized gain nor realized loss, so the transaction is without tax consequence.

## ILLUSTRATIVE PROBLEMS

The following problems illustrate how the checklist can be used to answer a question involving property dispositions.

---

### ■ PROBLEM 6.1 ■

---

T is a professional truck driver. In order to purchase Blackacre, a parcel of undeveloped real property on sale for $100,000, T borrowed $90,000 from Bank. To secure T's repayment obligation to Bank, T gave Bank a mortgage on Blackacre (if T defaults on the repayment obligation, Bank is entitled to Blackacre). T used the loan proceeds, together with $10,000 of T's own cash, to purchase the property. T held Blackacre at all times for investment purposes.

One year later, T paid off $15,000 of the Bank loan, reducing the principal balance of the Bank loan to $75,000.

T then decided to construct a building on Blackacre. T incurred total costs of $60,000 to develop and construct the building. Shortly thereafter, T sold Blackacre, subject to the Bank mortgage, to an unrelated purchaser for $200,000. At the time of the sale, the principal balance of the Bank loan was still $75,000.

What are the federal income tax consequences of these events to T?

---

### Analysis

---

T's sale of Blackacre is a realization event that triggers application of the formula for gain or loss under IRC § 1001(a). To determine the consequences of the sale to T, one must first determine T's amount realized under IRC § 1001(b). T's amount realized upon the sale of Blackacre is $275,000. This is the sum of the amount of cash received ($200,000) plus the amount of the liability secured by Blackacre ($75,000). *Tufts v. Commissioner*.

The $275,000 amount realized is netted against T's adjusted basis in Blackacre to determine whether T realizes gain or loss.

Under § 1012, T's original basis (cost) in Blackacre is $100,000 because T paid $10,000 of cash and became liable to repay Bank $90,000 in order to acquire the property. *Crane v. Commissioner.* When T pays $15,000 of the loan back to Bank, there is no change to T's basis because the total cost incurred to acquire Blackacre has not changed. (Instead of paying $10,000 cash and owing $90,000 to Bank, T now has paid $25,000 and owes $75,000 to Bank—in either case the total cost to T remains $100,000).

T's basis is then increased by the $60,000 spent to improve the property with the addition of a building. IRC § 1016(a)(1). This brings T's adjusted basis to $160,000 at the time of T's sale. Therefore, T's realized gain is $115,000, the excess of the $275,000 amount realized over the $160,000 adjusted basis. This realized gain is recognized under IRC § 1001(c) because no nonrecognition provisions applies.

---

## ■ PROBLEM 6.2 ■

---

To reward T for superior performance on the job, T's employer, E, promised to pay a $10,000 bonus to T. E lacked cash at the time, so E transferred $10,000 worth of Costco stock to T. E's adjusted basis in the shares at the time of the transfer to T was $13,000. Six months later, T sold the Costco stock to an unrelated buyer for $12,000 cash.

What are the federal income tax consequences of these events to T?

### Analysis

---

To satisfy an obligation to pay compensation to T, E transferred property worth $10,000 in which E had an adjusted basis of $13,000. E's transfer to T is a realization event to E just as if E had sold the shares for cash and transferred the sale proceeds to T as compensation. Accordingly, E realizes a $3,000 loss from the transfer (E's amount realized is the relief from the obligation to pay $10,000 to T, and E's basis in the stock is $3,000). Because this is a loss incurred in E's business, the $3,000 realized loss is deductible. IRC § 165(c)(1). Because the loss arises from the sale or exchange of a capital asset, the Costco stock, the loss will be characterized as a capital loss to E.

Meanwhile, T has gross income under IRC § 61(a)(1) of $10,000, the fair market value of the Costco shares at the time of T's receipt. T takes a $10,000 basis in the shares because his "tax cost" to acquire the stock is having to include the $10,000 of compensation in T's gross income. *Philadelphia Park Amusement Co. v. United States*. Thus, when T sells the stock to the unrelated buyer for $12,000, T realizes a $2,000 gain ($12,000 amount realizes less $10,000 adjusted basis). The realized gain is recognized under IRC § 1001(c) because no nonrecognition provision applies.

## ■ PROBLEM 6.3 ■

In Year One, T, an attorney with extra cash to invest, purchased an apartment building as an investment. At no point has this rental activity been a trade or business for T. T paid $500,000 for the building and another $100,000 to remodel the property to make it more suitable for renting. T was entitled to claim a depreciation deduction of $30,000 with respect to the building for Year One, but T forgot to claim this deduction on T's federal income tax return for Year One. At the end of Year One, T sold the building to an unrelated buyer for $620,000.

What are the federal income tax consequences of these events to T?

## Analysis

T's sale of the apartment building is a realization event that triggers application of the formula for gain or loss under IRC § 1001(a). To determine the consequences of the sale to T, one must first determine T's amount realized under IRC § 1001(b). T's amount realized upon the sale of the building is $620,000, the amount of cash received from the buyer.

Under § 1012, T's original basis (cost) in the building was $500,000, but the $100,000 spent to remodel the property is added to T's basis under IRC § 1016(a)(1). This brings T's adjusted basis to $600,000. T was entitled to claim a $30,000 depreciation deduction with respect to the building but did not do so. Still, IRC § 1016(a)(2) requires a $30,000 reduction to T's adjusted basis because when it comes to depreciation deductions a taxpayer's basis is reduced by the greater of the amount of depreciation allowed (here, zero) and the amount allowable (here, $30,000). Therefore, T's adjusted basis at the time of sale is $570,000, meaning T's realized gain is $50,000, the excess of the $620,000 amount realized over the $570,000 adjusted basis. This realized gain is recognized under IRC § 1001(c) because no nonrecognition provisions applies.

## POINTS TO REMEMBER

- The basic formula for computing gain or loss under IRC § 1001(a) (amount realized less adjusted basis) applies upon any sale or other disposition of property except by gift.

- Debt incurred to acquire property is added to the taxpayer's basis in the property.

- When a taxpayer disposes of property that secures a liability, the amount of the liability is included in the taxpayer's "amount realized."

- A taxpayer's basis is, generally, his or her unrecovered cost in the property. It is computed by taking the original cost, adding the cost of any permanent improvements or additions to the property, and subtracting the amount of any depreciation deductions with respect to the property (the greater of the amount allowed as a depreciation deduction or the amount allowable as a depreciation deduction).

- A realized gain is recognized (added to gross income) unless a specific nonrecognition provision applies. A realized loss is recognized (deductible) only if the loss is described in IRC § 165(c) (business losses, investment losses, and casualty or theft losses of personal-use property).

*

# CHAPTER 7

# Nonrecognition Transactions

As discussed in Chapter 6, IRC § 1001(c) provides that all realized gains and losses must be recognized "except as otherwise provided in this subtitle." While the general rule of recognition applies in most cases, there are actually several exceptions sprinkled throughout the Code. This Chapter considers four of the most significant nonrecognition provisions applicable to individuals: IRC § 1031 (like-kind exchanges); IRC § 1033 (involuntary conversions); IRC § 1041 (transfers between spouses and certain former spouses); and IRC § 121 (gain on the sale of a principal residence).

Nonrecognition provisions generally share two common themes. First, nonrecognition is conferred because the transaction usually involves a mere change in the form of an investment and not a change in the substance of that investment. In a like-kind exchange of real estate, for example, the *form* of the taxpayer's investment has changed (the taxpayer now owns a different parcel of real estate) but the *substance* of the investment (land ownership) has not.

The second common theme to nonrecognition provisions is that the realized gain or loss usually carries over into the new asset. When the new asset is sold or exchanged in a taxable transaction, the realized gain or loss from the first transaction will then be recognized. Preservation of the unrecognized gain or loss is accomplished by giving the new asset a cost basis equal to the adjusted basis of the old asset. Thus, whenever you see a nonrecognition provision, you should expect to see some basis mechanism within that provision that preserves the unrecognized gain or loss.

Some commentators believe that if a Code section excluding gain or loss does not fit within these two common themes, then that section is not a pure "nonrecognition provision." They would quibble with the inclusion of the IRC § 121 exclusion for gain from the sale of a principal residence in this Chapter because the exclusion is not premised on a "mere change in form," and the exclusion does not require the taxpayer to adjust the basis of other assets to preserve the unrecognized gain. But since IRC § 121 excludes certain realized gains, it seemed most fitting to include that exclusion in this Chapter and not in Chapter 5.

## NONRECOGNITION TRANSACTIONS REVIEW

*Like-Kind Exchanges.* If a taxpayer exchanges one asset for another asset that is of "like kind," no realized gain or loss is recognized. Any such gain or loss is generally preserved in the new asset by giving the taxpayer a basis in the new asset equal to his or her basis in the property exchanged. A "like-kind exchange" is any transaction where the properties exchanged have the same nature or character. Most like-kind exchanges involve real property, but it is also possible to have a like-kind exchange of tangible personal property (a passenger car for another passenger car) or even intangible property (a copyright in a song for a copyright in a different song).

As explained above, the principal justification for nonrecognition in a like-kind exchange is that the taxpayer has not changed the substantive nature of his or her investment; instead, only the exact form of the investment has changed. For instance, if a landlord swaps one apartment building for another apartment building, one can justify nonrecognition on the grounds that the landlord remains invested in rental real estate after the exchange.

As long as any gain or loss from the old property is carried over into the new property, there is no serious harm in letting the landlord change the form of his or her investment. When one considers the breadth of IRC § 1031(a), however, some of this justification is lost. A taxpayer can, for example, swap an acre of farmland for a metropolitan apartment building and qualify for nonrecognition under IRC § 1031(a).

IRC § 1031(a)(1) provides that if a taxpayer exchanges property held for business or investment purposes solely for property "of like kind" that will be held for business or investment purposes, no gain or loss is recognized. If a taxpayer receives both like-kind property and other property in the exchange (cash or property not of like kind), IRC § 1031(b) states that the taxpayer must recognize gain (but not loss) to the extent of the value of the other property.

If a transaction qualifies under IRC § 1031, the taxpayer will generally take a basis in the new property that preserves any unrecognized gain or loss. The formula for computing the taxpayer's basis in the new property is set forth in the first sentence of IRC § 1031(d).

*Involuntary Conversions.* To illustrate the need for IRC § 1033, suppose an earthquake destroys a taxpayer's business property and the taxpayer receives insurance proceeds equal to the value of the building immediately before the disaster. If the property had a low basis, the receipt of cash compensation would cause the taxpayer to realize a substantial gain. Because the taxpayer receives cash, IRC § 1031 would not apply even if the taxpayer used the proceeds to purchase property of like kind. If the gain is recognized, the taxpayer might be unable to purchase similar property of equivalent value because a portion of the proceeds will be used to pay the associated tax liability. IRC § 1033 is thus required to avoid recognition of gain in this and similar cases.

In order for IRC § 1033 to apply, there must be an involuntary conversion of the taxpayer's property. IRC § 1033(a) identifies four events that give rise to an involuntary conversion: (1) destruction in whole or in part; (2) theft; (3) seizure; and (4) requisition or condemnation (or threat or imminence thereof). If an involuntary conversion has occurred, one must determine whether the property was converted into property "similar or related in service or use" to the converted property or into money or other property. If the property is converted into similar-use property (a rare event), then IRC § 1033(a)(1) provides for complete nonrecognition of gain. If the property is converted into money or other, dissimilar property, then the taxpayer may still be able to avoid recognizing all or a portion of the realized gain under IRC § 1033(a)(2), so long as the taxpayer purchases similar-use property within the prescribed time period.

The key to nonrecognition, therefore, is the taxpayer's acquiring similar-use property. The Code does not define property "similar or related in service or use," and the regulations offer little guidance, listing merely three transactions where similar-use property is not acquired by a taxpayer. See Treas. Reg. § 1.1033(a)–2(c)(9). About the most we can glean from the statute is that there is no requirement that similar-use property be held for business or investment purposes. Thus, the involuntary conversion of personal-use property can also qualify for nonrecognition under IRC § 1033 if the taxpayer acquires similar-use property.

As one would expect with a nonrecognition provision, any unrecognized gain upon an involuntary conversion is preserved in the basis of the acquired property. If a taxpayer receives similar-use property upon the conversion and gain is not recognized under IRC § 1033(a)(1), then the taxpayer's basis in the similar-use property is generally the same as the taxpayer's basis in the converted property. See IRC § 1033(b)(1). If the taxpayer purchases similar-use property and the realized gain from the converted property is not recognized (in whole or in part) under IRC § 1033(a)(2), then the taxpayer's basis is the cost of the similar-use property reduced by the amount of unrecognized gain. See IRC § 1033(b)(2).

*Transfers Between Spouses and Former Spouses.* In *United States v. Davis*, 370 U.S. 65, the Court held that a taxpayer had to recognize gain upon the transfer of stock to his spouse pursuant to a separation agreement. The moral of the case is that the transfer of appreciated property in satisfaction of a legal obligation is a realization event for federal income tax purposes. See Chapter 6. Congress understood the moral, perhaps, but it clearly felt the specific result in *Davis* was wrong. So it enacted IRC § 1041 to overrule *Davis* in the context of inter-spousal transfers. Under IRC § 1041(a), no gain or loss is recognized on a transfer of property to a spouse. The nonrecognition rule also applies to transfer between former spouses if they are "incident to a divorce." IRC § 1041(c)(1) automatically deems all transfers within one year of the divorce to be "incident to the divorce," and IRC § 1041(c)(2) includes all transfers "related to the cessation of the marriage" as being incident to the divorce. Just like other nonrecognition transactions, IRC § 1041(b) preserves the gain or loss in the hands of the recipient spouse by giving the recipient spouse a basis in the transferred property equal to the transferor spouse's basis.

*Sale of Principal Residence.* Prior to 1997, the applicable rules upon the sale of a taxpayer's home were substantially more complicated. In those days, taxpayers could avoid recognizing gain from the sale of a home as long as they acquired a new residence within two years of the sale. The catch was that the taxpayer's basis in the new home had to reflect the unrecognized gain from the sale of the old home. In addition, a special rule gave taxpayers age 55 or over a one-time exclusion of up to $125,000 of gain from the sale of a residence. This added benefit helped taxpayers who sought to "buy down" to a less expensive home once their children had grown and left home. Under the prior regime, then, taxpayers who did not buy new homes that were at least as expensive as their old homes had to recognize at least a portion of their realized gains unless they qualified for the one-time exclusion for taxpayers who reached age 55.

The current regime is much simpler. For one thing, everything is contained in a single Code section, IRC § 121, instead of two Code sections. Moreover, we no longer care what a taxpayer does with the sale proceeds, and we no longer force deferral of unrecognized gains into the basis of any subsequently acquired residence. Only taxpayers with extraordinary gains and those who flunk the statutory requirements of IRC § 121 will face taxation of gains from home sales.

A taxpayer may exclude up to $250,000 of realized gain from the sale or exchange of the taxpayers' principal residence. The taxpayer need not be living in the home at the time of the sale; IRC § 121(a) only requires that the taxpayer have owned and used the property as his or her personal residence "for periods aggregating 2 years or more" during the five-year period prior to the date of sale. Practitioners often refer to the IRC § 121(a) requirements as the "ownership test" and the "use test." Even where a taxpayer meets the ownership test and the use test, however, the IRC § 121 exclusion is not available if the taxpayer has made prior use of the exclusion within the two-year period ending on the date of sale.

Married couples filing joint returns can exclude up to $500,000 of realized gain provided either spouse meets the ownership test, both spouses meet the use test, and neither spouse is ineligible for the exclusion because of the prior use of the exclusion within the two years prior to the sale.

If a taxpayer cannot meet all of the requirements for the IRC § 121(a) exclusion, a "reduced exclusion" under IRC § 121(c) will still apply as long as the sale is due to a change in place of employment, health, or "unforeseen circumstances," generally defined as events outside the control of the taxpayer that were not reasonably foreseeable upon acquisition of the property.

Any gain in excess of the applicable limitation will likely be recognized. If the property was held for more than one year, any such recognized gain will very likely qualify as long-term capital gain.

 ## NONRECOGNITION TRANSACTIONS
CHECKLIST

The following checklist will help you determine whether a particular nonrecognition provision applies to the taxpayer's realized gain or loss.

## A. LIKE-KIND EXCHANGES (IRC § 1031)

Use this Part A to determine if the transaction qualifies for nonrecognition under IRC § 1031. Remember that IRC § 1031 is not elective; if the transaction fits within IRC § 1031, nonrecognition will result even if the taxpayer would prefer to recognize the realized gain or loss.

1. **Old Property Held for Business or Investment**—Was the property surrendered by the taxpayer held for use in a business or investment activity?

   a. **Yes**—If yes, continue in this Part A unless the property surrendered is expressly excluded from IRC § 1031 treatment under IRC § 1031(a)(2). Examples of property ineligible for IRC § 1031 nonrecognition include inventory items held for sale to customers, marketable securities, promissory notes, and partnership interests.

   b. **No**—If no, then IRC § 1031 does not apply. Property held by the taxpayer for personal use is not eligible for IRC § 1031 treatment. This includes the taxpayer's residence, personal automobile, and personal effects like a television.

2. **Exchange for Like–Kind Property**—Is the property acquired in the exchange of "like-kind" with the property surrendered?

   a. **General Definition**—The Code contains no guidance as to whether an exchange involves property of like kind. The regulations provide that the term "like kind" refers to "the nature or character of the property and not to its grade or quality." Thus, for example, improved real property and unimproved real property are of like kind because they share the same nature or character (they are both interests in land) even though they have different grades or qualities.

   b. **Real Property**—Nearly every exchange of real property for other real property will qualify. The regulations state that "[t]he fact that any real estate involved is improved or unimproved is not material, for that facts relates only to the grade or quality of the property and not its kind or class." Treas. Reg. § 1.1031(a)–1(b). Thus, an exchange of unimproved land for improved land is a like-kind exchange. See Treas. Reg. § 1.1031(a)–1(c)(2).

c. **Personal Property**—Exchanges of personal property (anything other than land, whether tangible or intangible) are subject to more restrictive rules. See Treas. Reg. § 1.1031(a)–2. Generally, *depreciable* personal property will be considered like-kind to other depreciable personal property that has the same "General Asset Class" used in assigning class lives for purposes of depreciation. For *intangible* property (and personal property not subject to depreciation), the more general test of "nature or character" applies.

d. **Yes**—If yes, continue in this Part A.

e. **No**—If no, then IRC § 1031 does not apply. Unless another nonrecognition provision applies, the realized gain or loss will be recognized.

3. **New Property Held for Business or Investment**—Is the like-kind property received in the exchange going to be held by the taxpayer for use in a business or investment activity?

a. **Yes**—If yes, then continue in this Part A. Note that there is no requirement that the taxpayer use the new property in the *same* activity in which the taxpayer used the old property. For example, a taxpayer can swap land used in his or her business for rental real estate that will be held for investment purposes. The only restriction is that the new property cannot be held for personal use. Presumably a taxpayer ultimately intending to use the acquired property for personal purposes may not simply hold the property for business or investment purposes for only a brief time; however, there is no firm guidance on this point.

b. **No**—If no, then IRC § 1031 does not apply. Unless another nonrecognition provision applies, the realized gain or loss will be recognized.

4. **Loss**—Does the taxpayer realize a loss in the transaction?

a. **Yes**—If yes, the realized loss is not recognized. IRC § 1031(a). This is true even if the taxpayer receives consideration in addition to the like-kind property. IRC § 1031(c). Go to A(6) below to determine the basis in the acquired property.

b. **No**—If no, continue in this Part A.

5. **Boot**—Does the taxpayer receive cash or some other property (referred to as "boot") in addition to the like-kind property?

   a. **Debt Relief is Treated as Boot**—If the old property is encumbered by debt, remember that the amount realized includes the amount of the debt no matter whether the debt is recourse or nonrecourse and no matter whether the other party formally assumes the debt or merely takes the property subject to the debt. In addition, the last sentence of IRC § 1031(d) treats such debt relief as money received by the taxpayer. Thus, where the taxpayer transfers property that secures a debt, the taxpayer is deemed to receive cash equal to the amount of the debt relief, meaning the taxpayer receives boot.

   b. **Yes**—If yes, then IRC § 1031(a)(1) does not apply. Instead, IRC § 1031(b) applies and the taxpayer recognizes gain to the extent of the value of the boot received. Under this rule, if the taxpayer's realized gain exceeds the value of the boot received, the amount of gain recognized is limited to the amount of boot received. If instead the realized gain is less than the amount of boot received, the entire realized gain is recognized but nothing more. Go to A(6) below to determine the basis in the acquired property.

   c. **No**—If no, then no portion of the gain is recognized. IRC § 1031(a). Go to A(6) below to determine the basis in the acquired property.

6. **Basis in Property Received**—A taxpayer's basis in property received in a like-kind exchange is computed under the formula provided in the first sentence of IRC § 1031(d):

---

Basis in Old Property
*Minus* Money Received
*Plus* Recognized Gain
*Minus* Recognized Loss
Basis in New Property

You can always check to make sure this result is correct by computing the consequences of a sale of the new property for fair market value immediately after the exchange. The amount of any realized gain or loss should equal the amount of gain or loss that was not recognized because of the application of IRC § 1031.

    a. **Debt Relief Treated as Money Received**—The last sentence of IRC § 1031(d) treats debt relief as money received by the taxpayer "for purposes of this section," meaning IRC § 1031. Thus any debt relief should be treated as "money received" for purposes of computing the basis of the new property received.

    b. **Taking on Extra Debt**—If the taxpayer takes the new property subject to a different liability, and if the amount of that liability exceeds the amount of the liability attached to the taxpayer's old property, then there is no net debt relief to the taxpayer. Accordingly, the taxpayer in such a situation is not deemed to receive any cash under IRC § 1031(d). See Treas. Reg. § 1.1031(d)–2, Example (2). The other party to the exchange, of course, will be deemed to receive cash because that party necessarily has been relieved of more debt than he or she is assuming in the transaction.

    c. **Basis in Other Property**—If the taxpayer received boot in addition to the like-kind property, the basis computed under the formula in the first sentence of IRC § 1031(d) must be apportioned between the like-kind property and the boot.

        i. **Boot Gets Fair Market Value Basis**—The second sentence of IRC § 1031(d) provides that any non-cash boot receives a basis equal to the fair market value of such property.

        ii. **Remaining Basis Goes to Like–Kind Property**—Any basis remaining after assigning a fair market value basis to the boot becomes the basis in the like-kind property received.

## B. INVOLUNTARY CONVERSIONS (IRC § 1033)

Use this Part B to determine if the transaction qualifies for nonrecognition under IRC § 1033.

1. **Involuntary Conversion**—Was there an involuntary conversion of the taxpayer's property?

   a. **Definition**—IRC § 1033(a) lists four events that give rise to an involuntary conversion: (1) destruction in whole or in part; (2) theft; (3) seizure; and (4) requisition or condemnation (or threat or imminence thereof). In case it matters, there is a difference between a "seizure" and a "requisition or condemnation:" the former refers to the confiscation of property by the government without payment of compensation (like impoundment of a vehicle, for example), while the latter refers to a taking where compensation would be paid but the property nevertheless is converted without the consent of the taxpayer.

   b. **Yes**—If yes, then continue in this Part B.

   c. **No**—If no, then IRC § 1033 does not apply. Unless another nonrecognition provision applies, the taxpayer will recognize the underlying gain or loss.

2. **Realized Gain**—Does the taxpayer realize a gain from the transaction?

   a. **Yes**—If yes, then continue in this Part B.

   b. **No**—If no, then IRC § 1033 does not apply. IRC § 1033 only applies to gains and not losses. So if the taxpayer realized a loss from the conversion, recognition of the loss will depend on the application of other loss limitation provisions. See Chapter 8.

3. **Conversion Into Similar–Use Property**—Was the taxpayer's property converted directly into property similar or related in service or use?

   a. **Similar or Related in Service or Use**—In determining whether property acquired by the taxpayer is "similar or related in service or use" to the involuntarily converted property, the Internal Revenue Service says that one should focus on "whether the properties are of a similar service to the taxpayer, the nature of the business risks connected with the properties, and what such properties demand of the taxpayer in the way of management, services and relations to his tenants." *Revenue Ruling 64–237.*

b. **Yes**—If yes, then the realized gain is not recognized. Proceed to B(5) to determine the taxpayer's basis in the new property.

c. **No**—If no, then continue in this Part B.

4. **Conversion Into Cash or Other Property**—Was the taxpayer's property converted into cash or other property not similar or related in service or use to the involuntarily converted property?

a. **Yes**—If yes, then the amount of gain recognized, if any, depends upon whether and when the taxpayer ultimately purchases property similar or related in service or use to the involuntarily converted property.

   i. **Purchase Within Two Full Taxable Years**—If the taxpayer acquires property similar or related in service or use to the involuntarily converted property (or a controlling interest in a corporation that owns such property) anytime during the period beginning on the date of the involuntary conversion and ending two years after the close of the taxable year in which the gain was realized, then the realized gain is recognized only to the extent the amount realized from the conversion exceeds the cost of such replacement property. IRC § 1033(a)(2)(A), (B). If this test is met, proceed to B(5) to determine the taxpayer's basis in the new property. If not, continue here to see if there is another avenue through which IRC § 1033 can apply.

   ii. **Three-Year Period for Business or Investment Real Property Seized or Condemned**—In the case of real property held for business or investment purposes that is seized, requisitioned or condemned, if the taxpayer acquires either property of like-kind or property similar or related in service or use to the involuntarily converted property (or a controlling interest in a corporation that owns such property) anytime during the period beginning on the date of such seizure, requisition or condemnation and ending *three* years after the close of the taxable year in which the gain was realized, then the realized gain is recognized only to the extent the amount realized from the conversion exceeds the cost of such replacement property. IRC § 1033(a)(2)(A), (a)(2)(B), (g)(1), (g)(4). If this test is met, proceed to B(5) to determine the taxpayer's basis in the new property. If not, continue here to see if there is another avenue through which IRC § 1033 can apply.

iii. **Principal Residence Converted by Presidentially Declared Disaster**—If the taxpayer's principal residence is involuntarily converted in a Presidentially declared disaster, and if the taxpayer acquires property similar or related in service or use to such residence anytime during the period beginning on the date of such conversion and ending *four* years after the close of the taxable year in which the gain was realized, then the realized gain is recognized only to the extent the amount realized from the conversion exceeds the cost of such replacement property. IRC § 1033(a)(2)(A), (a)(2)(B), (h)(1)(B). If this test is met, proceed to B(5) to determine the taxpayer's basis in the new property. If not, then IRC § 1033 does not apply because no replacement property was purchased within the required time-frame. Accordingly, any realized gain will be recognized in full.

b. **No**—If no, then IRC § 1033 does not apply to any extent. Unless another nonrecognition provision applies, the realized gain must be recognized.

5. **Basis in Replacement Property**—Was the replacement property acquired in a transaction described in IRC § 1033(a)(1) (where the taxpayer's property was converted directly into property similar or related in service or use)?

a. **Yes**—If yes, then the taxpayer's basis in the replacement property is equal to the taxpayer's basis in the involuntarily converted property, minus any money received by the taxpayer that was not used to purchase replacement property (if any), plus any gain recognized by the taxpayer in the transaction, minus any loss recognized by the taxpayer in the transaction. IRC § 1033(b)(1).

b. **No**—If no, then the taxpayer's basis in the replacement property is equal to the cost of the replacement property minus any realized gain that is not recognized. IRC § 1033(b)(2). If the replacement property consists of more than one asset, this basis is to be apportioned among the assets proportionately according to their relative costs.

## C. PROPERTY TRANSFERS BETWEEN SPOUSES AND EX–SPOUSES (IRC § 1041)

Use this Part C anytime a taxpayer realizes a gain or loss from the transfer of property to a spouse, a former spouse, or a third party on behalf of a spouse or former spouse.

1. **Transfer to Spouse**—Did the gain or loss arise from the transfer of property from an individual to (or in trust for the benefit of) such individual's spouse?

   a. **Yes**—If yes, then such gain or loss is not recognized, provided that the spouse is a United States citizen or resident. IRC § 1041(a)(1), (d). The transferee spouse is deemed to receive the property by gift, IRC § 1041(b)(1), meaning he or she does not have gross income. IRC § 102(a). In addition, the transferee spouse takes a basis in the property equal to the transferor spouse's adjusted basis in the property at the time of the transfer. IRC § 1041(b)(2).

   b. **No**—If no, then continue in this Part C.

2. **Transfer to Former Spouse Within One Year of Divorce**—Did the gain or loss arise from the transfer of property from an individual to (or in trust for the benefit of) such individual's former spouse within one year after the date on which the marriage ceased?

   a. **Yes**—If yes, then the transfer is "incident to the divorce," IRC § 1041(c)(1), meaning the gain or loss is not recognized, provided that the former spouse is a United States citizen or resident. IRC § 1041(a)(1), (d). The former spouse is deemed to receive the property by gift, IRC § 1041(b)(1), meaning he or she does not have gross income. IRC § 102(a). In addition, the former spouse takes a basis in the property equal to the transferor's adjusted basis in the property at the time of the transfer. IRC § 1041(b)(2).

b.  **No**—If no, then continue in this Part C.

3.  **Transfer to Former Spouse Within Six Years of Divorce and Pursuant to Instrument**—Did the gain or loss arise from the transfer of property from an individual to (or in trust for the benefit of) such individual's former spouse pursuant to a divorce or separation instrument within six years after the date on which the marriage ceased?

a.  **Yes**—If yes, then the transfer is "related to the cessation of the marriage," Treas. Reg. § 1.1041–1T(b), Q & A 7. It is therefore "incident to the divorce," IRC § 1041(c)(2), meaning the gain or loss is not recognized as long as the former spouse is a United States citizen or resident. IRC § 1041(a)(1), (d). The former spouse is deemed to receive the property by gift, IRC § 1041(b)(1), meaning he or she does not have gross income. IRC § 102(a). In addition, the former spouse takes a basis in the property equal to the transferor's adjusted basis in the property at the time of the transfer. IRC § 1041(b)(2).

b.  **No**—If no, then continue in this Part C.

4.  **Transfer to Former Spouse to Effect Division of Marital Property**—Did the gain or loss arise from the transfer of property from an individual to (or in trust for the benefit of) such individual's former spouse in order to effect the division of property owned by the former spouses at the time the marriage ceased?

a.  **Yes**—If yes, then the transfer may be "related to the cessation of the marriage" if the parties can show that it was burdensome to comply with the one- and six-year periods described in C(2) and C(3) above. Treas. Reg. § 1.1041–1T(b), Q & A 7. If successful, the transfer will be considered "incident to the divorce," IRC § 1041(c)(2), meaning the gain or loss is not recognized as long as the former spouse is a United States citizen or resident. IRC

§ 1041(a)(1), (d). The former spouse is deemed to receive the property by gift, IRC § 1041(b)(1), meaning he or she does not have gross income. IRC § 102(a). In addition, the former spouse takes a basis in the property equal to the transferor's adjusted basis in the property at the time of the transfer. IRC § 1041(b)(2).

   b.  **No**—If no, then continue in this Part C.

5.  **Transfer to Third Party Pursuant to Spouse's Written Request**—Did the gain or loss arise from the transfer of property from an individual to a third party either pursuant to the written request of the transferor's spouse or former spouse or pursuant to a divorce or separation instrument?

   a.  **Yes**—If yes, then such transfer is deemed to be a transfer to the spouse or former spouse. Treas. Reg. § 1.1041–1T(c), Q & A 9. Thus, any realized gain or loss to the transferor is not recognized if the other elements of IRC § 1041 are met. If IRC § 1041 applies, the transferee is deemed to have received the property by gift, IRC § 1041(b)(1), meaning he or she does not have gross income. IRC § 102(a). In addition, the transferee takes a basis in the property equal to the transferor's adjusted basis in the property at the time of the transfer. IRC § 1041(b)(2). The transferee is then deemed to have transferred the property to the third party, the tax consequences of which will depend on the facts surrounding such transfer. Treas. Reg. § 1.1041–1T(c), Q & A 9.

   b.  **No**—If no, then IRC § 1041 does not apply to the transfer. Unless another nonrecognition provision applies, the realized gain or loss will be recognized.

## D.  GAIN ON SALE OF PRINCIPAL RESIDENCE (IRC § 121)

To qualify for the IRC § 121 exclusion, selling taxpayers must meet the three basic requirements covered in D(1)–(3) below. If all requirements are met, the applicable exclusion amount determined in D(4) applies. If any of these requirements is not met, the taxpayer's only hope is to qualify for the reduced exclusion discussed in D(5).

1.  **Ownership Test**—Did the taxpayer own the residence for a total period of two years (730 days) in the five-year period

(1,825 days) prior to the date of the sale? See IRC § 121(a). Remember that the 730 days of ownership need not be consecutive; as long as the taxpayer owned the property for a total of 730 days in the 1,825 days prior to the sale, the ownership test is met.

a. **Imputing Ownership of Spouse or Ex–Spouse**—If the taxpayer received the property in a transaction described in IRC § 1041 (transactions between spouses and transactions between former spouses that are incident to divorce, see Part C of this checklist), then the taxpayer's ownership period includes all of the days the transferor (the spouse or former spouse) owned the property. IRC § 121(d)(3)(A).

b. **Property Acquired from a Decedent**—When a decedent's estate sells the decedent's residence, it may claim the period of the decedent's ownership and use even though the estate is generally a separate taxable entity. IRC § 121(d)(11)(A). Likewise, a sale of a decedent's home by a trust that was a "qualified revocable trust" before the decedent's death can qualify for the IRC § 121(a) exclusion and the decedent's ownership and use will be attributed to the trust. IRC § 121(d)(11)(C).

c. **Yes**—If yes, continue in this Part D.

d. **No**—If no, then the IRC § 121(a) exclusion does not apply. Go to D(5) below.

2. **Use Test**—Did the taxpayer use the residence as his or her principal residence for a total period of two years (730 days) in the 5–year period (1,825 days) prior to the date of the sale?

a. **Consecutive Days Not Required**—Again, there is no requirement that the taxpayer use the property as his or her personal residence for at least 730 consecutive days; nonconcurrent periods of use within the five-year pre-sale period are aggregated to determine whether the use test is met. See Treas. Reg. § 1.121–1(c)(1).

b. **Principal Residence**—If the taxpayer uses more than one home during the year, determining whether the home that is sold is the taxpayer's "principal" residence depends on all the facts and circumstances. Generally, the taxpayer's principal residence is the one he or she uses a majority of the time during a taxable year. Treas. Reg. § 1.121–1(a)(2). But other factors count too, including the principal place of abode of the taxpayer's family members, the address listed on the taxpayer's tax returns, and the address used for bills and other correspondence.

c. **Short Temporary Absences**—The taxpayer is deemed to continue using a residence during "short temporary absences" like vacations or other seasonal absences. Treas. Reg. § 1.121–1(c)(2)(i). An example in the regulations, however, indicates that a college professor is not deemed to be using his residence during his one-year abroad on a sabbatical leave. See Treas. Reg. § 1.121–1(c)(4), Example 4.

d. **Use by Former Spouse Pursuant to Divorce Decree**—A taxpayer is treated as using a home he or she owns during such times that the taxpayer's spouse or former spouse is granted use of the property under a divorce or separation instrument. IRC § 121(d)(3)(B).

e. **Use During Periods of Care Away from Home**—A taxpayer may be deemed to continue using a property as his or her principal residence during periods when he or she in fact resides in a licensed care facility. IRC § 121(d)(7). To qualify for this special rule, the taxpayer must be physically or mentally incapable of self-care and must have in fact used the property as his or her principal residence for at least 365 days during the 1,825 days prior to the property's sale.

f. **Yes**—If yes, continue in this Part D.

g. **No**—If no, then the IRC § 121(a) exclusion does not apply. Go to D(5) below.

3. **Once–Every–Two–Years Test**—Did the taxpayer make prior use of the IRC § 121 exclusion within the two-year period (730 days) prior to the date of the sale?

a. **Yes**—If yes, the IRC § 121(a) exclusion is not available for the current sale. IRC § 121(b)(3)(A). Go to D(5) below.

b. **No**—If no, all of the requirements for the IRC § 121(a) are met. Continue in this Part D.

4. **Applicable Exclusion Limitation**—Is the taxpayer married and filing a joint return for the year of the sale?

a. **Yes**—If yes, then the taxpayer can exclude up to $500,000 of realized gain from the sale of the residence, but only if these three requirements are met (if any of these requirements is not met, IRC § 121(b)(2)(B) provides that the maximum amount excludible is the sum of the maximum amounts each spouse could exclude separately if they were unmarried):

    i. **Either Owns**—At least one of the spouses must meet the ownership test. IRC § 121(b)(2)(A)(i).

    ii. **Both Use**—Both spouses must meet the use test. IRC § 121(b)(2)(A)(ii).

    iii. **Neither Ineligible**—Neither spouse can be ineligible for the exclusion because of a prior use of the IRC § 121(a) exclusion within the two years prior to the current sale. IRC § 121(b)(2)(A)(iii).

Note that if the taxpayer claimed depreciation deductions with respect to the property anytime after May 6, 1997, the IRC § 121(a) exclusion does not apply to the extent of that prior depreciation (i.e., the amount of prior depreciation deductions must be included in gross income). IRC § 121(d)(6). This rule will usually apply where the taxpayer used part of the property as a home office and claimed depreciation deductions with respect to that part of the property.

b. **No**—If no, then the taxpayer can exclude from gross income up to $250,000 of realized gain from the sale of the principal residence. IRC § 121(b)(1). Note that if the taxpayer claimed depreciation deductions with respect to the property anytime after May 6, 1997, the IRC § 121(a) exclusion does not apply to the extent of that prior depreciation (i.e., the amount of prior depreciation deductions must be included in gross income). IRC § 121(d)(6). This rule will usually apply where the taxpayer used part of the property as a home office and claimed depreciation deductions with respect to that part of the property.

5. **Reduced Exclusion Limitation**—Was the taxpayer's sale of the home due to a change in place of employment, health, or unforeseen circumstances?

　　a. **Unforeseen Circumstances**—The Code does not define this term, but the regulations provide that a sale is due to unforeseen circumstances "if the primary reason for the sale or exchange is the occurrence of an event that the taxpayer could not reasonably have anticipated before purchasing and occupying the residence." Treas. Reg. § 1.121–3(e)(1). The regulations also list a number of specific events that qualify automatically as unforeseen circumstances, including disasters, death, divorce, and multiple births from the same pregnancy. Treas. Reg. § 1.121–3(e)(2). The same regulation indicates that a preference for a new home or changed financial circumstances will not qualify as an unforeseen circumstance.

　　b. **Yes**—If yes, then a reduced exclusion limitation applies. IRC § 121(c)(2). The amount of the reduced exclusion limitation may be determined by the following formula:

$$\frac{[\text{Lesser of: (i) actual ownership and use; or (ii) period since prior sale}]}{2 \text{ years}} \times \begin{array}{c}\text{applicable}\\\text{exclusion}\\\text{limit}\end{array} = \begin{array}{c}\text{reduced exclusion}\\\text{limitation}\end{array}$$

See IRC § 121(c)(1). In this formula, "actual ownership and use" refers to the total number of days during the five-year period prior to the sale during which the taxpayer "owned and used" the property as his or her principal residence. The "period since prior sale" refers to the number of days between the most recent prior sale by the taxpayer to which the IRC § 121(a) exclusion applied and the date of the sale at issue. The "applicable exclusion limit" is either $250,000, $500,000, or whatever figure serves as the exclusion amount as identified in Part B above. Note that if the reduced exclusion limitation exceeds the taxpayer's realized gain from the sale of the residence, the entire gain is excluded. The reduction, in other words, applies to the applicable limitation on the exclusion and not the exclusion itself.

c. **No**—If no, then the realized gain is recognized unless another nonrecognition provision applies.

## ILLUSTRATIVE PROBLEMS

Here are several problems designed to show how the checklist can be used to answer a question involving these nonrecognition provisions.

## ■ PROBLEM 7.1 ■

T transfers a parcel of undeveloped real property worth $100,000 (adjusted basis of $30,000) to an unrelated party in exchange for an office building worth $100,000. T held the raw land as an investment and intends to use the office building in T's business activity.

What are the federal income tax consequences to T?

### Analysis

T realizes a gain of $70,000 on this transaction (T's amount realized is $100,000, the fair market value of the building, and T's adjusted basis in the raw land is $30,000). None of this gain is recognized, however, because IRC § 1031(a)(1) applies. Specifically, T exchanged investment property for business property and the two parcels of real estate are of "like kind." Although the property received is an office building and the property surrendered is raw land, those differences relate only to the grade or quality of the property and not the underlying nature of the assets (both are interests in real property).

T's basis in the office building will be $30,000, the same basis T had in the raw land. This makes sense because if T sells the building the next day for its $100,000 fair market value, T will realize and recognize $70,000 of gain, the amount of realized gain that was not recognized on the exchange of the raw land.

---

## ■ PROBLEM 7.2 ■

---

T transfers a parcel of undeveloped real property worth $100,000 (adjusted basis of $30,000) to an unrelated party in exchange for an office building worth $60,000, $25,000 in cash, and $15,000 worth of X Corporation stock. T held the raw land as an investment and intends to use the office building in T's business activity.

What are the federal income tax consequences to T?

### Analysis

---

T's amount realized in this transaction is $100,000, consisting of the fair market value of the building, the fair market value of the stock, and the cash. T's adjusted basis in the raw land is $30,000, so T's realized gain is $70,000. The transaction qualifies as a like-kind exchange because T exchanges raw land for an office building and the two parcels of real estate are of "like kind." Although the property received is an office building and the property surrendered is raw land, those differences relate only to the grade or quality of the property and not the underlying nature of the assets (both are interests in real property). T held the raw land for investment purposes and intends to hold the office building for business purposes, so the basic elements of IRC § 1031 are met.

T does not qualify for complete nonrecognition, however, because T receives boot (the cash and the stock) in addition to the like-kind property. Under IRC § 1031(b), T recognizes gain to the extent of the value of the boot received. T received $25,000 in cash and X Corporation stock worth $15,000, for a total of $40,000. Thus, T must recognize $40,000 of the $70,000 realized gain.

T's basis in the property received will be $45,000, computed as the basis T had in the raw land ($30,000), minus the cash received ($25,000), plus the gain recognized ($40,000). Of this amount, $15,000 is assigned to the X Corporation stock so that T has a fair market value basis in the shares. See IRC § 1031(d). The remaining $30,000 of basis becomes T's basis in the office building. This makes sense because if T sells the building the next day for its $60,000 fair market value, T will realize and recognize $30,000 of gain, the amount of realized gain that was not recognized on the exchange of the raw land.

---

## ■ PROBLEM 7.3 ■

---

T transfers a parcel of undeveloped real property worth $120,000 (adjusted basis of $30,000) that secures a $20,000 nonrecourse loan to an unrelated party in exchange for an office building worth $80,000 and $20,000 in cash. The other party expressly assumed the nonrecourse liability. T held the raw land as an investment and intends to use the office building in T's business activity.

What are the federal income tax consequences to T?

### Analysis

---

T's amount realized in this transaction is $120,000, consisting of the $80,000 fair market value of the building, the $20,000 of cash, and the $20,000 of debt relief under *Crane v. Commissioner*. T's adjusted basis in the raw land is $30,000, so T's realized gain is $90,000. The transaction qualifies as a like-kind exchange because T exchanges raw land for an office building and the two parcels of real estate are of "like kind." Although the property received is an office building and the property surrendered is raw land, those differences relate only to the grade or quality of the property and not the underlying nature of the assets (both are interests in real property). T held the raw land for investment purposes and intends to hold the office building for business purposes, so the basic elements of IRC § 1031 are met.

T does not qualify for complete nonrecognition, however, because T receives boot (the cash and relief from the nonrecourse debt) in addition to the like-kind property. Under IRC § 1031(d), the other party's assumption of the $20,000 debt is treated as money received by T. And under IRC § 1031(b), T must recognize gain to the extent of the value of the boot received. T received a total of $40,000 in cash ($20,000 of real cash and $20,000 of deemed cash in the form of debt relief). Thus, T must recognize $40,000 of the $90,000 realized gain.

T's basis in the office building will be $30,000, computed as the basis T had in the raw land ($30,000), minus the "cash" received ($40,000), plus the gain recognized ($40,000). This makes sense because if T sells the building the next day for its $80,000 fair market value, T will realize and recognize $50,000 of gain, the amount of realized gain that was not recognized on the exchange of the raw land.

---

## ■ PROBLEM 7.4 ■

---

In Year One, T's house was completely destroyed when a fire raced through a neighboring forest and engulfed the T's home. T's basis in the home was $300,000 and it was worth $650,000 at the time of the loss. Fortunately, the home was insured. In Year Two, T received $650,000 from Insurance Company to compensate for the loss of the home. In Year Four, T purchased a new home in a cheaper neighborhood for $500,000.

What are the federal income tax consequences to T?

### Analysis

---

T has no gain or loss in Year One (the year of the fire). T did not receive any insurance proceeds in Year One so there cannot be a gain. T cannot claim a loss for Year One because T has a reasonable expectation of recovery from Insurance Company as of the end of Year One.

When T received the $650,000 from Insurance Company in Year Two, T realized a gain of $350,000 (the excess of the insurance proceeds over T's basis in the home). If recognized, this would be a "personal casualty gain" for Year Two. (See Chapter 8). But because T acquired another residence before the end of Year Four (two full taxable years after the year in which the gain is realized), IRC § 1033(a)(2)(A) applies, meaning T will only have to recognize the $150,000 by which the amount realized from the conversion ($650,000) exceeds the cost of the replacement property ($500,000). The extended, four-year replacement period for principal residences does not apply here because there is no evidence that the fire was a Presidentially declared disaster.

Because IRC § 1033(a)(2)(A) applies, T's basis in the new home will be the $500,000 cost minus the $200,000 of realized gain that was not recognized. Thus T's basis in the new home is $300,000.

---

## ■ PROBLEM 7.5 ■

---

T and S divorced in Year One. Their divorce decree requires T to transfer Blackacre, a parcel of real property worth $100,000 in Year One, to S. T's adjusted basis in Blackacre is $30,000. In Year Four, when the value of Blackacre was $120,000, T transferred title to Blackacre to S. In Year Five, S sold Blackacre to an unrelated individual for $125,000.

What are the federal income tax consequences to T and S?

### Analysis

---

T's transfer of Blackacre to S is a realization event because it represents the satisfaction of T's legal obligation to transfer property to S. *United States v. Davis*. T realizes a $90,000 gain from the transfer in Year Four (amount realized of $120,000 less basis of $30,000).

T will not recognize this gain, however, because IRC § 1041(a) applies. Specifically, T's transfer of Blackacre is "related to the cessation of the marriage" between T and S because T transfers Blackacre to S pursuant to a divorce or separation instrument within six years of the end of their marriage. Treas. Reg. § 1.1041–1T(b), Q & A 7. The transfer is therefore "incident to the divorce," IRC § 1041(c)(2), meaning IRC § 1041(a) applies.

S is deemed to receive Blackacre by gift, IRC § 1041(b)(1), meaning S does not have gross income. IRC § 102(a). In addition, S takes T's $30,000 basis in the property. IRC § 1041(b)(2). Consequently, when S sells Blackacre to an unrelated buyer in Year Five for $125,000, S realizes and recognizes a gain of $95,000 ($125,000 amount realized less $30,000 adjusted basis).

## ■ PROBLEM 7.6 ■

T and T's spouse, S, purchased their home at the beginning of Year One for $200,000. They immediately moved into the home and stayed there until the end of Year Eight. At that time, they sold the home to an unrelated purchaser for $500,000. T and S will file a joint return for Year Eight.

What are the federal income tax consequences to T?

### Analysis

T and S realize a gain of $300,000 from the sale of their home (amount realized of $500,000 less their $200,000 basis). This gain is excluded from their gross income on the Year Eight joint return because IRC § 121(a) applies. Specifically, T and S both owned the home throughout the five-year period ending on the date of the sale even though they are only required to own the home for periods aggregating two years or more during such time (the "ownership test"). In addition, both T and S used the house as their principal residence throughout the same five-year pre-sale period although it is only necessary that they make such use of their home for periods aggregating two years or more during this time (the "use test"). Finally, neither T nor S appear to have made prior use of the IRC § 121 exclusion within the two years prior to the sale.

Normally the IRC § 121 exclusion is limited to $250,000. But because T and S will file jointly for Year Eight, they may qualify for a $500,000 exclusion limitation under IRC § 121(b). Indeed, T and S do qualify for the higher exclusion limit on these facts: at least one spouse meets the ownership test, both spouses meet the use, and neither has made prior use of the IRC § 121 exclusion within the two years prior to the Year Eight sale at issue. Accordingly, they may exclude the entire $300,000 realized gain from their gross income.

---

## ■ PROBLEM 7.7 ■

---

T purchased a home in New York at the beginning of Year One for $200,000 and immediately moved in to the property. Several months later, T's employer promoted T to regional manager. As part of the promotion, T's employer insisted that T move to Los Angeles. T was thus forced to sell the New York home. At the beginning of Year Two, exactly one year after acquiring the home, T sold the property to an unrelated purchaser for $250,000.

What are the federal income tax consequences to T?

### Analysis

---

T's sale of the home in Year Two triggers a realized gain of $50,000 (amount realized of $250,000 less T's $200,000 basis). Normally T could not exclude this gain under IRC § 121 because IRC § 121(a) requires that T own and use the property as his principal residence for periods aggregating two years or more during the five-year period prior to the sale. On these facts, T only owned and used the home as a principal residence for a total of one year.

IRC § 121(c), however, provides a reduced exclusion limitation that applies if T is disqualified from the IRC § 121(a) exclusion because of a change in place of employment, health, or unforeseen circumstances. In this case, T sold the property because of a change in the place of T's employment: T's employer required T to move from New York to Los Angeles. Consequently, the reduced exclusion limitation applies.

The maximum amount that T can exclude from gross income under IRC § 121(c) is a fraction of the $250,000 limitation normally applicable if the IRC § 121(a) elements are met. In this case, T owned and used the home as T's principal residence for one year, which is one-half of the requisite two years of ownership and use needed to claim the regular exclusion. Accordingly, T may exclude up to $125,000 (one-half of $250,000) of gain. Since T's realized gain is only $50,000, all of the gain may be excluded because it is entirely within this reduced exclusion limitation amount.

## POINTS TO REMEMBER

- IRC § 1031 is not elective; if the elements of a like-kind exchange are present, the taxpayer has no choice but to apply IRC § 1031 to determine the tax consequences.

- Almost all land-for-land exchanges will qualify as like-kind exchanges. Be more suspicious of exchanges involving tangible personal property or intangible property.

- If the taxpayer receives both like-kind property and other property in exchange for an asset (including cash), all or a portion of the realized gain will be recognized but no loss will be recognized.

- Debt relief is treated as money received by the taxpayer for purposes of a like-kind exchange.

- The basis that the taxpayer takes in the new property received in a like-kind exchange will preserve any unrecognized gain or loss from the disposition of the old property.

- IRC § 1033 only applies to realized gains and not to realized losses.

- Generally a taxpayer has the rest of the year plus two more full taxable years to acquire replacement property that is "similar or related in service or use" to involuntarily converted property in order for IRC § 1033 to apply.

• The basis that the taxpayer takes in the replacement property acquired in a transaction to which IRC § 1033 applies will preserve any unrecognized gain or loss from the conversion of the old property.

• IRC § 1041 will apply only to property transfers between spouses and former spouses. Cash transfers between former spouses may qualify as "alimony" but they will certainly not qualify under IRC § 1041.

• IRC § 1041 will provide nonrecognition treatment to any property transfers between spouses, any property transfers between former spouses if within one year of divorce, and any property transfers between spouses pursuant to a divorce or separation instrument made within six years of the divorce. Beyond that, a taxpayer will need to be able to rebut a presumption that a transfer to a former spouse is not related to the cessation of the marriage.

• A taxpayer must meet both the ownership test and the use test in order to claim the IRC § 121(a) exclusion. If the taxpayer fails either of these tests, consider whether the reduced exclusion limitation in IRC § 121(c) applies. If not, then any realized gain is recognized.

• In addition to the ownership and use tests, the taxpayer must meet an additional requirement: no prior use of the IRC § 121 exclusion within the two years prior to the sale. The reduced exclusion limitation can apply here too if the taxpayer fails this additional requirement.

• The reduced exclusion limitation under IRC § 121(c) is available only if the taxpayer's sale of a principal residence is attributable to a change in place of employment, health, or unforeseen circumstances. Whether a sale is caused by "unforeseen circumstances" depends on the facts, but the regulations do identify some events that are deemed to be unforeseen circumstances.

- The maximum amount excludable under IRC § 121 is generally $250,000, but a $500,000 limit applies to married couples that file jointly provided either spouse meets the ownership test, both spouses meet the use test, and neither spouse is ineligible because of a prior use of the exclusion within the two years prior to the sale.

# CHAPTER 8

# Loss Limits

R ecall from Chapter 6 that an individual taxpayer's realized loss is recognized if it is described in IRC § 165(c). There are, however, other Code provisions that take an otherwise deductible loss and render it nondeductible. This Chapter considers four of these special loss limitation rules, as well as a detailed examination of the rules applicable to casualty and theft losses allowable under IRC § 165(c)(3).

## LOSS LIMITS REVIEW

*At-Risk Rules.* Taxpayers with substantial amounts of gross income look for ways to generate deductions without having to incur the cost associated with the deduction. Prior to 1976, there was an easy technique for accomplishing this. To illustrate, suppose a taxpayer with salary income of $200,000 borrows $1 million from a bank on a nonrecourse basis in to purchase depreciable property for use in a new business venture. The taxpayer's basis in the depreciable property, thanks to *Crane v. Commissioner*, 331 U.S. 1 (1947), starts at $1 million. See Chapter 6. The taxpayer will receive a substantial depreciation deduction in the year of purchase that might fully offset the salary income. The problem, from a tax policy standpoint, is that the taxpayer can simply walk away from the debt to the bank without personal liability. The bank will be able to foreclose against the property but nothing else. The taxpayer loses the building, but the taxpayer is not sad because he or she never paid any out-of-pocket costs for the property in the first place.

Congress added IRC § 465 in 1976 to prevent taxpayers from getting away with this and similar schemes. IRC § 465 generally provides that the amount of any net loss (otherwise allowable for the year) which may be deducted in connection with a business or investment activity cannot exceed the aggregate amount with respect to which the taxpayer is at risk in such activity at the close of the taxable year. Losses disallowed under this rule are treated as deductions with respect to the activity in the following year. So if a taxpayer's amount at risk increases in later years, he or she can obtain the benefit of previously disallowed losses to the extent that such increases in the amount at risk exceed net losses in later years.

In general, a taxpayer is "at risk" with respect to an activity to the extent of the taxpayer's cash and the adjusted basis of other property contributed to the activity, as well as any amounts borrowed for use in the activity with respect to which the taxpayer has personal liability for payment from his personal assets. A taxpayer's at risk amount also generally includes amounts borrowed for use in the activity which are secured by property other than property used in the activity. But a taxpayer generally will not be at risk with respect to any other nonrecourse debt, a rule that effectively thwarts the planning technique described above.

*Passive Activity Losses.* The at-risk rules in IRC § 465 proved helpful in stopping many tax shelters of the day, but it was incomplete. While IRC § 465 adequately ensnared those who were claiming deductions beyond the extent to which they bore a risk of loss, it did not address those shelters where wealthy taxpayers could manipulate the realization rule to tremendous advantage. Suppose, for example, another taxpayer with a large annual salary. He or she would like to generate deductions to offset the large amount of salary income each year, but does not want to devote much time or effort to a new activity. So the taxpayer invests in an apartment building, borrowing $1 million on a recourse basis from a bank to purchase the building. Although the building will generate rental income, the expenses from the activity (taxes, insurance, repairs, and the like—not to mention the interest on the bank loan) will consume much of that amount. When you figure in depreciation, a purely paper deduction that has no present cost to the taxpayer, the activity now produces a net loss each year for many years. IRC § 465 would not apply in this example because the taxpayer is "at risk" with respect to the $1 million recourse loan. Voila! The taxpayer has substantial net losses to offset the salary income, all at little effort and with very little cost to the taxpayer.

In 1986, Congress dealt a crippling blow to this strategy with the enactment of IRC § 469. In general, IRC § 469(a) permits taxpayers to deduct losses from "passive activities" only to the extent of the taxpayer's aggregate income from all passive activities. Under IRC § 469(b), any disallowed passive losses carry over to the next taxable year. A "passive activity," in general, is any business activity in which the taxpayer does not "materially participate." See IRC § 469(c)(1). A taxpayer is deemed to materially participate in an activity if the taxpayer meets any one of several tests contained in the regulations.

Returning to the example, then, the deductions for depreciation and other expenses will be disallowed to the extent they exceed the income from the rental activity each year. When the taxpayer finally sells the building and thus disposes of his or her entire interest in the rental activity, any losses disallowed under IRC § 469 from prior years can be claimed then. In effect, then, IRC § 469 postpones the deduction of excessive losses from passive activities until the taxpayer has enough income from that activity or until the taxpayer finally realizes gain or loss on the disposition of the assets used in the activity. This timing limitation makes the tax shelter scheme much less attractive to wealthy taxpayers.

*Wash Sales of Stocks or Securities.* Suppose a taxpayer purchases 100 shares of stock in ACME Corporation, a publicly-traded company, for $10,000. Eighteen months later, the stock has declined in value to $4,000. The taxpayer is confident that the stock value will rebound and eventually surpass the original purchase price. But the taxpayer is thinking about using the momentary decline in value to an advantage: sell the stock now, claim a $6,000 loss, and then immediately buy back the shares for $4,000. Eventually, if the stock returns to its original $10,000 value, the taxpayer can sell the stock for a $6,000 gain. In the aggregate, of course, the transaction has produced neither gain nor loss, but if the two transactions are respected for tax purposes, the taxpayer accelerates a deduction (which is good because the tax savings can be invested sooner, so the taxpayer comes out ahead from a time value of money perspective) and defers a corresponding item of income (also good because the longer the taxpayer defers the gain, the more the taxpayer can benefit from the growth of the investment).

IRC § 1091(a) frustrates this simple technique by disallowing the loss from a sale of stock or securities if the taxpayer acquires or contracts to acquire substantially the same stock or securities within a certain window of time. In addition, IRC § 1091(d) gives the taxpayer a basis in the new stock or securities equal to the basis the taxpayer had in the old stock or securities plus any excess of the price of the new stock over the selling price of the old stock (or minus any excess of the selling price of the old stock over the price of the new stock). As a result, the taxpayer who engages in a "wash sale" of stock or securities will be treated as though the original block of stock or securities was never sold.

*Transactions with Related Parties.* Another strategy for accelerating a loss while keeping control of an asset involves the use of related parties. Suppose a taxpayer holds an asset that originally cost $10,000 but has declined in value to $4,000. If the taxpayer believes that the asset will regain its value, there is an incentive to engage in a little chicanery akin to the wash sale: sell the asset to a related person (like a corporation that the taxpayer controls or the taxpayer's child) for fair market value. If the taxpayer immediately buys the asset back from the related party, of course, the Internal Revenue Service could successfully argue that the entire transaction is a scam. So for the plan to work, the related person will have to keep the asset. That might be acceptable to the taxpayer since the asset will stay "within the family" under the taxpayer's control. Thus, by manipulating the realization rule, the taxpayer can obtain a very significant benefit that the Internal Revenue Service would not be able to attack absent statutory arsenal.

IRC § 267(a) prevents this easy manipulation by disallowing any otherwise deductible loss if the loss results from the sale or exchange of property to a related person. The key, obviously, is determining whether the buyer is related to the taxpayer. Section 267(b) spells out several specific relationships that will trigger disallowance of the loss. Note that if the related party later sells the asset at a gain, the related person can offset the taxpayer's disallowed loss under IRC § 267(a) against such gain. IRC § 267(d).

*Casualty and Theft Losses Involving Personal–Use Property.* As explained in Chapter 6, IRC § 165(c)(3) permits a deduction for losses sustained with respect to property held for personal use that arise from a casualty or theft. Thefts are easy to spot, but casualties can be a bit trickier. The Internal Revenue Service insists that a casualty must be an event that is both "sudden" and "unexpected or unusual." *Revenue Ruling 79–174.* A gradual destruction of the property, then, would not qualify as a casualty. Nor would a foreseeable event like a flood in a low-lying area that experiences floods every other year.

There are three important limitations on the deduction for casualty and theft losses involving personal-use property. First, the regulations provide that the amount of the loss is measured as the lesser of the taxpayer's basis in the asset immediately before the loss and the loss in value to the property caused by the casualty or theft. Treas. Reg. § 1.165–7(b)(1). So if a personal-use asset worth $4,000 in which the taxpayer's basis is $9,000 is completely lost in a fire, the gross deduction amount starts at $4,000, not $9,000. Second, IRC § 165(h)(1) imposes a $100 per-casualty limitation: only the gross deduction amount in excess of this very modest threshold is deductible. Finally, if the taxpayer's personal casualty losses for the year—after application of the $100 speed bump—exceed the taxpayer's personal casualty gains (which arise where, for instance, the insurance received by the taxpayer for the loss of the asset exceeds the taxpayer's basis in the asset immediately before the casualty or theft), the personal casualty losses are deductible to the

extent of the personal casualty gains plus so much of such excess as
exceeds ten percent of the taxpayer's adjusted gross income. IRC
§ 165(h)(2)(A).

## LOSS LIMITS CHECKLIST

This checklist will assist in determining whether a realized loss is
recognized.

**A. AT-RISK LIMITATION (IRC § 465)**

1.  **Loss From Activity**—Does the taxpayer have more deductions
    from a particular activity than income from the activity for the
    taxable year?

    a.  **Yes**—If yes, then the taxpayer has a "loss" to which IRC
        § 465 may apply. IRC § 465(d). Continue in this Part A.

    b.  **No**—If no, then IRC § 465 does not apply.

2.  **Activity to Which IRC § 465 Applies**—Does the loss arise
    from a business or investment activity of the taxpayer?

    a.  **Yes**—If yes, the loss may be subject to IRC § 465. IRC
        § 465(c)(1), (c)(3)(A). Continue in this Part A.

    b.  **No**—If no, then IRC § 465 does not apply.

3.  **Loss Limited to Amount At Risk**—Does the amount of the loss
    from the activity exceed the amount by which the taxpayer is
    "at risk" for such activity as of the end of the taxable year?

    a.  **At-Risk Amount**—Generally, the taxpayer's "at-risk"
        amount for a particular activity is the sum of four things:

        i.   **Cash Contributions**—The amount of money contrib-
             uted by the taxpayer to the activity. IRC
             § 465(b)(1)(A). Thus, for example, if the taxpayer
             uses $10,000 of cash to purchase an asset for use in the
             activity, the taxpayer is at risk as to the $10,000.

        ii.  **Property Contributions**—The adjusted basis of prop-
             erty contributed by the taxpayer to the activity. IRC
             § 465(b)(1)(A). Thus, for example, if the taxpayer

begins using an asset in the activity, the taxpayer is at risk to the extent of the asset's adjusted basis.

iii. **Amounts Borrowed on Recourse Basis**—The total amount borrowed on a recourse basis from a disinterested person for use in the activity. IRC § 465(b)(1)(B), (b)(2)(A). Recall that a recourse debt is one for which the taxpayer is personally liable; if the property specifically securing the debt is insufficient to satisfy the amount owed to the lender upon default, the taxpayer will be required to transfer other non-exempt assets to the lender to pay off the remaining amount owed. A "disinterested person" is one whose only interest in the activity is as a creditor or shareholder and who is not related to a person who has a more involved interest in the activity. IRC § 465(b)(3).

iv. **Amounts Borrowed on Nonrecourse Basis to Extent of Other Pledged Assets**—The total amount borrowed on a nonrecourse basis from a disinterested person for use in the activity, but only to the extent of the net fair market value of the taxpayer's interest in the property not used in the activity that specifically secures the debt. IRC § 465(b)(1)(B), (b)(2)(B).

b. **Yes**—If yes, the loss is deductible only to the extent of the amount by which the taxpayer is at risk. The excess loss is not deductible in the current year, IRC § 465(a)(1), but it will carry over to the next taxable year. IRC § 465(a)(2). Going forward, the amount of the allowable loss serves to reduce the amount by which the taxpayer is at risk for subsequent taxable years. IRC § 465(b)(5).

c. **No**—If no, then IRC § 465 does not apply and the loss remains deductible in full. But consider whether another loss limitation in this checklist applies. Going forward, the amount of the allowable loss serves to reduce the amount by which the taxpayer is at risk for subsequent taxable years. IRC § 465(b)(5).

**B.** **PASSIVE ACTIVITY LOSSES (IRC § 469)**

1. **Passive Activities**—Did the taxpayer engage in one or more "passive activities" during the taxable year?

a.  **Definition**—A passive activity is any activity that involved the conduct of a trade or business in which the taxpayer does not "materially participate," IRC § 469(c)(1), or any rental activity not engaged in by a taxpayer in the real property business. IRC § 469(c)(2), (c)(7).

b.  **Material Participation**—A taxpayer "materially participates" in an activity if he or she is involved in the operations of the activity on a regular, continuous, and substantial basis. IRC § 461(h)(1). The regulations offer objective tests for determining whether a taxpayer materially participates in an activity. Treas. Reg. § 1.469–5T(a) lists seven situations where a taxpayer will be deemed to materially participate in an activity: (i) participation in the activity for more than 500 hours in the taxable year; (ii) participation in the activity for 500 hours or less during the taxable year, but such participation constitutes substantially all of the participation in the activity by everyone involved in that activity; (iii) participation in the activity for more than 100 hours in the taxable year, provided the taxpayer's participation equals or exceeds the hours of participation by anyone else involved in that activity; (iv) participation in the activity for more than 100 hours in the taxable year, provided the taxpayer's participation in that activity *and* all other "significant participation activities" (those business activities in which the taxpayer participates for more than 100 hours but no more than 500 hours) in the same year totals more than 500 hours in the taxable year; (v) material participation in the activity for any five of the ten taxable years immediately prior to the taxable year at issue; (vi) material participation in an activity involving the performance of personal services for any three of the five taxable years immediately prior to the taxable year at issue; or (vii) participation in the activity for more than 100 hours in the taxable year provided that, based on all of the facts and circumstances, the taxpayer participates in the activity on a regular, continuous, and substantial basis.

c.  **Yes**—If yes, then IRC § 469 may apply. Continue in this Part B.

d. **No**—If no, then IRC § 469 does not apply and the loss remains deductible in full. But consider whether another loss limitation in this checklist applies.

2. **Aggregate Loss From Passive Activities**—Does the taxpayer have more deductions from all passive activities for the taxable year than income from all passive activities for the taxable year?

   a. **Yes**—If yes, then the taxpayer has a "passive activity loss" to the extent such deductions exceed such income. IRC § 469(d)(1). The passive activity loss is disallowed for the taxable year, IRC § 469(a), but the amount of the disallowed loss is treated as a deduction allocable to such passive activities in the next taxable year. IRC § 469(b).

   b. **No**—If no, then IRC § 469 does not apply and the loss remains deductible in full. But consider whether another loss limitation in this checklist applies.

C. **WASH SALES OF STOCK OR SECURITIES (IRC § 1091)**

1. **Sale of Stock or Securities**—Does the loss arise from the sale or other disposition of stock or securities (or from contracts or options to buy or sell stock or securities)?

   a. **Yes**—If yes, then continue in this Part C.

   b. **No**—If no, then IRC § 1091 does not apply. But consider whether another loss limitation in this checklist applies.

2. **Commitment to Purchase Substantially Identical Stock or Securities**—Did the taxpayer acquire or commit to acquire substantially identical stock or securities within the 61–day period that begins 30 days before the sale or disposition and ends 30 days after such sale or disposition?

   a. **Yes**—If yes, then continue in this Part C.

   b. **No**—If no, then IRC § 1091 does not apply. But consider whether another loss limitation in this checklist applies.

3. **Not a Dealer**—Is the taxpayer a dealer in stock or securities?

   a. **Yes**—If yes, then IRC § 1091 does not apply if the sale or disposition is made in the ordinary course of the taxpayer's business. But consider whether another loss limitation in this checklist applies. If the transaction was not made in the ordinary course of the taxpayer's business, then see the analysis below as if the answer to this question was "no."

b. **No**—If no, then no deduction is allowed for the loss. IRC § 1091(a). In addition, the taxpayer's basis in the stock or securities subsequently acquired (the "new stock") will be equal to the adjusted basis of the stock of securities the disposition of which gave rise to the disallowed loss (the "old stock"), increased or decreased by the difference between the price at which the new stock was acquired and the price at which the old stock was sold or otherwise disposed of. IRC § 1091(d); Treas. Reg. § 1.1091–2(a), Example (1).

## D. TRANSACTIONS WITH RELATED PARTIES (IRC § 267(a)(1))

1. **Related Party**—Does the loss arise from the sale or exchange of property, directly or indirectly, between related persons?

   a. **Definition**—IRC § 267(b) lists the relationships that give rise to related party status. These include: (i) an individual and members of his or her family (defined in IRC § 267(c)(4) to mean only siblings, a spouse, ancestors, and lineal descendants); (ii) a corporation and a shareholder that owns more than half of the shares by value (keeping in mind that under IRC § 267(c)(1)–(2) a shareholder is deemed to own any shares held by members of his or her family as well as a proportionate share of any shares held by a partnership of which he or she is a partner and an estate or trust of which he or she is a beneficiary); (iii) the grantor and trustee of a trust; (iv) the trustee of a trust and any beneficiary of such trust; and (iv) a corporation and a partnership if the same person holds controlling interests in each.

   b. **Yes**—If yes, then continue in this Part D.

   c. **No**—If no, then IRC § 267(a)(1) does not apply.

2. **Transfers Between Spouses and Former Spouses**—Does the loss arise from a sale or exchange transaction to which IRC § 1041 applies? See Chapter 7.

    a.  **Yes**—If yes, then IRC § 267(a)(1) does not apply. IRC § 267(g). Instead, the transaction is governed wholly by IRC § 1041.

    b.  **No**—If no, then the loss is disallowed. IRC § 267(a)(1). Note that if the related party transferee subsequently sells or exchanges the property at a gain, the related party transferee recognizes the gain only to the extent it exceeds the amount of the taxpayer's disallowed loss. IRC § 267(d). In other words, the related party transferee can claim the taxpayer's disallowed loss to reduce the amount of gain her or she would otherwise recognize.

**E. CASUALTY & THEFT LOSSES OF PERSONAL–USE PROPERTY (IRC § 165(h))**

This Part E applies to any property of the taxpayer that has been damaged or lost from a casualty or theft.

    **1.**  **Casualty or Theft**—Did a casualty or theft occur?

        a.  **Definition**—The statute lists fires, storms, and shipwrecks as casualties. IRC § 165(c)(3). The Tax Court has held that a casualty results from an external force applied to property that the taxpayer is powerless to prevent. Carpenter v. Commissioner, T.C. Memo. 1966–228. The Internal Revenue Service has held that a casualty is an event that is both "sudden" and "unexpected or unusual." *Revenue Ruling 79–174.*

        b.  **Yes**—If yes, then continue in this Part E.

        c.  **No**—If no, then any loss is realized not subject to the extra limitations in IRC § 165(h).

    **2.**  **Personal–Use Property**—Was the property lost in the casualty or theft property used in the taxpayer's business or property held from a transaction entered into for profit?

        a.  **Yes**—If yes, then the loss is deductible under IRC § 165(c)(1) (in the case of property used in a trade or business) or IRC § 165(c)(2) (in the case of property held from a transaction entered into for profit). The additional limitations on casualty and theft losses only apply to property held for personal use, so IRC § 165(h) does not apply.

        b.  **No**—If no, then continue in this Part E.

3.  **Gross Loss**—Does the taxpayer's adjusted basis in the property immediately before the casualty or theft exceed the loss in value to the property caused by the casualty or theft?

    a.  **Yes**—If yes, then the gross amount of the loss is limited to the loss in value to the property. Treas. Reg. § 1.165–7(b)(1). Continue in this Part E.

    b.  **No**—If no, then the gross amount of the loss is equal to the taxpayer's adjusted basis in the property. Treas. Reg. § 1.165–7(b)(1). Continue in this Part E.

4.  **Insurance**—Did the taxpayer receive insurance or any other compensation for the loss?

    a.  **Yes**—If yes, then the amount of insurance or other compensation received is subtracted from the gross amount of the loss determined in Part E(3) above. Continue in this Part E. If the amount of insurance or other compensation received exceeds the taxpayer's adjusted basis in the property, a "personal casualty gain" results. In that case, skip to Part E(6) below.

    b.  **No**—If no, then no adjustment is made to the gross amount of the loss determined in Part E(3) above. Continue in this Part E.

5.  **$100 Limitation**—Does the gross amount of the loss, adjusted as applicable under Part E(4) above, exceed $100?

    a.  **Yes**—If yes, then the gross deduction amount from the casualty or theft is equal to the amount of such excess. IRC § 165(h)(1). Continue in this Part E.

    b.  **No**—If no, then there is no deduction for the loss. IRC § 165(h)(1).

6.  **Personal Casualty Losses vs. Personal Casualty Gains**—Does the total amount of all of the taxpayer's "personal casualty losses" for the year exceed the total amount of all of the taxpayer's "personal casualty gains" for the year?

    a.  **Personal Casualty Losses**—"Personal casualty losses" means all of the casualty and theft losses that have survived through Part E(5) of this checklist. IRC § 165(h)(3)(B).

b. **Personal Casualty Gains**—"Personal casualty gains" means the recognized gains from all casualties and thefts involving personal-use property. IRC § 165(h)(3)(A). Generally speaking, such gains would be identified in Part E(4) of this checklist.

c. **Yes**—If yes, then the personal casualty losses are deductible to the extent of the personal casualty gains plus so much of such excess as exceeds ten percent of the taxpayer's adjusted gross income. IRC § 165(h)(2)(A). Expressed in formula form:

---

Personal Casualty Losses
*Minus* Personal Casualty Gains
*Equals* Excess
*Minus* 10% of Adjusted Gross Income
*Equals* Deductible Excess
*Plus* Personal Casualty Gains
*Equals* Total Amount of IRC § 165(c)(3) Deduction

---

The portion of the personal casualty losses equal to the amount of personal casualty gains is treated as an above-the-line deduction. IRC § 165(h)(4)(A). The deductible portion of the excess personal casualty losses is a regular itemized deduction. IRC § 67(b)(3).

d. **No**—If no, then all of the personal casualty gains and personal casualty losses are treated as gains and losses, respectively, from the sale or exchange of capital assets. IRC § 165(h)(2)(B). See Chapter 9.

## ILLUSTRATIVE PROBLEMS

The following problems are designed to show how the checklist helps in analyzing a question involving the loss limitations discussed in this Chapter.

---

## ■ PROBLEM 8.1 ■

---

T is a surgeon who earns a substantial salary income. T borrows $800,000 on a nonrecourse basis from Bank and uses the loan proceeds plus $200,000 of T's own money to purchase an office building that T rents out to businesses. T does not materially participate in this activity. For the current year, T collects $100,000 in rents but pays $30,000 in maintenance expenses attributable to the building and $60,000 of interest on the Bank loan. T's depreciation deduction on the building for the current year is $40,000.

What are the federal income tax consequences of these events to T?

## Analysis

The Bank loan to T is not gross income because of T's obligation to repay Bank. T's basis in the building is $1,000,000, consisting of the $200,000 paid out of pocket plus the $800,000 nonrecourse loan. *Crane v. Commissioner*. (See Chapter 6.)

All of the expenses described in the problem are deductible because the activity of operating and leasing an office building is an investment activity for T. It would not be a trade or business for T because T is not involved in the activity on a regular, continuous, and substantial basis. *Commissioner v. Groetzinger*. T could therefore deduct the interest expense as "investment interest" and the maintenance expenses under IRC § 212(2). The depreciation is deductible under IRC § 167 because the building is subject to wear and tear and T holds the building for investment.

The activity generates a net loss for the year because total expenses of $130,000 exceed the $100,000 of rental income. The net loss is disallowed under IRC § 465 if T is not "at risk" to the extent of at least $30,000 for this activity. T's amount at risk on these facts is $200,000, the amount of cash T has contributed toward the activity. T is not at risk with respect to any portion of the nonrecourse debt, however, because that debt is not secured by any property outside of the property used in the rental activity. Still, IRC § 465 will not disallow T's net loss here because T is sufficiently at risk just from the cash contribution. In the next year, however, this $30,000 net loss will reduce T's at-risk amount from $200,000 to $170,000. IRC § 465(b)(5). This could affect the deductibility of future net losses.

Although IRC § 465 does not disallow the net loss, IRC § 469(a) does. The activity is a "passive activity" for T because it is a rental activity and T is not a taxpayer engaged in the real property business. IRC § 469(c)(2). T has more deductions than income from this passive activity, so a passive activity loss exists. IRC § 469(d)(1). Based only on these facts, there are no other passive activities to consider. Therefore, the $30,000 passive activity loss is disallowed for the current year. IRC § 469(a). The loss will carry over to the next year and be treated as a deduction allocable to the office rental activity in that year. IRC § 469(b).

---

### ■ PROBLEM 8.2 ■

---

When T returned home from a ten-day vacation, T discovered that T's home entertainment system had been stolen. T purchased the system two years before the theft for $5,000. It was worth $3,000 at the time of the theft. T was uninsured for the loss and has no idea as to the identity of the thief. T's adjusted gross income for the year of the theft was $25,000.

What are the federal income tax consequences of these events to T?

### Analysis

---

T sustained a loss in the theft because T received no insurance and has no reasonable expectation of recovering the home entertainment system. The home entertainment system was an asset held for personal use. IRC § 165(c)(3) permits a deduction for casualty and theft losses of personal-use property, so T will be able to deduct the loss.

The amount of the loss is measured as the lesser of T's basis in the item ($5,000) or the decline in value. Since the property has been stolen, the entire $3,000 value is lost. Thus the gross deduction amount is $3,000. T received no insurance proceeds or other compensation that would reduce this amount. IRC § 165(h)(1) trims $100 off of this amount, so the deduction amount is $2,900.

T does not have any other casualty losses on these facts, nor does T have any personal casualty gains. Thus, the $2,900 personal casualty loss is deductible to the extent it exceeds ten percent of T's adjusted gross income. IRC § 165(h)(2)(A). Ten percent of T's $25,000 adjusted gross income is $2,500. Therefore, T can deduct $400 of the theft loss. This will be a regular itemized deduction under IRC § 67(b)(3) and will be spared from any phase-out to itemized deductions under IRC § 68. IRC § 68(c)(3).

## POINTS TO REMEMBER

- Whenever a taxpayer has a net loss (deductions exceed gross income) from an activity consider whether and to what extent the at-risk rules in IRC § 465 and the passive loss rules in IRC § 469 apply.

- Any deductions disallowed under IRC §§ 465 and 469 will carry over to the next taxable year.

- If a taxpayer's loss is disallowed under IRC § 267(a), the related party may be able to use that disallowed loss upon the related party's disposition of the asset.

- Any insurance or other compensation received by the taxpayer will reduce the amount of the gross deduction for casualty and theft losses of personal-use property under IRC § 165(c)(3).

CHAPTER 9

# Characterization of Gains and Losses

A ll people are created equally, but not all income is taxed equally. IRC § 1(h) sets forth a series of preferential tax rates for so-called "net capital gain." Very generally, a taxpayer will be subject to the lower rates of IRC § 1(h) on gains from the sale or exchange of "capital assets" held for more than one year. Accordingly, upon any disposition where a taxpayer recognizes gain, one must "characterize" (or "flavor") the gain as either ordinary income or capital gain. Likewise, because capital losses are deductible generally to the extent of capital gains, if a taxpayer recognizes a loss upon the sale or exchange of property, the loss must be characterized as either ordinary loss or capital loss. This chapter considers how recognized gains and losses are flavored are federal income tax purposes.

## CHARACTERIZATION OF GAINS AND LOSSES REVIEW

A capital gain and a capital loss can arise only from the sale or exchange of a capital asset. IRC § 1221(a) provides that a capital asset is any asset *except* for certain specifically designated items. The statute then lists eight types of assets that are not capital assets. Accordingly, if a taxpayer sells an asset described in any of IRC

§ 1221(a)(1)–(8), the resulting gain or loss is ordinary and not capital gain or loss. In addition, capital gain or loss can arise only from a "sale or exchange," and not any other disposition like a gift or an involuntary conversion of the property.

If a taxpayer has a capital gain or loss, one must determine whether the gain or loss is "short-term" or "long-term" in nature. The Code provides a one-year rule for this purpose: capital assets held for one year or less before sale or exchange generate short-term capital gain or loss, while capital assets held for more than one year generate long-term capital gain or loss. This distinction is crucial because only long-term capital gains can be subject to tax at the preferential rates in IRC § 1(h). Specifically, a taxpayer seeking to use the preferential tax rates of IRC § 1(h) must have a "net capital gain" for the taxable year, meaning an excess of net long-term capital gain over net short-term capital loss. If there is no such excess, the preferential rates of IRC § 1(h) will not come into play; any capital gains subject to tax will be treated just like ordinary income. Thus, for example, a taxpayer whose only capital gain for the year is from the sale of a capital asset held for eight months must treat that gain as ordinary income.

Thus far reference has been limited to two forms of income or loss: ordinary and capital. There is, however, a third, temporary form of income and loss, so-called "IRC § 1231 gains and losses." Although IRC § 1221(a)(2) excludes from the definition of capital asset the depreciable property and real property used in a taxpayer's business, such property may, if held for more than one year, qualify for preferential treatment under IRC § 1231. IRC § 1231 is a win-win rule: it states that if a taxpayer's "IRC § 1231 gains" for the year exceed the taxpayer's "IRC § 1231 losses" for the year, all such gains and losses will be treated as long-term capital gains and long-term capital losses. This is good because the net IRC § 1231 gain will be taxed at a preferential rate under IRC § 1(h). On the other hand, if a taxpayer's IRC § 1231 gains for the year do not exceed the taxpayer's IRC § 1231 losses for the year, all such gains and losses will be treated as ordinary gains and losses. This too is good because any net IRC § 1231 loss will be treated as ordinary loss which can offset all forms of income. In effect, IRC § 1231 gain and IRC § 1231 loss are the best possible flavors of income and loss because they will always receive the best possible treatment at the end of the year.

To compute whether a taxpayer has a net IRC § 1231 gain or loss for the taxable year, practitioners speak of placing all IRC § 1231 gains and losses into a "hotchpot" and then netting the gains against the losses at the end of the year. A special rule provides that certain types of gains and losses will be added to the hotchpot only if there are more gains than losses of those certain types for the year. Practitioners thus speak of a "sub-hotchpot" (or "firepot") for these gains and losses to be placed before deciding whether they are added to the main hotchpot. The checklist in this chapter will help you identify whether a particular gain or loss item should be placed in the firepot or the main hotchpot, and it will also help in determining what to do with each of those pots at the end of the year.

If a taxpayer has IRC § 1231 gain or loss from a disposition of an asset that was subject to depreciation, the concept of "depreciation recapture" comes into play. Depreciation recapture is premised on the theory that it would be a double benefit to a taxpayer to permit depreciation deductions from property used in a trade or business to offset ordinary income and then let gain attributable to depreciation deductions be treated as long-term capital gain. Absent IRC § 1245, this could result. A taxpayer, for example, could purchase a piece of equipment for use in the taxpayer's business and depreciate the cost of the equipment over its useful life. These deductions will offset ordinary income. But if the taxpayer then sells the fully-depreciated equipment for any consideration, the taxpayer would have gain that will qualify as IRC § 1231 gain because the property will have been held for more than one year. If that is the only item of IRC § 1231 gain for the taxable year, the gain will be treated as long-term capital gain and will be subject to tax at a preferential rate. IRC § 1245 generally provides that gain attributable to prior depreciation deductions is characterized as ordinary income unless a specific exception applies.

# CHARACTERIZATION OF GAINS AND LOSSES CHECKLIST

This checklist will assist in determining the character and tax treatment of a taxpayer's recognized gains and losses.

## A. CAPITAL GAINS AND LOSSES

1. **Capital Asset**—Did the taxpayer dispose of a capital asset? Capital gains and losses arise only upon the sale or exchange of a "capital asset."

    a. **List of Non–Capital Assets**—Under IRC § 1221(a), any asset is a capital asset *except* for the assets specifically described in IRC § 1221(a). So if an asset is described in IRC § 1221(a), it is not a capital asset; if the asset does not fit within any of the specific categories identified in IRC § 1221(a), it is a capital asset.

        i. **Inventory**—An item of the taxpayer's inventory is not a capital asset. IRC § 1221(a)(1). Thus, for example, a guitar sold by a taxpayer in the business of manufacturing, wholesaling, or retailing musical instruments would not be a capital asset.

        ii. **Property Held for Sale to Customers**—Property held by the taxpayer primarily for sale to customers in the ordinary course of the taxpayer's business is not a capital asset. IRC § 1221(a)(1). Under this rule, then, a parcel of real estate is not a capital asset in the hands of a taxpayer who normally sells such parcels to customers as part of the taxpayer's business. But that same parcel of real estate would be a capital asset in the hands of a taxpayer not in the business of selling real estate who held the property for investment purposes. Courts trying to distinguish between real property held for investment purposes (a capital asset) and real property held for sale to customers in the ordinary course of business (not a capital asset) will often examine these factors: (1) the nature and purpose of the acquisition of the property; (2) the length of ownership; (3) the frequency and substantiality of sales; (4) the extent of taxpayer's efforts in subdividing, developing and advertising the property; (5) whether the taxpayer used a business office or selling agents; and (6) the time and effort habitually spent by the taxpayer in sales. See *Byram v. United States*, 705 F.2d 1418 (5th Cir. 1983).

iii. **Depreciable Property Used in Business**—Tangible property used in the taxpayer's business that is subject to depreciation deductions is not a capital asset. IRC § 1221(a)(2). As explained in Part B, however, such property could qualify for the benefit of IRC § 1231.

iv. **Real Property Used in Business**—Real property used in the taxpayer's business is not a capital asset. IRC § 1221(a)(2). Thus, for example, office and factory buildings are not capital assets if the taxpayer uses those buildings in the taxpayer's trade or business. As explained in Part B, however, such property may qualify for the benefit of IRC § 1231.

v. **Certain Compositions**—Copyrights, literary compositions, musical compositions, artistic compositions, letters, memos, and similar assets are not capital assets in the hands of their creators, those for whom such property was prepared or produced, and those whose basis in such assets are determined in whole or in part with reference to the basis of such property in the hands of the creator or a person for whom such property was prepared or produced. IRC § 1221(a)(3). A taxpayer can elect to treat a musical composition or a copyright in a musical work as a capital asset if the taxpayer is the creator of the work, the person for whom the work was created, or a person whose basis in the work is determined with reference to the basis of such property in the hands of its creator or the person for whom it was created. IRC § 1221(b)(3). A taxpayer will want to make the IRC § 1221(b)(3) election if there is a sale or exchange of the musical work held for more than one year at a gain, since such gain would qualify as long-term capital gain. If the work sells for a loss, however, the taxpayer will not want to make the election because under the general rule of IRC § 1221(a)(3) the sale will generate ordinary loss.

vi. **Business Receivables**—Accounts receivable and notes receivable derived in the ordinary course of the taxpayer's business for services rendered or from the sale of inventory property or other property held for sale to customers are not capital assets. IRC § 1221(a)(4). An "account receivable" is any right to payment from the provision of goods or services. Thus, when a lawyer bills a client for legal services performed on the client's behalf, the lawyer has an account receivable. In the lawyer's hands, the account receivable is not a capital asset.

vii. **Government Publications**—Any publication of the United States government acquired other than by purchase at the price at which it is offered for sale to the public is not a capital asset in the hands of the person who received such publication from the government or a person whose basis in such publication is determined in whole or in part with reference to the basis of such publication in the hands of the person who received the publication from the government. IRC § 1221(a)(5).

viii. **Commodities Derivative Financial Instruments**— Any "commodities derivative financial instrument" is not a capital asset in the hands of a "commodities derivatives dealer" unless the instrument has no connection to the dealer's business and such instrument is clearly identified as such by the dealer before acquisition. IRC § 1221(a)(6). These special terms are defined in IRC § 1221(b)(1).

ix. **Hedging Transactions**—Any "hedging transaction" that is identified as such before it is acquired is not a capital asset. IRC § 1221(a)(7). A hedging transaction is any transaction entered into by the taxpayer as part of the taxpayer's business primarily to manage risks related to price changes and currency fluctuations affecting the taxpayer's business property. See IRC § 1221(b)(2).

    x.  **Business Supplies**—Supplies regularly used or consumed by the taxpayer in the taxpayer's business are not capital asset. IRC § 1221(a)(8). Thus, for example, a sale of paper, staples, toner cartridges, and pencils used in the taxpayer's business will produce ordinary gain or loss. Likewise, a sale of gasoline by a taxpayer that requires fuel to run the taxpayer's business equipment will give rise to ordinary income or loss.

  b.  **Construe the List Literally**—Although one can generally conclude that assets held for business use are not capital assets and assets held for investment or personal use are capital assets, one should not construe the list of non-capital assets in IRC § 1221(a) with this framework in mind. Instead, courts are instructed to give the terms in IRC § 1221(a) their plain meaning and not to consider the broader thematic ties of the items described in the list. *Arkansas Best Corporation v. Commissioner*, 485 U.S. 212 (1988). In *Arkansas Best*, the Court held that stock in a bank held by a holding company was a capital asset because, even though the stock was an essential component of the holding company's business, it was not an asset described in IRC § 1221(a).

  c.  **Rights to Ordinary Income Not Capital Assets**—Footnote 5 of the *Arkansas Best* case preserved a line of cases standing for the proposition that the definition of capital asset "does not include claims or rights to ordinary income." Thus, for example, if a taxpayer sells his or her rights to future rental income from an asset, any resulting gain is ordinary income and not capital gain even though "rights to rental income" is not listed in IRC § 1221(a). In a recent line of cases, courts have consistently applied this doctrine to conclude that the sale of rights to future payments under a state lottery create ordinary income and not capital gain. See *Davis v. Commissioner*, 119 T.C. 1 (2002).

d. **Yes**—If yes, then continue in this Part A.

e. **No**—If no, then the resulting gain or loss is not capital gain or loss. Proceed to Part B of this checklist.

2. **Sale or Exchange**—Did the taxpayer dispose of the capital asset by a sale or exchange?

a. **Definition**—A bilateral transaction involving an exchange of assets is easy to spot, and such an exchange will obviously meet the "sale or exchange" requirement. The other extreme is just as obvious—there is no sale or exchange if a taxpayer abandons a capital asset, if the asset is stolen, or if the asset is gifted to the taxpayer's beneficiary. Certain transactions, while perhaps not technically sales or exchanges, are nonetheless treated as if they are because they are economically equivalent to sale or exchange transactions.

   i. **Satisfaction of Pecuniary Bequest**—If an estate transfers a capital asset in satisfaction of its obligation to make a pecuniary bequest (a specific dollar amount) to the decedent's beneficiary, the estate is deemed to have "sold" the property because it is the equivalent of selling the property and paying cash to the beneficiary. *Kenan v. Commissioner*, 114 F.2d 217 (2d Cir. 1940).

   ii. **Personal Casualty Gains**—If a taxpayer receives insurance for the involuntary loss of a personal-use asset by casualty or theft, a "personal casualty gain" results if the amount of insurance received exceeds the taxpayer's adjusted basis in the asset. IRC § 165(h)(3)(A). If a taxpayer's personal casualty gains for the year exceed his or her personal casualty losses for the year, all such gains and losses are deemed to arise from sales or exchanges of capital assets. IRC § 165(h)(2)(B). See Chapter 8 for more discussion of the rules related to casualty and theft losses.

b. **Yes**—If yes, then the resulting gain or loss is capital gain or loss. Continue in this Part A.

c. **No**—If no, then the resulting gain or loss is not capital gain or loss. Proceed to Part B of this checklist.

3. **Long–Term or Short–Term**—Did the taxpayer hold the capital asset for more than one year before its sale or exchange?

a. **Tacking**—In some instances the length of time a taxpayer holds a capital asset (the taxpayer's "holding period") includes the length of time someone else held the property or the length of time the taxpayer held some other property.

i. **Carryover Holding Period**—Where a taxpayer exchanges one capital asset (the "old capital asset") for another (the "new capital asset"), the taxpayer's holding period in the new capital asset includes the taxpayer's holding period for the old capital asset if the taxpayer's basis in the new capital asset is the same (in whole or in part) as the taxpayer's basis in the old capital asset. IRC § 1223(1). This will be the case, for example, in a like-kind exchange of capital assets under IRC § 1031, the tax-free transfer of a capital asset to a corporation in exchange for its stock under IRC § 351, the tax-free transfer of a capital asset to a partnership in exchange for an interest in the partnership under IRC § 721, and the involuntary conversion of a capital asset under IRC § 1033.

ii. **Transfer of Another's Holding Period**—If the taxpayer's basis in the capital asset is determined with reference to the basis of such property in the hands of its transferor, the taxpayer's holding period includes the holding period of the transferor. IRC § 1223(2). For instance, if the taxpayer received the capital asset by gift from a donor, the taxpayer's holding period in the capital asset includes the donor's holding period in the same asset because the taxpayer took the donor's basis in the capital asset under IRC § 1015(a).

iii. **Long–Term Holding Period on Property Acquired from Decedent**—If the taxpayer acquired the capital asset from a decedent and took a stepped-up basis in the asset under IRC § 1014, the taxpayer is deemed to have held the asset for more than one year even if the asset is sold within one year of the decedent's death. IRC § 1223(9).

b. **Yes**—If yes, the gain or loss is long-term capital gain or loss. IRC § 1222(3)–(4). Proceed to Part E of this checklist to determine how such gain or loss will be taxed.

c. **No**—If no, then the gain or loss is short-term capital gain or loss. IRC § 1222(1)–(2). Proceed to Part E of this checklist to determine how such gain or loss will be taxed.

## B. IRC § 1231 GAINS AND LOSSES

**1. Property Used in the Trade or Business**—Did the taxpayer sell or exchange "property used in the trade or business?"

a. **Definition**—An asset qualifies as "property used in the trade or business" if it has each of the following four characteristics [IRC § 1231(b)(1)]:

   i. **Used in Taxpayer's Business**—The property must have been used in the taxpayer's business activity.

   ii. **Depreciable Tangible Property or Real Estate**—The property must either be depreciable under IRC § 167 (see Chapter 4) or be real property.

   iii. **Held More Than One Year**—The taxpayer must have held the property for more than one year.

   iv. **Not Excepted Out**—The property must not be inventory in the hands of the taxpayer, property held by the taxpayer for sale to customers in the taxpayer's business, property described in IRC § 1221(a)(3) (copyrights and other artistic works), or property described in IRC § 1221(a)(5) (certain government publications).

b. **Certain Assets Included**—Property used in the trade or business includes certain timber, coal, and iron ore. IRC § 1231(b)(2). The term also includes certain cattle, horses, and livestock, but not any poultry. IRC § 1231(b)(3). It also includes any unharvested crop on land used in the taxpayer's business if the taxpayer sells both the land and the crop at the same time. IRC § 1231(b)(4).

    c. **Yes**—If yes, the gain or loss is IRC § 1231 gain or loss and should be placed into the main hotchpot, IRC § 1231(a)(3)(A)(i), unless the gain or loss arises from a casualty or theft (in which case it belongs in the firepot, as discussed in B(2) below). Continue in this Part B.

    d. **No**—If no, continue in this Part B.

2. **Firepot Gains and Losses**—Did the taxpayer recognize gain or loss from a casualty to or theft of either "property used in the trade or business" or a capital asset held for more than one year in connection with the taxpayer's business or an investment activity?

    a. **Yes**—If yes, the gain or loss should be placed into the "firepot." IRC § 1231(a)(4)(C). Whether such items ultimately pass into the main hotchpot depends upon whether there is a net gain in the firepot or a net loss.

        i. **Firepot Losses Exceed Firepot Gains**—If, at the end of the year, the losses in the firepot exceed the gains in the firepot, IRC § 1231 does not apply to any of the items in the firepot. Instead, such items will be treated as ordinary income or loss (even the capital assets in the firepot will be treated as ordinary income or loss because there was no "sale or exchange" of these assets). Continue in this Part B to see if there are other items of IRC § 1231 gain or loss for the year.

        ii. **Firepot Gains Equal or Exceed Firepot Losses**—If, at the end of the year, the gains in the firepot equal or exceed the losses in the firepot, then all of the firepot items are treated as IRC § 1231 gains and losses and are added to the main hotchpot. Continue in this Part B.

    b. **No**—If no, continue in this Part B.

3. **Other Involuntary Conversions**—Did the taxpayer recognize gain or loss from the involuntary conversion by seizure, requisition, or condemnation of either "property used in the

trade or business" or a capital asset held for more than one year in connection with the taxpayer's business or an investment activity?

a. **Yes**—If yes, the gain or loss is IRC § 1231 gain or loss and should be placed into the main hotchpot. IRC § 1231(a)(3)(A)(ii). Continue in this Part B.

b. **No**—If no, then continue in this Part B only if, up to this point, the taxpayer has some item of IRC § 1231 gain or loss. If there is no such item, proceed to Part E of this checklist.

4. **Recapture of Net Ordinary Losses**—In the five prior taxable years, has the taxpayer had a "net IRC § 1231 loss?"

a. **Definitions**—A taxpayer has a "net IRC § 1231 loss" for any given taxable year in which the IRC § 1231 losses exceed the IRC § 1231 gains. IRC § 1231(c)(4). Under IRC § 1231(a)(2), such net IRC § 1231 losses are treated as ordinary loss. Not surprisingly, a taxpayer has a "net IRC § 1231 gain" for any given taxable year in which the IRC § 1231 gains exceed the IRC § 1231 losses. IRC § 1231(c)(3).

b. **Yes**—If yes, then if the recapture rules of IRC § 1231(c) may apply in the current year. If the total net IRC § 1231 losses for five prior taxable years exceed the total net IRC § 1231 gains for such prior taxable years after the first year in which the taxpayer has a net IRC § 1231 loss, then the taxpayer has "non-recaptured net IRC § 1231 losses" to the extent such losses have not already been subject to this recapture rule. IRC § 1231(c)(2). If the taxpayer has a net IRC § 1231 gain in the current year, therefore, such gain must be treated as ordinary income to the extent such gain does not exceed the non-recaptured net IRC § 1231 losses. IRC § 1231(c)(1). For the tax treatment of any remaining portion of the IRC § 1231 gain not subject to this recapture rule, continue in this Part B.

c. **No**—If no, then continue in this Part B.

5. **Main Hotchpot Gains and Losses**—Do the IRC § 1231 gains in the main hotchpot exceed the IRC § 1231 losses for the taxable year?

a. **Yes**—If yes, then all such gains and losses are treated as long-term capital gains and long-term capital losses, subject the exceptions for non-recaptured net IRC § 1231 losses described above and for depreciation recapture described in Part C below. IRC § 1231(a)(1). Proceed to Part C of this checklist.

b. **No**—If no, then all such gains and losses are treated as ordinary income and loss. IRC § 1231(a)(2).

C. **DEPRECIATION RECAPTURE ON PERSONAL PROPERTY (NOT REAL ESTATE)**

1. **IRC § 1245 Property**—Has the taxpayer disposed of IRC § 1245 property? IRC § 1245 property is any property which is or was depreciable and is either personal property (anything other than real property) or certain very limited forms of real property set forth in the statute. IRC § 1245(a)(3).

    a. **Yes**—If yes, continue in this Part C.

    b. **No**—If no, proceed to Part D of this checklist.

2. **Recomputed Basis**—What is the taxpayer's recomputed basis in the property? Recomputed basis is the sum of the adjusted basis of the property at the time of the taxpayer's disposition plus all prior depreciation and amortization deductions allowed or allowable to the taxpayer or to any other person with respect to the property. IRC § 1245(a)(2)(A). This includes any amounts that were treated as expenses pursuant to an election under IRC § 179. IRC § 1245(a)(2)(C). If the taxpayer can prove that the amount allowed as a depreciation deduction for any prior taxable year was less than the amount allowable under the law as of that time, only the amount actually allowed as depreciation will be added to adjusted basis in determining the taxpayer's recomputed basis. IRC § 1245(a)(2)(B).

3. **Recapture as Ordinary Income**—Did the taxpayer dispose of the IRC § 1245 property by sale, exchange, or involuntary conversion?

    a. **Yes**—If yes, then unless an exception in C(4) below applies, the taxpayer must, under IRC § 1245(a)(1), recognize as ordinary income the smaller of the following amounts (any remaining gain will be characterized under the normal rules set forth in Parts A and B above):

i.   **Gain Attributable to Prior Depreciation Deductions**—The excess of the recomputed basis of the property over the adjusted basis of such property.

ii.  **Realized Gain**—The excess of the amount realized over the adjusted basis of such property.

Proceed to Part D of this checklist.

b.   **No**—If no, then unless an exception in C(4) below applies, the taxpayer must, under IRC § 1245(a)(1), recognize as ordinary income the excess of the fair market value of the property over the adjusted basis of such property at the time of disposition. Proceed to Part D of this checklist.

4.   **Exceptions and Limits**—IRC § 1245 forces the recognition of ordinary income even if another Code provision would otherwise provide for nonrecognition. IRC § 1245(d). Nonetheless, if the taxpayer's disposition is described in IRC § 1245(b), the general rule of IRC § 1245(a) will not apply or will have limited application.

a.   **Gifts**—Depreciation recapture does not apply to dispositions by gift. IRC § 1245(b)(1). Instead, the amount that otherwise would have been recaptured will be saved until there is a non-gift disposition by the donee. At that time the donee will face recapture to the extent there is gain attributable to depreciation that has been allowed to the donee "or to any other person" (i.e., the donor).

b.   **Bequests**—Depreciation recapture generally does not apply to any transfers at death. IRC § 1245(b)(2).

c.   **Certain Nonrecognition Transactions**—In the case of certain nonrecognition transactions—like those under IRC §§ 351 (transfers to controlled corporations) and 721 (transfers to partnerships)—the amount of depreciation recapture is limited to the amount of any recognized gain to the transferor. IRC § 1245(b)(3). In the case of a like-kind exchange under IRC § 1031 or an involuntary conversion under IRC § 1033, the amount of depreciation recapture is limited to the sum of any recognized gain under those provisions plus the value of any non-IRC § 1245 property received by the taxpayer that is not taken into account as part of the taxpayer's recognized gain. IRC § 1245(b)(4).

### D. DEPRECIATION RECAPTURE ON BUILDINGS

1. **IRC § 1250 Property**—Has the taxpayer disposed of depreciable real property? Examples include office buildings, factory buildings, and other real estate used in the taxpayer's business or investment activity and which was subject to depreciation.

   a. **Yes**—If yes, note that IRC § 1245 generally does not apply; instead the property is referred to as "IRC § 1250 property" and is subject to its own recapture rule. IRC § 1250(c). Continue in this Part D.

   b. **No**—If no, proceed to Part E of this checklist.

2. **Additional Depreciation Recaptured**—Does the total depreciation taken on the IRC § 1250 property exceed the total depreciation that would have been allowed if the taxpayer used the straight line method of depreciation?

   a. **Yes**—If yes, then generally the amount of such excess must be recognized and treated as ordinary income. IRC § 1250(a)(1)(A), (b). Any remaining gain can still qualify as IRC § 1231 gain.

      i. **The Dinosaur Rule**—Since 1986, taxpayers have been required to depreciate real estate using the straight-line method. IRC § 168(b)(3). Thus, any depreciable real estate placed in service since 1986 will not be subject to depreciation recapture because there is no "additional depreciation." Accordingly, IRC § 1250 today applies only to buildings that were placed in service before 1986. As time goes by, therefore, IRC § 1250 recapture will become increasingly rare.

      ii. **The Payback**—Although modern depreciable real property will not be subject to depreciation recapture, Congress has generally provided that any gains from the sale or exchange of depreciable real estate held for more than one year will, to the extent they are treated as long-term capital gains, be subject to a less preferential rate of tax under IRC § 1(h): instead of the 15 percent rate normally applicable to such gains, any "unrecaptured IRC § 1250 gain" will be taxed at a rate of 25 percent. See Part E below.

b.  **No**—If no, then IRC § 1250 does not apply. As explained above, however, any gains from the sale or exchange of depreciable real estate held for more than one year will, to the extent they are treated as long-term capital gains, be subject to a less preferential rate of tax under IRC § 1(h): instead of the 15 percent rate normally applicable to such gains, any "unrecaptured IRC § 1250 gain" will be taxed at a rate of 25 percent. See Part E below.

**E.  NET CAPITAL GAIN AND THE PREFERENTIAL TAX RATES**

1.  **Net Long–Term Capital Gain or Loss**—Does the taxpayer have a net long-term capital gain or a net long-term capital loss for the taxable year? Take all of the taxpayer's long-term capital gains and long-term capital losses for the year and net them against each other. If the taxpayer has more long-term capital gains than long-term capital losses, the taxpayer has a net long-term capital gain for the year. IRC § 1222(7). Likewise, if the taxpayer has more long-term capital losses than long-term capital gains, the taxpayer has a net long-term capital loss for the year. IRC § 1222(8).

2.  **Net Short–Term Capital Gain or Loss**—Does the taxpayer have a net short-term capital gain or a net short-term capital loss for the taxable year? Take all of the taxpayer's short-term capital gains and short-term capital losses for the year and net them against each other. If the taxpayer has more short-term capital gains than short-term capital losses, the taxpayer has a net short-term capital gain for the year. IRC § 1222(5). Likewise, if the taxpayer has more short-term capital losses than short-term capital gains, the taxpayer has a net short-term capital loss for the year. IRC § 1222(6).

3.  **Net Capital Gain**—Does the taxpayer have a "net capital gain" for the taxable year?

a. **Net Capital Gain**—The taxpayer has a "net capital gain" if there is an excess of net long-term capital gain over net short-term capital loss for the taxable year. IRC § 1222(11).

b. **Yes**—If yes, the net capital gain will be taxed at the preferential tax rates set forth in IRC § 1(h). These rates can be summarized generally as follows:

   i. **28% on Collectibles and IRC § 1202 Stock**—If the taxpayer's ordinary income already consumes all of the tax brackets below 28 percent, that portion of the net capital gain attributable to "collectibles gain" and "section 1202 gain" will be taxed at a flat rate of 28 percent. IRC § 1(h)(1)(E). Collectibles gain is the taxable gain from the sale or exchange of a collectible (like a work of art, antique, jewelry, stamp collection, wine collection, or the like) held for more than one year. IRC § 1(h)(5)(A). Section 1202 gain is the taxable gain from the sale or exchange of IRC § 1202 stock. IRC § 1(h)(7). In order to be IRC § 1202 stock, among other things, such stock must have been held for more than five years.

   ii. **25% on Unrecaptured IRC § 1250 Gain**—If the taxpayer's ordinary income already consumes all of the tax brackets below 25 percent, that portion of the net capital gain attributable to prior depreciation deductions on real estate (office buildings and factory buildings, for example) will be taxed at a flat rate of 25 percent. IRC § 1(h)(1)(D).

   iii. **15% on Adjusted Net Capital Gain**—If the taxpayer's ordinary income already consumes all of the tax brackets below 15 percent, the taxpayer's "adjusted net capital gain" (generally meaning the taxpayer's net capital gain other than the collectibles, IRC § 1202 stock, and unrecaptured IRC § 1250 gain, see IRC § 1(h)(3)) will be taxed at a flat rate of 15 percent. IRC § 1(h)(1)(C).

   iv. **5% or 0% Rate on Adjusted Net Capital Gain for Low–Income Taxpayers**—If the taxpayer's ordinary income does not completely consume all of the tax brackets below 15 percent, then the adjusted net capital gain will be taxed at a rate of five percent until the combined amount of the taxpayer's ordinary income and adjusted net capital gain exceeds the ceiling of the taxpayer's 15–percent tax bracket. IRC § 1(h)(1)(B). For the years 2008, 2009, and 2010, however, this five-percent rate is reduced to zero percent.

c. **No**—If no, then to the extent capital gains exceed capital losses for the taxable year, such gains and losses will be treated like ordinary income and losses. In other words, no preferential tax rates will apply. If capital losses exceed capital gains for the taxable year, proceed to Part F of this checklist.

## F. CARRYOVER OF NET CAPITAL LOSS

1. **Net Capital Loss**—Does the taxpayer have a net capital loss for the taxable year?

   a. **Definition**—The taxpayer has a "net capital loss" if all of the taxpayer's capital losses (long-term and short-term) exceed the deductible amount of such capital losses for the year. IRC § 1222(10).

      i. **Deductible Amount of Capital Losses for Individuals**—In the case of an individual, a taxpayer's capital losses for a taxable year are deductible to the extent of the taxpayer's capital gains for the year (long-term and short-term) plus up to $3,000 of the excess of such losses over such gains. IRC § 1211(b). This is often referred to as the "$3,000 bonus" for individuals.

      ii. **Deductible Amount of Capital Losses for Corporations**—In the case of a corporation, its capital losses for a taxable year are deductible to the extent of its capital gains for the year (long-term and short-term). Unlike the $3,000 bonus for individuals, no portion of any excess of such losses over such gains may be used by a corporation to offset its ordinary income for the year. IRC § 1211(a).

    b. **Yes**—If yes, continue in this Part F.

    c. **No**—If no, then stop.

2. **Carryover Long–Term Capital Loss**—To what extent does the taxpayer's net long-term capital loss for the taxable year exceed the net short-term capital gain? Any such excess shall be treated as long-term capital loss in the next taxable year. IRC § 1212(b)(1)(B).

    a. **$3,000 Bonus Treated as Short–Term Capital Gain**—In determining the flavor of any capital loss carryover, the $3,000 bonus amount is generally treated as short-term capital gain. IRC § 1212(b)(2)(A). This serves to increase any net short-term capital gain or, indeed, convert a small net short-term capital loss into a net short-term capital gain.

    b. **Limit on Amount Treated as Short–Term Capital Gain**—If the taxpayer's "adjusted taxable income" is less than the $3,000 bonus amount used in determining the deductible amount of capital loss for the year, then only the adjusted taxable income is treated as short-term capital gain for purposes of computing the capital loss carryover. IRC § 1212(b)(2)(A). A taxpayer's adjusted taxable income is the sum of the taxpayer's taxable income, the amount of any deduction for personal exemptions claimed by the taxpayer, and the deductible amount of capital loss for the year. IRC § 1212(b)(2)(B).

3. **Carryover Short–Term Capital Loss**—To what extent does the taxpayer's net short-term capital loss for the taxable year exceed the net long-term capital gain? Any such excess shall be treated as short-term capital loss in the next taxable year. IRC § 1212(b)(1)(A).

    a. **$3,000 Bonus Treated as Short–Term Capital Gain**—In determining the flavor of any capital loss carryover, the $3,000 bonus amount is generally treated as short-term capital gain. IRC § 1212(b)(2)(A). This serves to reduce any net short-term capital loss and could even turn a net short-term capital loss into a net short-term capital gain.

    b. **Limit on Amount Treated as Short–Term Capital Gain**—If the taxpayer's "adjusted taxable income" is less than the $3,000 bonus amount used in determining the deductible amount of capital loss for the year, then only the adjusted taxable income is treated as short-term capital gain for purposes of computing the capital loss carryover. IRC § 1212(b)(2)(A). A taxpayer's adjusted taxable income is the sum of the taxpayer's taxable income, the amount of any deduction for personal exemptions claimed by the taxpayer, and the deductible amount of capital loss for the year. IRC § 1212(b)(2)(B).

## ILLUSTRATIVE PROBLEMS

The following problems demonstrate how the checklist can be used to answer a question involving the character of recognized gains and losses.

---

## ■ PROBLEM 9.1 ■

---

During the most recent taxable year, T recognized the following gains and losses:

- $20,000 gain from the sale of inventory to customers of T's full-time business activity;

- $10,000 gain from the sale of General Electric stock held for three years;

- $4,000 gain from the sale of Blackacre, a parcel of undeveloped real property, held as an investment for nine months;

- $2,000 loss from the sale of a painting T purchased at auction and held for fifteen years; and

- $7,000 loss from the sale of Blue Star Airlines stock held for six months.

What are the federal income tax consequences to T?

### Analysis

---

Since all of the gains and losses are recognized, each must be characterized for federal income tax purposes. The gain from the sale of the inventory will be taxed as ordinary income because T's inventory is property held for sale to customers and thus not a capital asset. IRC § 1221(a)(1). The gain from the sale of the GE stock is a long-term capital gain because it is gain from the sale of a capital asset (the stock) held for more than one year. The gain from the sale of Blackacre is a short-term capital gain, for, while unimproved property held for investment purposes is a capital asset, T held the property for not more than one year before its sale. The loss from the sale of the painting is a long-term capital loss because the painting is a capital asset and it was held for more than one year. Finally, the loss from the sale of Blue Star stock is a short-term capital loss, again because the stock (a capital asset) was held for not more than one year.

For the most recent year, therefore, T has a net capital gain of $5,000. This is computed by subtracting the $3,000 net short-term capital loss from T's $8,000 net long-term capital gain:

|  | LONG-TERM | SHORT–TERM |
| --- | --- | --- |
| GAIN | 10,000 | 4,000 |
| LOSS | (2,000) | (7,000) |
| NET | 8,000 | (3,000) |

The $5,000 net capital gain will be taxed at a preferential rate under IRC § 1(h). Generally, T will pay tax of 15 percent on this net capital gain, but the rate could be reduced to five percent (or zero percent if the most recent taxable year is 2008, 2009, or 2010) if T's ordinary income does not completely consume the 10– and 15–percent tax brackets.

---

## ■ PROBLEM 9.2 ■

---

Assume the same facts as Problem 9.1, and also assume that T sold the following items in the same year:

- T sold a forklift used in T's business for $25,000. T originally purchased the forklift three years ago for

$20,000 and properly claimed a total of $15,000 in depreciation deductions with respect to the forklift.

- T's factory building was completely destroyed in a fire. T purchased the building ten years ago for $780,000 and properly claimed $200,000 in depreciation deductions using the straight line method with respect to the property. The building was insured but for less than its value, so T collected only $600,000 in insurance for the loss of the building. T spent the insurance proceeds on other parts of his business; T did not use any portion of the proceeds to acquire property similar or related in service or use to the destroyed factory building.

- T sold a photocopier used in T's business for $10,000. T originally purchased the copier two years ago for $25,000 and properly claimed a total of $10,000 in depreciation deductions with respect to the copier.

What are the federal income tax consequences to T?

## Analysis

Nothing changes with respect to the specific items described in Example 9.1, but the three transactions described in this Example each have consequences for T. T's sale of the forklift results in a realized gain of $20,000: the amount realized is the $25,000 of cash received and T's adjusted basis in the forklift at the time of sale was $5,000 ($20,000 purchase price less $15,000 in depreciation deductions). This realized gain is recognized, so it must be characterized. The forklift is depreciable property used in the taxpayer's business so it does not qualify as a capital asset. IRC § 1221(a)(2). However, the forklift is "property used in the trade or business" for purposes of IRC § 1231 (it was depreciable property held for more than one year in T's business), so the $20,000 gain is, preliminarily, IRC § 1231 gain. But the forklift is also IRC § 1245 property because it is depreciable personal property. This means depreciation recapture will apply. $15,000 of T's $20,000 gain is attributable to depreciation deductions (put differently, T's "re-computed basis" in the forklift is $20,000, and that exceeds T's adjusted basis by $15,000), so that portion of the gain must be treated as ordinary income. The remaining $5,000 of gain is IRC § 1231 gain that will, for now, be placed into the main hotchpot.

T realized a gain of $20,000 by collecting $600,000 of insurance on the loss of a factory building in which T's adjusted basis was $580,000 ($780,000 purchase price less $200,000 in depreciation deductions). The gain is recognized because T does not qualify for nonrecognition under any provision of the Code. The factory building is "property used in the trade or business" for purposes of IRC § 1231 because it was depreciable real property used in T's business and held for more than one year. Because the gain arises from a casualty, however, the $20,000 must initially be placed into the "firepot" (or "sub-hotchpot") for now. There is no depreciation recapture here because IRC § 1245 applies only to personal property and limited forms of real property not relevant here and because IRC § 1250 would apply only if T had claimed depreciation deductions in excess of the amount T could claim under the straight line method, and T did not do so here.

T's sale of the copier results in a realized loss of $5,000: the amount realized is the $10,000 of cash received and T's adjusted basis in the copier at the time of sale was $15,000 ($25,000 purchase price less $10,000 in depreciation deductions). This realized loss is recognized because it is a loss incurred in T's business. IRC § 165(c)(1). The copier is depreciable property used in the taxpayer's business so it does not qualify as a capital asset. IRC § 1221(a)(2). However, the copier is "property used in the trade or business" for purposes of IRC § 1231 (it was depreciable property held for more than one year in T's business), so the $5,000 loss is IRC § 1231 loss that will be placed into the main hotchpot. IRC § 1245 does not apply to loss property, so recapture is not an issue.

As there are no other items, the netting process can begin. First, there is only one item in the firepot: the $20,000 gain from the factory building. Therefore, because firepot gains for the year exceeds firepot losses, IRC § 1231 applies to everything in the firepot. Thus, this gain passes to the main hotchpot.

The main hotchpot consists of two gain items (the $20,000 from the factory and the $5,000 from the forklift) and one loss item (the $5,000 from the copier). Because the IRC § 1231 gains (total of $25,000) exceed the IRC § 1231 losses (total of $5,000), all three items are treated as long-term capital gains and losses. When these items are folded in with the other items of capital gain and loss for the year, T ends up with a net capital gain of $25,000:

|          | LONG-TERM | SHORT–TERM |
|----------|-----------|------------|
| **GAIN** | 35,000    | 4,000      |
| **LOSS** | (7,000)   | (7,000)    |
| **NET**  | 28,000    | (3,000)    |

The $25,000 net capital gain will be taxed at a preferential rate under IRC § 1(h). $20,000 of the $25,000 net capital gain is attributable to the factory building, and this represents "unrecaptured IRC § 1250 gain." Therefore, this $20,000 portion will generally be subject to a preferential rate of 25 percent while the remaining $5,000 will generally be taxed at 15 percent.

---

## ■ PROBLEM 9.3 ■

---

Assume the same facts as Problem 9.1, and also assume that T recognized a $15,000 loss from the sale of ACME stock held for ten months.

What are the federal income tax consequences to T?

### Analysis

---

Nothing changes with respect to the specific items described in Example 9.1. The $15,000 loss from the sale ACME stock is short-term capital loss because T held the stock for not more than one year.

For the most recent year, therefore, T has a net long-term capital gain of $8,000 and a net short-term capital loss of $18,000:

| | LONG-TERM | SHORT–TERM |
|---|---|---|
| **GAIN** | 10,000 | 4,000 |
| **LOSS** | (2,000) | (22,000) |
| **NET** | 8,000 | (18,000) |

T can deduct capital losses to the extent of capital gains plus up to $3,000. IRC § 1211(b). Accordingly, T can deduct $17,000 of the total $24,000 in capital losses because T had total capital gains of $14,000. The remaining $7,000 is T's "net capital loss" for the year. As the chart above indicates, the entire $7,000 net capital loss will carry over as to short-term capital loss to the next taxable year. This is because the net-short term capital loss (reduced to $15,000 thanks to the $3,000 bonus from IRC § 1211(b)) exceeds the net long-term capital gain by $7,000 and because there is no net long-term capital loss for the year.

## POINTS TO REMEMBER

- There must be a "sale or exchange" of a capital asset in order to generate capital gain or loss.

- IRC § 1221(a) sets forth the list of items that are not capital assets. Any asset not listed in IRC § 1221(a) is generally a capital asset.

- Depreciable property used in a taxpayer's trade or business is not a capital asset, but if it is held for more than one year it will subject to very preferential treatment under IRC § 1231.

- Anytime a taxpayer has IRC § 1231 gain attributable to prior depreciation deductions, one should consider the possible application of IRC § 1245 or IRC § 1250.

- IRC § 1250, the depreciation recapture rule for buildings and other depreciable real property, only applies to the extent the taxpayer used something other than the straight line method for computing depreciation deductions. This is increasingly rare, as straight line depreciation has been required for depreciable real property for over 20 years now.

\*

# CHAPTER 10

# Timing

From a practical perspective, the material considered in this final Chapter is among the most important in all of the federal income tax. Timing, as they say, is everything. The other Chapters have mostly considered *what* constitutes income and, to a lesser extent, *who* has the income. Now we consider *when* the taxpayer must include an item in gross income or claim a deduction for a particular item.

## TIMING REVIEW

The threshold issue for every question involving timing relates to the taxpayer's method of accounting. There are two dominant accounting methods: the cash method and the accrual method. Under the cash method, a taxpayer has income upon receipt of the item and a deduction when the item is paid. Under the accrual method, a taxpayer has income when the item is earned and a deduction when the item is owed.

A taxpayer's accounting method is dictated by how the taxpayer maintains books and records. Since most individuals use a checkbook ledger or similar records for keeping track of finances, most individuals use the cash method. Think about it: most of us think we have income when we receive payment, not just when payment is promised or guaranteed. Likewise, most of us do not consider a liability to be satisfied until it is paid; it is not enough that we have legal liability to make the payment. The cash method recognizes these conventions.

Most corporations, however, have bookkeepers that keep the company's records according to generally accepted accounting principles. These principles generally recognize income once all events have occurred that fix the company's right to the item. Likewise, they recognize an expense once all events have occurred that fix the company's obligation to make a payment. The accrual method for tax purposes is consistent with these principles, as they focus less on the actual inflow and outflow of cash and more on when the rights and liabilities are established.

In your federal income tax it is safe to assume that an individual uses the cash method and that a corporation uses the accrual method. If that is not the case, the fact pattern of a problem will specifically provide otherwise.

Assuming the taxpayer uses the cash method, one must determine when receipt (in the case of income) and payment (in the case of deductions) occur. A taxpayer has income under the cash method when he or she is in actual or constructive receipt of the income item. It should be obvious but sometimes this gets people mixed up: just because it's called the "cash method," it does not mean that only cash is included in gross income. A cash method taxpayer has gross income upon actual or constructive receipt of income in any form, whether in cash, property, services, or other economic benefits. There is one basic exception, however: a cash method taxpayer generally does not have gross income upon receipt of a promissory note because the note represents a mere promise of future payment. Only in those cases where the note itself is so strong as to be a cash equivalent does the receipt of a note cause inclusion for the taxpayer on the cash method. Part A of the checklist considers the notions of actual receipt, constructive receipt, and promissory notes that are cash equivalents.

The cash method taxpayer claims a deduction for an item only when it is actually paid. Part B of the checklist below helps you determine when actual payment has been made. It also considers the problem of advance expense payments. A taxpayer with a large amount of income for the current year may seek to prepay some of the expenses the taxpayer would otherwise incur early in the next year to help reduce the current year's taxable income. In modest amounts, this represents good tax planning. But taxpayers could get greedy: instead of prepaying next year's expenses, why not prepay the expenses for the next several years? This can actually make sense if there is sufficient cash on hand this year and the taxpayer expects to be in lower tax brackets in the later years. As Part B of the checklist indicates, there is a limit as to how far a cash method taxpayer can go in claiming a deduction for prepaid expenses.

The regulations provide that an accrual method taxpayer has income "when all the events have occurred that fix the right to receive the income and the amount of the income can be determined with reasonable accuracy." Treas. Reg. § 1.446–1(c)(1)(ii)(A). Practitioners refer to this rule as the "all-events test." Notice that it is the right to income, not its receipt, that is determinative for the all-events test. Nonetheless, an accrual method taxpayer is generally required to include an income item that has been received before it has been earned. Part C of the checklist considers this and other nuances to the all-events test, such as whether the taxpayer's good faith doubts as to the collectibility of an income item owed affects inclusion and whether the payor's good faith objection to the liability for payment affects inclusion.

Part D of the checklist looks at the timing of deductions for accrual method taxpayers. Here a similar but more detailed "all-events test" applies. In order for an accrual method taxpayer to claim a deduction, "all the events [must occur] that establish the fact of the liability, the amount of the liability [must be] determined with reasonable accuracy, and economic performance [must have] occurred with respect to the liability." Treas. Reg. § 1.461–1(a)(2)(i). Logically, then, Part D of the checklist walks through each of these requirements in turn.

Parts E and F of the checklist consider two doctrines that can be grouped under the heading of "error correction." When a taxpayer deducts a cost in one year and then recovers the cost in a later year because of refund, restoration, or the like, there is an issue as to how to handle these inconsistent events. One approach would be to require the taxpayer to amend the prior return and erase the deduction because it later proved to be mistaken. Alternatively, the taxpayer could be required to leave the prior return alone and account for the error in the year of recovery by including the recovery in gross income. As Part E of the checklist demonstrates, this latter approach is the one chosen by Congress and the Internal Revenue Service. Under the so-called "tax benefit rule," a taxpayer must include the recovery of a prior deduction item in gross income to the extent the prior deduction actually reduced the taxpayer's federal income tax liability. Authority to exclude that portion of a recovery that did not produce a tax savings is found in IRC § 111(a).

Part F of the checklist considers the mirror image of the tax benefit rule: what happens when a taxpayer previously included an amount in gross income but in a later year restores all or a portion of that amount because it turned out the taxpayer was not entitled to the amount received earlier? IRC § 1341 provides a generous rule, if it applies. If IRC § 1341 applies, the taxpayer can, in the year of restoration, either claim the deduction for the restoration or claim a credit equal to the extra tax the taxpayer paid in the prior year attributable to the prior inclusion of the income item. In general, a taxpayer will prefer the deduction if tax rates are higher in the year of restoration than they were in the prior year of inclusion, but will prefer the credit if tax rates in the year of restoration are lower. Whether IRC § 1341 applies and, if so, how it applies are at play in Part F of the checklist.

 ## TIMING CHECKLIST

This checklist will assist in considering the issues of timing depending on whether the taxpayer uses the cash method or the accrual method.

### A. CASH METHOD–INCOME

This Part A of the checklist concerns the timing of income items for a cash method taxpayer. Recall that a cash method taxpayer generally has income upon receipt of the income item. Thus the key is to establish when receipt has occurred.

1.  **Actual Receipt**—Is the taxpayer in actual receipt of the item of income (cash or property)?

    a.  **Yes**—If yes, then include the item in the taxpayer's gross income for the year of receipt.

    b.  **No**—If no, continue in this Part A.

2.  **Constructive Receipt**—Is the taxpayer in constructive receipt of the item of income?

    a.  **Definition**—A taxpayer is in constructive receipt of an item if it has been "credited to his account, set apart for him, or otherwise made available so that he may draw upon it at any time, or so that he could have drawn upon it during the taxable year if notice of intention to withdraw had been given." Treas. Reg. § 1.451–2. The taxpayer must have notice that the income item is available and subject to the taxpayer's control. *Davis v. Commissioner*, T.C. Memo. 1978–12. A taxpayer is not in constructive receipt of income from services just because the services have been performed; any agreement to defer the receipt of income negotiated at arm's-length and entered into prior to the originally scheduled date for payment will be respected. *Veit v. Commissioner*, 8 T.C. 809 (1947).

    b.  **Yes**—If yes, then include the item in the taxpayer's gross income for the year of constructive receipt.

    c.  **No**—If no, continue in this Part A.

3.  **Cash Equivalence**—Is the taxpayer in receipt from a solvent obligor an unconditional and assignable promissory note that is not subject to set-offs and is of a kind that is frequently transferred to lenders or investors at a discount not substantially greater than the generally prevailing rate for the use of money?

a. **Yes**—If yes, then the promissory note will be treated as the equivalent of cash and will be included in the taxpayer's gross income for the year in which the taxpayer receives the note. *Cowden v. Commissioner*, 289 F.2d 20 (5th Cir. 1961).

b. **No**—If no, then the taxpayer does not yet have gross income from the income item.

## B. CASH METHOD—DEDUCTIONS

Recall that a cash method taxpayer generally may claim a deduction in the taxable year in which the deduction item is paid. The typical issues at play here are whether the taxpayer has made a payment and the appropriate treatment of advance payments for expenses attributable to future years.

1. **Actual Payment Required**—Did the taxpayer actually pay the cost giving rise to the deduction? Actual payment can occur by cash payment, by the transfer of property, or by the performance of services. Payment by check is considered to occur when the check is delivered, as long as the check is honored when presented for payment. *Estate of Spiegel v. Commissioner*, 12 T.C. 524 (1949). Payment by credit card is deemed to occur at the point of sale, not when the taxpayer is billed or when the bill is paid. *Revenue Ruling 78–38*.

   a. **Yes**—If yes, then continue in this Part B.

   b. **No**—If no, there is no deduction yet. Although a cash method taxpayer can be in constructive receipt of income, there is no way for a taxpayer to make a "constructive payment" of a deduction item. Thus, for example, transferring a promissory note is not considered to be payment of the deduction item. *Vander Poel v. Commissioner*, 8 T.C. 407 (1947). There is no deduction until the note is paid. *Helvering v. Price*, 309 U.S. 409 (1940).

2. **Advance Payments**—Has the taxpayer paid a deductible expense attributable to a subsequent taxable year? This could occur, for example, if the taxpayer in the current year pays next year's rent expense for property leased in the taxpayer's business.

    a. **Yes**—If yes, then the taxpayer may deduct the expense in the year of payment only if the total benefit obtained through the payment does not last more than 12 months and does not extend beyond the end of the taxable year after the year of payment. See Treas. Reg. § 1.1263(a)–4(f)(1).

    b. **No**—If no, then the entire amount paid by the taxpayer can be deducted in the year of payment.

### C. ACCRUAL METHOD—INCOME

This Part C concerns the timing of gross income for an accrual method taxpayer. Remember that the general rule is that an accrual method taxpayer has income when it is earned and not necessarily when payment is received.

  **1.** **All Events**—Have all events occurred that fix the taxpayer's right to receive the income?

    a. **"Earlier of" Test**—The Internal Revenue Service's position is that "[a]ll the events that fix the right to receive income occur when (1) the required performance occurs, (2) payment therefor is due, or (3) payment therefor is made, whichever happens earliest." *Revenue Ruling 74–607.* So once one of these three events has occurred, the question is answered in the affirmative.

    b. **Yes**—If yes, continue in this Part C.

    c. **No**—If no, then the accrual method taxpayer does not yet have gross income.

  **2.** **Reasonable Accuracy**—Can the amount of the taxpayer's income be determined with reasonable accuracy?

    a. **Yes**—If yes, then the accrual method taxpayer generally has gross income. Treas. Reg. § 1.446–1(c)(1)(ii)(A). Continue in this Part C, however, to see if any exceptions apply.

    b. **No**—If no, then the accrual method taxpayer does not yet have gross income.

  **3.** **Doubts as to Collection**—Does the taxpayer reasonably believe that he or she will not be able to collect the income item owed at the time the requirements in C(1) and C(2) above are met?

a. **Yes**—If yes, then the taxpayer need not accrue the income until collection of the income is no longer in doubt. *Clifton Manufacturing Company v. Commissioner*, 137 F.2d 290 (4th Cir. 1943). Note, however, that if the taxpayer's doubt arises after the requirements in C(1) and C(2) are met, the taxpayer must still accrue the income. *Spring City Foundry Company v. Commissioner*, 292 U.S. 182 (1934).

b. **No**—If no, then the accrual method taxpayer still has income, but continue in this Part C to see if another exception applies.

4. **Contested Income**—Does the party under obligation to pay the income item to the taxpayer dispute its obligation to pay?

a. **Yes**—If yes, then the taxpayer does not accrue the income while the dispute remains. *Lamm v. Commissioner*, 873 F.2d 194 (8th Cir. 1989). The taxpayer will have income when the dispute is resolved, whether from the other party conceding liability to pay or from a final judgment in favor of the taxpayer. If the other party is willing to pay a portion of the contested income to the taxpayer, the taxpayer does not accrue that portion of the income if the taxpayer's acceptance would compromise the taxpayer's claim to the full amount. *Maryland Shipbuilding and Drydock Company v. United States*, 409 F.2d 1363 (Ct. Cl. 1969).

b. **No**—If no, then the accrual method taxpayer still has income, but continue in this Part C to see if another exception applies.

5. **Advance Payments**—Has the taxpayer received payment in advance of either the taxpayer's performance or the due date for payment?

a. **Yes**—If yes, then the "earlier of" test described in C(1) above indicates that the accrual method taxpayer has gross income upon receipt of the advance payment. The Supreme Court has endorsed the rule that an accrual method service-provider has gross income from the receipt of an advance payment even though the taxpayer has not earned the income. *Schlude v. Commissioner*, 372 U.S. 128 (1963). There are, however, two exceptions to this rule. If either of these exceptions applies, the taxpayer can defer inclusion of the income until performance or the due date for payment, whichever is earlier.

    i.  **Identifiable Dates of Performance**—If the taxpayer will provide services on specific, identifiable future dates, the income can be deferred until those dates. In *Artnell Company v. Commissioner*, 400 F.2d 981 (7th Cir. 1968), the owners of the Chicago White Sox were allowed to defer advance payments for season tickets received in 1962 to the specific dates on which games were played in 1963. The court determined that reporting the payments in 1963 would provide a clearer reflection of the taxpayer's income than requiring the taxpayer to include the payments in 1962.

    ii.  **One-Year Deferral Method**—An accrual method taxpayer may elect to report advance payments using the "Deferral Method" described in *Revenue Procedure 2004–34*. Under this method, the taxpayer includes the advance payment in gross income for the year of receipt but only to the extent such payment is "recognized in revenues" for bookkeeping purposes in that year. The remaining amount of the advance payment is gross income in the first taxable year after the year of receipt. The Deferral Method can apply to advance payments for services and the sale of most goods; it expressly cannot apply to advance payments of interest, for rents, or for insurance coverage, to name a few.

  b.  **No**—If no, then the accrual method taxpayer still has income, as no other exception applies.

### D. ACCRUAL METHOD—DEDUCTIONS

Recall that an accrual method taxpayer may claim a deduction when the item is owed, not necessarily when the item is paid. This Part D examines the requirements for deduction more fully and also considers the impact of a taxpayer's contesting liability for payment.

    **1.**  **All Events**—Have all events occurred that establish the taxpayer's liability to pay the deduction item?

      a.  **Yes**—If yes, continue in this Part D.

b.  **No**—If no, then the accrual method taxpayer cannot yet claim a deduction. Treas. Reg. § 1.461–1(a)(2)(i).

c.  **Contested Liability**—If the taxpayer in good faith contests a deductible liability supposedly owed to another party, the taxpayer's liability is not yet established so a deduction cannot be claimed for the liability. *Dixie Pine Products Company v. Commissioner*, 320 U.S. 516 (1944). If the taxpayer contesting a deductible liability nonetheless transfers cash or property to that other party in order to, for example, stop the accrual of interest or penalties, the taxpayer may claim a deduction for such payment in the year of payment even though the dispute remains. IRC § 461(f).

2.  **Reasonable Accuracy**—Can the amount of the taxpayer's liability be determined with reasonable accuracy?

a.  **Yes**—If yes, continue in this Part D.

b.  **No**—If no, then the accrual method taxpayer cannot yet claim a deduction. Treas. Reg. § 1.461–1(a)(2)(i).

3.  **Economic Performance**—Has economic performance occurred with respect to the liability?

a.  **Definition**—IRC § 461(h)(1) generally provides that an accrual method taxpayer cannot claim a deduction for an item until "economic performance with respect to such item occurs." The specific time at which economic performance occurs depends upon the nature of the transaction giving rise to the deduction.

   i.   **Services, Property or Use Provided to Taxpayer**—If the deduction arises out of another party's providing services, property, or the use of property to the taxpayer, economic performance occurs as such services or property are provided or as the taxpayer uses such property. IRC § 461(h)(2)(A). Thus, for example, if an accrual method landlord contracts with a landscaper to have the landscaper perform monthly services at the landlord's business property, economic performance occurs as the landscaper provides such services. This means the landlord cannot claim a deduction for the monthly amount owed to the land-scaper until the landscaper has performed.

ii. **Services or Property Provided by Taxpayer**—If the deduction arises out of the taxpayer's obligation to provide services or property to another party, economic performance occurs as such services or property are provided. IRC § 461(h)(2)(B). For example, if a taxpayer incurs the deductible future obligation to engage in environmental cleanup of the taxpayer's property because of some hazardous activity conducted on the property by the taxpayer, there is no deduction until the taxpayer actually performs the cleanup work even though the taxpayer's liability to do so has already fixed and even though the taxpayer might be able to estimate the amount the taxpayer will have to pay with reasonable accuracy.

iii. **Workers Compensation and Tort Liabilities**—If the deduction arises from the taxpayer's obligation under any workers compensation act or under tort liability to make a payment to another person, economic performance occurs as such payments are actually made. IRC § 461(h)(2)(C). In effect, this rule places the accrual method taxpayer on the cash method for purposes of these deductions.

iv. **Recurring Items Exception**—If economic performance of a deduction item occurs within a reasonable period after the close of the year in which the requirements of D(1) and D(2) above are met (the "year of all events"), but not more than 8.5 months after the close of the year of all events, and if such item is recurring in nature and the taxpayer consistently treats such items as being incurred in the year of all events, then economic performance is deemed to occur in the year of all events, but only if such item is not a material item or if the accrual of such item in the year of all events results in a clearer reflection of income than accruing such item in the year in which economic performance otherwise occurs. IRC § 461(h)(3)(A). This exception is not available for workers compensation or tort liabilities described in D(3)(a)(iii) above.

b. **Yes**—If yes, then the accrual method taxpayer may claim the deduction. Treas. Reg. § 1.461–1(a)(2)(i).

c. **No**—If no, then the accrual method taxpayer cannot yet claim a deduction. Treas. Reg. § 1.461–1(a)(2)(i).

### E. TAX BENEFIT RULE (IRC § 111)

Use this Part E when the taxpayer claimed a deduction for a cost in a prior year that has been recovered by the taxpayer in a later year.

1. **Recovery**—Did the taxpayer recover an item that was deducted in a prior taxable year?

    a. **Fundamental Inconsistency**—Note that there are several forms of recovery: reimbursement, refund, restoration, and judgment to name a few. Formally, any event that is fundamentally inconsistent with the prior deduction constitutes a recovery. *Hillsboro National Bank v. Commissioner*, 460 U.S. 370 (1983). For example, if a taxpayer deducted the cost of supplies as a business expense in a prior taxable year and then, in the following year, converted the supplies to personal use, that action is fundamentally inconsistent with the premise for the prior deduction (that such supplies would be consumed in the taxpayer's business), so there is a "recovery" of the prior deduction.

    b. **Yes**—If yes, then continue in this Part E.

    c. **No**—If no, then the tax benefit rule does not apply.

2. **Benefit from Prior Deduction**—Did the prior deduction result in a savings of federal income tax?

    a. **Yes**—If yes, the taxpayer must include the amount recovered to the extent the prior deduction resulted in a savings of federal income tax. IRC § 111(a).

        i. **Change in Rates Irrelevant**—It does not matter if, for example, the taxpayer's marginal rate in the year of deduction was lower than the taxpayer's marginal rate in the year of recovery. The taxpayer must still include the recovery in gross income to the extent the deduction in the prior year saved tax. *Alice Phelan Sullivan Corporation v. United States*, 381 F.2d 399 (Ct. Cl. 1967).

    ii. **Erroneous Deduction Exception Mostly Rejected—** The Tax Court has held that if the prior deduction was improper, the taxpayer need not include the recovery in gross income. *Canelo v. Commissioner*, 53 T.C. 217 (1969). But four circuit courts of appeals have rejected or criticized this rule, concluding that the taxpayer must still report the recovery as gross income because there was a prior benefit to the taxpayer. See *Unvert v. Commissioner*, 656 F.2d 483 (9th Cir. 1981).

  b. **No**—If no, then the recovery is fully excluded from the taxpayer's gross income. IRC § 111(a).

## F. RESTORATION OF A CLAIM OF RIGHT (IRC § 1341)

Use this Part F when the taxpayer has, in the taxable year at issue, restored an amount included in gross income in a prior taxable year.

  **1. Prior Inclusion Under Claim of Right**—Did the taxpayer include the item in gross income in a prior taxable year because it appeared that the taxpayer had an unrestricted right to such item?

    a. **Yes**—If yes, then continue in this Part F.

    b. **No**—If no, then IRC § 1341 does not apply. IRC § 1341(a)(1).

  **2. Prior Inclusion Wrong**—Was it established after the close of the year of inclusion that the taxpayer did not have an unrestricted right to all or a portion of such income item?

    a. **Yes**—If yes, then continue in this Part F.

    b. **No**—If no, then IRC § 1341 does not apply. IRC § 1341(a)(2).

  **3. Deduction Allowed**—Is the taxpayer entitled to a deduction for the amount restored? Note that IRC § 1341 does not authorize a deduction itself; there must be some other authority for the deduction. If the prior inclusion was related to the taxpayer's business, it is very likely the restoration cost would give rise to a deduction under IRC § 162(a), for it is an ordinary and necessary business expense to refund amounts that ultimately prove to be incorrectly received.

   a. **Yes**—If yes, then continue in this Part F.

   b. **No**—If no, then IRC § 1341 does not apply. IRC § 1341(a)(2).

4. **Deduction Exceeds $3,000**—Does the amount of the deduction exceed $3,000?

   a. **Yes**—If yes, then continue in this Part F.

   b. **No**—If no, then IRC § 1341 does not apply. IRC § 1341(a)(3).

5. **Credit for Extra Tax in Prior Year v. Deduction in Year of Payment**—Would it be more beneficial for the taxpayer to claim a credit in the year at payment for the extra tax paid on the income item in the prior year of inclusion instead of claiming the deduction in the year of payment?

   a. **Yes**—If yes, then compute the taxpayer's tax liability for the year of payment by ignoring the deduction and instead giving the taxpayer a credit equal to the tax savings that would have resulted in the prior year of inclusion if the income item had been excluded. IRC § 1341(a)(5).

   b. **No**—If no, then compute the taxpayer's tax liability for the year of payment by claiming the deduction. IRC § 1341(a)(4).

## ILLUSTRATIVE PROBLEMS

Here are three problems designed to show how the checklist helps in analyzing a question involving the cash and accrual methods as well as the error correction topics discussed in this Chapter.

---

## ■ PROBLEM 10.1 ■

---

T is a cash method taxpayer who operates a life coaching business. T meets with clients to set and achieve their personal goals using techniques in leadership training, management consulting, and other disciplines. In October of Year One, T received $24,000 from a client for two years worth of coaching sessions. Under the contract, T agrees to meet with the client at the client's demand from October of Year One through September of Year Three.

T leases commercial office space for use in T's coaching business. In November of Year One, T paid the entire rent for Year Two ($30,000) to the landlord.

On December 30 of Year One, another client telephoned T and offered to pay the $1,000 that she owed T for prior coaching sessions. Although the client offered to pay the bill in person, T asked the client to mail the payment instead. T knew that if the payment were mailed it would not be received until Year Two, and T hoped to avoid inclusion of the $1,000 until that time.

## Analysis

As a cash method taxpayer, T has gross income upon actual or constructive receipt of an item of income. T received a $24,000 payment from a client for coaching services that will be performed in Years One, Two, and Three. Although T has not yet fully performed under the contract, T must include the entire $24,000 in gross income for Year One, the year of receipt.

A cash method taxpayer generally may claim a deduction in the year in which a deductible expense is actually paid. Here, T actually paid the rent for Year Two in Year One. Perhaps T anticipates having more income in Year One than in Year Two, so T hopes that by paying the Year Two rent expense in Year One the deduction may be claimed on the Year One return. T's plan will work: under Treas. Reg. § 1.1263(a)–4(f)(1), T may deduct the rent expense in Year One because the total benefit obtained through the payment does not last more than 12 months and does not extend beyond the end of Year Two.

T is in constructive receipt of the $1,000 payment from the other client in Year One. Under these facts, T is essentially turning his or her back on the income. It is clear from the conduct of the client that the money was available for T to take, but instead T hoped to defer inclusion of the income until Year Two by having the client send a check in the mail. Since T was effectively in control of the income in Year One, T should have to report it as gross income on the return for Year One.

---

## ■ PROBLEM 10.2 ■

---

T is an accrual method taxpayer who operates a life coaching business. T meets with clients to set and achieve their personal goals using techniques in leadership training, management consulting, and other disciplines. In October of Year One, T received $24,000 from a client for two years worth of coaching sessions. Under the contract, T agrees to meet with the client at the client's demand from October of Year One through September of Year Three.

T leases commercial office space for use in T's coaching business. In November of Year One, T paid the entire rent for Year Two ($30,000) to the landlord.

On December 30 of Year One, another client telephoned T and offered to pay the $1,000 that she owed T for prior coaching sessions in Year One. Although the client offered to pay the bill in person, T asked the client to mail the payment instead. T knew that if the payment were mailed it would not be received until Year Two, and T hoped to avoid inclusion of the $1,000 until that time.

### Analysis

---

As an accrual method taxpayer, T has gross income when all events have occurred that fix the right to receive the income and the amount of the income can be determined with reasonable accuracy. Generally, all events that fix the right to receive payment for services is deemed to occur upon the earlier of the taxpayer's performance, the due date for the payment, or receipt of the payment. Here, T received a $24,000 payment from a client for coaching services in Year One. Accordingly, the general rule would require T to include the entire advance payment in gross income for Year One. The services will be performed on the demand of the client and not on specific fixed dates, so the exception in the *Artnell* case does not apply. However, under the "Deferral Method" set forth in *Revenue Procedure 2004–34*, T can elect to include the $3,000 portion allocable to October, November, and December of Year One in T's gross income for Year One and the remaining $21,000 in T's gross income for Year Two.

An accrual method taxpayer generally may claim a deduction in the year in which all events have occurred that establish the taxpayer's liability for payment, the amount can be determined with reasonable accuracy, and economic performance of the liability has occurred. IRC § 461(h)(2)(A) provides that if the deduction arises from the taxpayer's use of property, economic performance occurs as the taxpayer uses the property. Accordingly, T cannot deduct the rent expense paid in Year One until Year Two because the payment represents T's use of the property in Year Two.

T must include the $1,000 income item from the other client in Year One. T's right to receive the income became fixed in Year One when T performed the coaching services, and the amount owed to T was obviously determinable with reasonable accuracy as of that time. The fact that the client may not pay until Year Two or that T might not receive payment until Year Two does not affect this analysis.

---

### ■ PROBLEM 10.3 ■

---

In Year One, T, a cash method taxpayer, received a $5,000 bonus from T's employer based on outstanding performance. Also in Year One, T paid $5,000 in state real property taxes. This was T's only deduction for the year, but since the standard deduction amount in Year One was $3,000, T itemized deductions and claimed the full $5,000 deduction for the taxes. Assume the applicable tax rate in Year One was 30 percent.

In Year Two, T learned for the first time that T's employer miscalculated the amount of the Year One bonus. It turned out that the bonus amount was only supposed to be $1,000, so T was forced to pay $4,000 to T's employer. Also in Year Two, the state in which T resides announced that due to budget surpluses it was refunding all real property taxes paid in Year One. Accordingly, T received $5,000 from the state in Year Two. Assume the applicable tax rare in Year Two was 20 percent.

## Analysis

T properly included the $5,000 bonus in gross income for Year One because as of the end that year it appeared that T had an unrestricted right to the money. T did not learn until Year Two that T was not entitled to the money. T's repayment of $4,000 to T's employer in Year Two should give rise to a deduction under IRC § 162(a), as one would think it would be customary for employees to restore excess compensation back to their employers. Because the deduction amount exceeds $3,000, all of the elements for IRC § 1341 are met, meaning T's tax liability for Year Two will be lesser of T's tax liability for the year with regard to the deduction and T's tax liability for the year without the deduction but with a credit for the extra tax paid in Year One. Assuming T had sufficient income in both Year One and Year Two, T is better off with the credit instead of the deduction. A deduction of $4,000 in Year Two will save T $800 in tax ($4,000 deduction x 20% tax rate). If T had not included the $4,000 portion in gross income for Year One, T would have saved $1,200 in tax ($4,000 extra income x 30% tax rate). Because the $1,200 tax savings from the credit is better than the $800 tax savings from the deduction, T should choose to claim the credit for the extra tax paid in Year One under IRC § 1341(a)(5).

T properly itemized the $5,000 state real property tax deduction under IRC § 164 on T's Year One return. When T receives the $5,000 payment back from the state, the tax benefit rule is triggered. Under the tax benefit rule, T must include the recovered tax payment in gross income to the extent the prior deduction saved T tax. The facts indicate that if T had not claimed the $5,000 deduction, T would have claimed a $3,000 standard deduction. Therefore, only $2,000 of the $5,000 deduction actually saved any federal income tax. Consequently, T must include only $2,000 of the $5,000 recovery; the balance is excluded from T's gross income under IRC § 111(a).

## POINTS TO REMEMBER

- Assume that every individual is a cash method taxpayer and that every corporation uses the accrual method unless a fact pattern specifically provides to the contrary. This assumption is based on the fact that most individuals do use the cash method and the majority of corporations use the accrual method.

- The cash method generally turns on receipt (for income items) and payment (for deduction items), while the accrual method generally turns on rights to receive payments (for income items) and obligations to make payments (for deduction items).

- If a cash method taxpayer appears to be deferring receipts until a later year, the question is whether the constructive receipt doctrine applies.

- The tax benefit rule and IRC § 111(a) concern a deduction in one year followed by its recovery in a later year. IRC § 1341, on the other hand, concerns the inclusion of income in one year followed by the taxpayer's restoration of the item to the payor in a later year.

†